The Girl in the Dark

The Girl in the Dark

The True Story of Runaway Child With a Secret.
A Devastating Discovery that Changes Everything.

ANGELA HART

bluebird
books for life

First published 2019 by Bluebird
an imprint of Pan Macmillan
20 New Wharf Road, London N1 9RR
Associated companies throughout the world
www.panmacmillan.com

ISBN 978-1-5290-0415-1

Certain details in this story, including names, places and dates, have been changed to protect the family's privacy.

1 3 5 7 9 8 6 4 2

A CIP catalogue record for this book is available from the British Library.

Typeset by Palimpsest Book Production Ltd, Falkirk, Stirlingshire
Printed and bound by CPI Group (UK) Ltd, Croydon, CR0 4YY

Visit www.panmacmillan.com to read more about all our books and to buy them. You will also find features, author interviews and news of any author events, and you can sign up for e-newsletters so that you're always first to hear about our new releases.

The Girl in the Dark

1

'How can we refuse?'

'I'll cut straight to the chase,' our support social worker said. Wilf was sounding much more stressed than usual. 'I need to place a young girl and I'm really hoping you can take her in. It's an emergency.'

We'd said goodbye to a boy who'd been staying with us on a short placement only a few hours earlier and I was enjoying the peace and quiet, though of course I didn't mind the interruption. This was our job, and if a child in difficulty needed a home then my husband Jonathan and I would always do our best to provide one.

'You know we'll help if we can.

I heard Wilf exhale deeply. 'Thank you, Angela. I was really hoping you'd say that. Thank you very much. I'm very grateful.' I thought he sounded quite desperate, which was unusual and made me worry about what we were letting ourselves in for. Wilf was in his fifties and was a very experienced social worker with nearly thirty years of service under his belt. We'd known him for quite a while now, but I'd never heard him like this before.

'Hold on, I haven't agreed to anything yet!' I said light-heartedly, attempting to dilute the tension I could detect down the phone line.

'Yes, of course. I realise you'll have to talk to Jonathan, but I don't mind admitting I really need you to take this girl in, as quickly as possible. I don't want to put you on the spot, but it's a very urgent case and I'm banking on you, to be honest.'

'I see. What's the situation?'

Wilf spoke rapidly, barely pausing for breath. He was an efficient, earnest man and he didn't mince his words. 'The girl is in a secure unit and if you don't take her she'll have to stay there until another specialist carer becomes available. She's twelve years old and locked up with young offenders, though she has no criminal record. She shouldn't be there, clearly, but we simply had nowhere else to place her at short notice.'

I listened quietly, feeling very worried for the girl, wanting to get her out of the unit as quickly as possible and wondering exactly how she'd ended up there.

Wilf went on to explain that the girl had run away from her foster carer's home on numerous occasions. This time she had been picked up by the police after going missing for several days and the foster carer subsequently refused to have her back.

'She's spent two nights in the unit already, which is far from ideal. I hate to put you under pressure, Angela, but I can't stress enough how urgently we want to move the girl.'

Wilf told me the name of the unit, which was well known in the region. Though it was designed for children aged twelve to eighteen I knew it wasn't meant to be an overspill facility for kids in care who had nowhere else to go. As far as I was aware, it was a detention centre for youngsters who'd got in trouble with the law, or those who were at risk of committing crimes and needed to be kept off the streets, either for their own good or for the safety of others. There was a high security section attached to the unit where youths accused of committing serious crimes were detained while on bail or awaiting a court appearance. The crimes were the sort of shocking and violent offences that often made headline news, giving the centre notoriety. I'd heard it called all kinds of names over the years, but typically it was described as a 'kids' prison'.

To my alarm, Wilf went on to explain that the girl was in this high security section, as there was no bed available in the main centre when she was taken in.

'So there you have it, Angela. She's locked up alongside young offenders, I'm afraid. I'm sure you can understand the urgency.'

I thought to myself, *You're not wrong there*. It was deeply shocking that an innocent twelve-year-old was being locked up alongside violent and dangerous youths.

'It shouldn't be happening,' Wilf went on. 'But I'm afraid it just goes to show how strapped we are for foster carers, and especially specialist carers. I'm sure we'd get a lot of stick if this story got out, but in the circumstances the emergency team had no option but to take her to the unit. It's put everybody in a very difficult situation, most of all the girl herself.'

Wilf reiterated that she had no criminal record, but added that she had a long history of absconding from care, going missing and being picked up by the police and returned to her foster carers. He explained that she came from a broken home and had been in care for over a year in total but didn't offer any further details at that stage.

'I'll speak to Jonathan straight away. I want to help, I'm sure he will feel the same way.'

'Thanks, Angela. It will only be a five-week placement, if that helps.' Placements rarely run to an exact timetable, which is inevitable when you're dealing with unpredictable kids, their often fickle or unreliable families and a care system that is perpetually stretched to breaking point. However, Wilf said this would be a maximum stay of five weeks, though he didn't explain why. I didn't know how he could be so confident about the timeframe in the circumstances, but I took him at his word.

Jonathan was outside, putting antifreeze in the car. It was a bitterly cold evening and there had been warnings of frozen fog and ice on the roads. I pulled on a coat and hat and went out to see him.

'How can we refuse?' he said straight away, his breath forming white clouds in the freezing air as he looked up from under the bonnet of our old estate car.

'I agree. It's only five weeks. Come what may, I'm sure we can cope with that.'

The truth was we didn't *want* to refuse, even though we both felt wary of dealing with a child who seemed so intent on running away. We'd never dealt with that scenario before, but we were prepared to do our best to help.

I phoned Wilf to tell him our decision. 'I can't thank you enough,' he said. His relief was palpable. 'I'll be back in touch as soon as possible with more details. We'd like you to visit Melissa at the unit first. Hopefully I can fix this up for tomorrow. Then we'll take it from there. Thank you again. You're a lifesaver. Please pass on my thanks to Jonathan too.'

I realised Wilf hadn't told me the girl's name until now, and when I hung up the phone I repeated it out loud. 'Melissa,' I said, looking at Jonathan, who had just come in from the cold and was standing in the hallway, rubbing his hands together to warm up. 'Wilf just said the girl's name is Melissa.'

The penny dropped for both of us at the same moment.

'Oh my God, it's the girl Lynne was looking after,' I exclaimed, putting my hand over my mouth to stifle a gasp. 'I can't believe I didn't work that out earlier!'

Jonathan sucked in a breath. 'What have we done?' He widened his eyes but then immediately looked for something positive to say, no doubt having seen the look of horror on my face.

'Come on, let's get the kettle on and draw up a battle plan!' he joked. 'We won't be defeated by a twelve-year-old girl!'

We sat in the kitchen drinking steaming-hot tea and

thinking back to everything our friend Lynne had told us about Melissa. She had done the training course to be a specialist teenage foster carer at the same time as Jonathan and me, and we'd got to know each other well. We now attended a regular support group with Lynne and other recently qualified specialist carers, where we were all encouraged to share our experiences in confidence with each other.

I cast my mind back to a session we'd had a couple of weeks earlier, when Lynne told the group she was exhausted. I could still picture her, looking very stressed and tired out.

'I'm at the end of my tether,' Lynne had sighed. 'I'm not sleeping properly because every time I hear a noise in the house I think it's her, up to her tricks again.'

The social worker leading the meeting encouraged Lynne to unload and share her story and Lynne went on to explain that the girl seemed 'hell-bent' on running off. At first, Melissa would pretend she needed to go to the corner shop, or to meet a friend, but then she'd simply not come home. Sometimes she returned of her own accord but other times she went missing for so long Lynne had to call the police. As time went on Melissa became more brazen, Lynne said. She would run off at all hours of the day or night without even bothering to make excuses, and she began to disappear for longer periods of time.

'It's a nightmare,' Lynne continued. 'I'm exhausted and I'm not sure I can take much more. She whistles too! I can't stand it!'

The course leader had reassured Lynne that she was doing everything right, but it was clear this was not much comfort. Jonathan recalled that Lynne had said she was feeling guilty about the effect the placement was having on her husband and two children, and that she was questioning her decision to become a specialist carer. She had dark circles under her eyes and said her husband was also feeling the strain and losing sleep.

Remembering that support meeting, and recalling how frustrated and defeated Lynne looked, I shuddered.

'It sounded like a complete nightmare, didn't it?' I said to Jonathan. 'And we've just volunteered to put ourselves in Lynne's shoes! We must be mad.'

'Mad, or optimistic?' he shrugged. 'Look, we've all but agreed to meet her now and we're not going to go back on our word, are we? Wilf could phone back any minute with the arrangements.'

I nodded. I knew that even though we'd have the chance to pull out once we'd met Melissa, as is always the case in such situations, if she was happy to come and live with us then it was highly unlikely we would refuse to take her in. How could we leave a young girl in a place like that?

'Maybe we can help turn things around for her,' Jonathan said. 'A fresh start might be just what Melissa needs. And as I recall, Lynne said she was a very nice girl, when she wasn't running off.'

'Did she? I can't remember that bit. I think that part of the story got overshadowed, not surprisingly. I can only remember how much of a nightmare it sounded. I'm going to give Lynne a call.'

*

'Are you joking?' was Lynne's reaction when I told her our news.

'No. We've agreed to go and meet her at the secure unit. I didn't put two and two together until we'd already set the ball rolling.'

Lynne groaned.

'The placement will only be for five weeks, while Social Services find something more permanent,' I went on. 'I'm sure we can manage that.'

'Well I was on my knees after just one week. I felt like running away myself!'

She laughed and I gamely joined in, though her attempt at humour didn't reduce my stress levels. I now felt even more worried than before.

I learned that Lynne had given Melissa a home for four weeks before deciding she could take no more. She explained how the beginning of the end came when Melissa began breaking out at night. With her two children in their beds, Lynne and her husband Nick had been horrified to wake up and discover Melissa had slipped out the back door, leaving the house unlocked as they slept.

'I couldn't sleep properly after she started doing that. I was always on alert through the night, listening for her. I felt helpless. I've known parents to lock kids in the house and hide the key to stop them disappearing overnight, but obviously as foster carers we can't do that, can we? All I could do was lie there, trying to detect if she was getting up and hoping I'd hear her if she started sneaking about. Maybe then I could talk her round, if I caught her trying to run off. That's what I thought, but it didn't work.'

We'd covered the issue of locked doors and windows in our specialist foster care training. Under no circumstances are foster carers allowed to lock children in rooms or houses, or anywhere else for that matter. Respecting human rights and adhering to health and safety guidelines are vitally important factors. Foster carers can be reprimanded for breaching the rules, however well-intentioned they may be.

'One evening Nick caught Melissa red-handed,' Lynne went on. 'He got to the back door just in time to see her making her way down the garden path. She wasn't running, she was simply walking away quite calmly. She was whistling to herself. Can you believe it? When he called after her she quickened her pace and then started to run. If it was one of our kids he'd have been able to at least catch her up and take hold of her arm to try to stop her from leaving, but of course Nick couldn't lay a finger on Melissa. It was all too much. I couldn't have her back in the end. The main problem was that I was too worried for my kids' safety. The placement was not sustainable at all.'

I told Lynne I didn't blame her. At least Jonathan and I didn't have kids of our own to worry about, and hopefully that might make it easier for us than it had been for her. I was looking for positives, though I was now under no illusion about what Jonathan and I were letting ourselves in for.

During the course of the phone conversation Lynne had also remarked that Melissa looked 'dishevelled' when she came home, but Lynne told me she didn't have a clue what Melissa got up to when she went missing. Seemingly, all that was known was that she hung around with a 'bad crowd'.

'It sounds like Melissa may prove to be our toughest challenge yet,' I said to Jonathan later.

It was the nineties and we had qualified as specialist carers only a short time prior to being asked to take in Melissa. Over the previous few weeks we'd looked after three teenage boys on short placements. Each had turned out to be less trouble than some of the kids who'd lived with us when we were dealing solely with so-called 'mainstream' children, rather than kids who needed extra help.

'Toughest challenge yet?' Jonathan said. 'Bring it on!' I knew my husband was as concerned as I was but was trying to look on the bright side and cheer me up.

'Bring it on,' I repeated, somewhat unconvincingly. I knew there was no point in dwelling on the negative now, though I had a very strong feeling we were going to have to draw on every ounce of our specialist training in order to cope with Melissa.

2

'Maybe we should stick to selling flowers?'

The phone rang not long after I'd finished telling Jonathan everything Lynne had passed on to me about Melissa. Though it was nearly eight o'clock by now, it was Wilf with the details for our visit to the unit the next day; it's not unusual for social workers to work on into the evening when they desperately need to place a child. He suggested that after the meeting, provided we were all in agreement, arrangements would be made for Melissa to move in with us as soon as possible, hopefully within a day or two.

'OK, that's fine,' I said. I was apprehensive but it was too late to change our minds now. I couldn't have lived with the thought of a young girl being locked in a unit like that when we had room in our house for her. As of that morning all three bedrooms on the top floor of our town house were empty. However difficult it may be to care for Melissa and keep her safe, the young girl deserved the chance to live in a normal home again, as quickly as possible.

I already knew roughly where the unit was but I carefully noted down the full address. Wilf explained that we had to report to the main security gate upon arrival. I told him I'd worked out that Melissa's former foster carer was my friend Lynne and that I'd learned a little more about her.

'It's very tough looking after a runner, but you and Jonathan are her best shot,' Wilf said. 'I think Melissa's very lucky you're willing to consider taking her in. I can't think of a better home for her. She's a sweet girl, too. I think you'll be pleasantly surprised when you meet her. I hope it all goes well.'

As soon as Wilf described Melissa as 'a sweet girl' I remembered how Jonathan had recalled Lynne telling the meeting she was a 'very nice girl, when she wasn't running off'. I'd forgotten to ask Lynne about this when I called her, as understandably my focus had been on Melissa's challenging behaviour. Now Wilf had used the word 'sweet' I found myself intrigued to meet her. How could this nice, sweet girl cause so much chaos? Why did she run away, and what was she running to? Or was she running *from* something? I wanted to know the answers.

'You never know,' I commented to Jonathan after the phone call with Wilf. 'This could be the placement that turns her life around. If Melissa's a nice, sweet girl by nature, how difficult can it be to get through to her?'

'Exactly. Let's hope this is a turning point.'

We were trying to reassure one another, of course. We had to be optimistic and approach this meeting feeling hopeful, not despondent. We were going to do our very best for Melissa and help her deal with whatever problems she had, and we wouldn't judge her on her history.

Wilf had given us as much information as he could about Melissa, but he had not been able to tell us why she ran away. Lynne didn't have an explanation either. All we'd heard so far was that Melissa mixed with the wrong crowd, but what made her go missing? Why would anybody want to be out on the streets in the dark and the cold? Where did she sleep and how did she survive when she disappeared for days on end?

Jonathan and I wondered if drugs and alcohol were involved as Lynne had told us that Melissa had started to come home looking 'dishevelled', though neither had been specifically mentioned. Was Melissa running away so she could be out drinking and smoking, or taking drugs? We didn't have a clue, and we had no idea just how much danger she was putting herself in by mixing with the wrong crowd.

The following morning, after arranging staff cover for our florist shop, Jonathan and I set off to the unit to meet Melissa. It was a fairly long drive and Jonathan and I chatted and reminisced about our fostering career.

It was 1993 now and we'd been fostering for about four years by this time. After a string of successful placements over the first three years, some involving extremely tricky teenagers who stayed long-term, a social worker we got on with particularly well had suggested we'd be ideal candidates to train as specialist carers for teenagers with complex needs.

'I think you'd be perfect,' she'd said very enthusiastically. 'I've seen how patient and understanding you are. Mainstream foster care simply doesn't work for all kids. Some need extra support and a closer eye kept on them. It doesn't mean they're bad kids. They are generally kids who've had bad things happen to them, and they need carers with a deeper knowledge of such things and the skills to tackle the repercussions of what's happened to them in the past. I think you and Jonathan should both do the training course together.'

Though we'd made a success of mainstream fostering, it had been more challenging than we'd ever imagined. Jonathan and I had had our doubts along the way and been tested to the limit in those early years, but we'd found it so rewarding we'd resolved to carry on for as long as we could manage. Working with teenagers had proved to be particularly gratifying. We felt we could connect with them and we'd also got used to having teenagers in the house. We always missed them when they'd gone, and so when we were approached about doing the specialist training course it wasn't a difficult decision for us to make. Just as we'd done when we first started fostering, Jonathan and I agreed that we would give it a try and see how it turned out. 'Nothing ventured, nothing gained' was our motto and attitude, and when we embarked on the year-long course we felt excited about the future. We were in our thirties then and were both open-minded and optimistic, daring to believe we had something to offer the most difficult of kids, and hoping we might even be able to change the lives of teenagers who needed that extra bit of support and understanding.

As we continued our car journey that day, Jonathan and I talked about the substantial amount of specialist training we'd had, attending fortnightly sessions over the previous twelve months. I think the closer we were to arriving at the unit, the more nervous and daunted we felt, because the more we reminisced. I can see now we were trying to build our confidence and buoy each other's spirits, reminding ourselves just how much training we'd had, and how we should be equipped to deal with the toughest foster placements imaginable – including a placement like Melissa's.

I'll never forget the first training session we attended. Jonathan and I, along with about twenty other foster carers, sat in a circle and had to take turns standing up and introducing ourselves. We both felt a bit self-conscious, never having done anything like that before, and to add to the stress you had to throw a foam ball to the person next to you when you'd finished saying your piece, to signify it was their turn to speak. When my turn came I dropped the ball and had the embarrassment of scrabbling under the coffee table in the middle to retrieve it. After that 'ice-breaker', one of the two social workers running the course stood up and gave an introductory speech.

'The teenagers you take in may have any manner of behavioural or emotional problems,' Marjory said. 'They may be violent, angry, aggressive, rude, disruptive, scared, anxious, confused, depressed or any combination of the above. They may have been physically, sexually or emotionally abused. They may be suffering from psychological problems, possibly linked to neglect or earlier childhood trauma. We will do our best to equip you to deal with all the challenges you may be faced with.'

You could have heard a pin drop in the room as the assembled foster carers swapped sideways glances. It sounded very alarming and serious indeed, particularly as we all knew from experience how difficult 'mainstream' kids could be. Could we really handle teenagers with problems so complex they needed specialist care? That was the question I imagined was on everybody's lips.

We launched straight into another activity, in which we each had to take turns saying a swear word. The challenge was to keep the chain going around the room. We had to pass a box of chocolates from one to the other at the same time, like pass the parcel, and when you had the chocolates in your hands it was your turn to say a swear word. The suggested words soon became more extreme, embarrassing and obscure as we went along, and if you couldn't think of a word (or couldn't bring yourself to say what came to your mind!) you were out. I blushed the first time I had to speak but I got used to it, and ultimately the exercise was a success. We all ended up giggling at the bizarre situation we were in, blurting out expletives to strangers.

Neither Jonathan nor I won the chocolates, which I wasn't unhappy about – not least because I was on a diet! The foster carer who won, with a word I don't think I'd even heard of before, said she wasn't sure whether to be proud or ashamed of her victory, which made everybody smile. The trainers were delighted with how we'd all responded. They told us the point of the exercise was to teach us that we mustn't be shocked by anything we may encounter. We might be exposed to the foulest language imaginable, but if we showed our shock then the kids may take our reaction as a victory. The best way was not to react at all, but to simply state, 'We don't allow bad language. Please watch what you are saying,' and remain unshaken, looking as if you'd heard it all before, even if you hadn't and were reeling with shock.

From that moment on I began to relax and really enjoy the course. Each session was extremely interesting and we picked up so many gems of information every time. It was clear that the training was invaluable, and not just in helping us deal with complex teenagers. Though Jonathan and I were being taught to specialise in the care of challenging teenagers – particularly those who had not progressed with other carers – we were still going to take in other foster children, as long as we had room in our house. We could both see that the knowledge we were gaining would benefit us as carers, as well as any of the children who stayed with us, regardless of their age or circumstances.

In one session, the two social workers taking the class told us that we couldn't be expected to like all the children we looked after, but that we had to remember that each child has something positive to offer and shows potential in something, even if that 'something' is not obvious at first. Our job as specialist carers was to find the positive and focus on that, and not to dwell on the negative. Similarly, we were taught that when kids arrive at our door we must never, ever pull a face at what they bring with them, or make a negative remark about how something smells. A black bin bag filled with dirty clothes or a stinky toy, or items that look like rubbish, might be incredibly important to a child. Something that smells bad to you might be a comfort to a child, reminding them of home, or inspiring a memory that means a lot to them. Making a critical comment could upset or alienate them.

When it's time to say goodbye to a child, we were taught to always aim for 'good goodbyes,' making them feel happy, safe and loved at the point of departure, so they would remember leaving our home in a positive way. Telling them they would be missed and that you'd enjoyed having them stay with you was important. If the reality was that you couldn't wait to see the back of them, you were to keep this to yourself and make sure you found at least one positive thing to say, whatever that may be.

At one memorable session the two social workers built a wall of shoeboxes. Those boxes at the bottom of the wall were labelled with the most basic of needs, such as food, water and shelter. As the wall stacked up, the boxes represented love, attention, trust, understanding, education, security and so on. When the wall was complete the social workers encouraged us to take turns in removing various different shoeboxes. The object was to show that the wall could still stand even with various blocks missing, the point being that on the surface children who have suffered trauma don't look any different to those who have received the correct care from birth. They are still standing, but in reality their behaviour and emotional reactions may be adversely affected by disadvantages and neglect they've suffered earlier in their life, which are not visible or obvious to outsiders looking in. Inside, the child could be crumbling or falling apart, despite the fact they are standing tall. I found this quite an eye-opener. Sessions like that spurred me on, and I felt I was learning to be the best carer I could be, even to the most difficult and challenging of teens.

Another of the memorable sessions Jonathan and I talked about that day was one we've discussed many times since, and it's still clear in my mind all these years on. It went like this. Each foster carer picked a description of a different character out of a hat and we were then told to line up against the wall at the far end of the Social Services meeting room where we were gathered. I represented a professional black female in a wheelchair, Jonathan was a middle-class, young, white, male university student and all the other members of the group played people of various ages and reflecting a wide range of religions, social classes, physical abilities, sexualities and races.

'Move one pace forward if you are guaranteed a meal on the table every evening,' one of the social workers said. Not everyone moved forward. 'Take another step if you can go out on your own in the evening, get in a taxi on your own and feel safe.'

Eventually it was Jonathan, playing the university student, who was the first person to reach the far wall. The aim was to demonstrate the need for us to view each new child with an open mind about the disadvantages he or she may be faced with. We should not compare their experiences to our own, expect them to react in the same way we might or assume they will have the same abilities as us, as they may not have had the same opportunities in life, or they may be affected by any number of issues that put them at a disadvantage to others. We learned, and accepted, that we may be called upon to look after kids who came from completely different worlds, with issues we had no personal experience of yet could still be trained to deal with. Crucially, we were taught never to judge a book by its cover. We had to get to know each child and not be swayed by any preconceptions we may have had based on our own views, by the image the child projected. I found this extremely interesting, and very useful. I wanted to learn more and more, and as the months went on I had a very powerful feeling that I was in the right place, doing what I was meant to do.

There had been times in the past, in the early years of our fostering careers, when Jonathan and I had both experienced insecurities about our ability to foster kids, but the course was filling us with confidence. This was our calling, and I couldn't imagine a day when we didn't foster.

Inevitably, there were some extremely difficult sessions to contend with and, looking back, we were still very naive, despite the fact we were feeling much more secure about our abilities. One week I had to leave the room when we were given training on sexual abuse because the scenario described was so upsetting. It was about a real case of a grandfather who had never abused before but inexplicably began to abuse his granddaughter. We were told exactly how it progressed, and how he brainwashed and blackmailed the young girl. I was fighting back tears. I excused myself and had to go outside for some fresh air, as I felt I could no longer breathe in the stuffy Social Services building. One of the social workers came out to check I was OK, as she or her colleague did when anyone left the room. When she spoke to me I gasped for breath and questioned whether I could carry on, and I seriously considered giving up that day. Jonathan helped. He told me I had so much to give and encouraged me to stick at it. Lynne was a big help too. 'Come on, Angela,' she said. 'You'll be fantastic. It's hard when you hear things like this, but it will get easier. There are a lot of kids who will lose out if you drop out now.' By this stage – more than halfway through the training course – about a third of the group had left, having decided it was not for them.

The following week it was me who was supporting Lynne, after we learned in some disturbing detail about children who groom and abuse other youngsters. Then it was Jonathan's turn to question his ability to carry on, when we heard stories about 'fire starters' (those children who deliberately set fire to things) and damaged kids who 'smear' (their own faeces on walls). I rallied him round when he faltered, reminding him we already had a history of coping well with a string of difficult teens, even without the excellent specialist training we were now receiving.

'I know, but are we really cut out for this?' he lamented.

'It's extreme, Angela. We are volunteering to invite incredibly damaged kids into our home and our lives. I'm really not sure I can go through with it. What are we doing?'

'You can't give up now,' I said to him. 'Think about Vicky.'

Vicky was a particularly challenging child who had lived with us for around three years before moving into her own flat the previous year. 'I am, and that's the trouble! I'm thinking about how hard it was at times, and in hindsight she was not that bad compared to the kids we're going to encounter now. Should we be putting ourselves through this? Maybe we should stick to selling flowers? Or just stay being mainstream foster carers?'

Our florist shop, a family business we'd inherited from my mother several years earlier, was doing very well. The rule with the specialist fostering service was that at least one of us would need to be a full-time carer. In his anxious state, Jonathan suggested he assume full responsibility for the shop while I became the main carer, but I knew this was not the way forward. I'd seen how we'd worked so well together over the previous few years, each wearing both hats and, vitally, supporting each other emotionally as well as on a practical level, both in the shop and in our fostering careers.

The most important thing, to my mind, was that the kids benefited from us working as a team. On many occasions I'd admired Jonathan's knack of defusing a situation with a joke or a well-timed, playful distraction. He was always great at playing with the kids, getting them outdoors and teaching them about cars and bikes, birds and gardening, and all sorts of things that were much more his forte than mine. He was endlessly engaging and inventive and still is, and they are qualities that are invaluable when looking after kids of all ages. They are also skills that are hard, if not impossible, to teach. He's a natural in that regard, and that's priceless and something I admire very much.

For my part, Jonathan always said I was a master of organisation, keeping the wheels of our lives turning with a constant flow of activities, holidays and practical suggestions and ideas to keep the kids busy, interested and learning something new each day. I think that's a pretty accurate description. I'm certainly one of life's doers, and I encourage every child to do at least one productive thing each day. That's how I was brought up, and I believe it's a good way to be.

At the same time, I was adamant I did not want to give up working in the shop and hand over the reins to Jonathan. It kept me at the heart of the community. I enjoyed running the florists and having an interest outside of fostering, and the kids profited from our shared involvement in it too. We gave each child who stayed with us the opportunity to work in the shop and earn some extra pocket money, and I often thought how useful it was for them to learn about the responsibilities that come with running a business. Jonathan and I were role models, showing the kids how hard work pays off and demonstrating that men and women's jobs were interchangeable.

I pointed all of this out to Jonathan when he had his crisis of confidence. I reminded him how we worked so well as a team, juggling the running of the shop with taking in up to three children at any one time. Some had been long-term, like Vicky, and others had come for short respite stays, ranging from a few days to a few weeks or months.

'Don't think about the hard times,' I said. 'Think about Vicky as she is now. Think about how far she's come. It's very likely she wouldn't be thriving like she is if she hadn't come to live with us at a crucial time in her life.'

When Vicky first moved in with us she was a troubled thirteen-year-old who was so terrified by her past she suffered alarming episodes when she froze with fear. She left when she was nearly seventeen and in a much-improved place, strong and capable of looking after herself in a flat supported by Social Services. We were still in touch with her – we still are to this day – and we continued to help her out in any way we could. I knew Jonathan could not deny the role we'd played in helping Vicky deal with her demons and learn to stand on her own two feet. As he did as I suggested and thought about Vicky, I saw a smile spread across his face. He didn't even have to tell me I'd got through to him. I smiled too as I pictured how well she now looked. I'm happy to say that Jonathan survived his wobble and we were back at training a fortnight later, and from that point on we never looked back.

The course fuelled my already strong desire to help disadvantaged kids. It was not their fault they had been born into a certain set of circumstances, and I wanted to help build them up again, until they were as tall and strong and emotionally stable as they could possibly be.

Back then, the damaging effect child abuse and neglect

can have on the brain and mental health was not understood in the way it is today. We'd never heard of attachment disorders, for example, along with many other conditions that are commonly known about more than twenty-five years on. Perhaps if I'd known then that my job as a specialist carer would lead to me looking after kids with severe autism, ADHD and a wide range of mental health issues over the years I'd have run a mile – just as Lynne jokingly suggested she had wanted to when looking after Melissa. I have no regrets, of course. I'm glad I stuck with specialist fostering, even if my commitment to the job in those early days was partly down to naivety about what I was really getting into!

After we completed the training we took in the three teenage boys I mentioned earlier. They came in quick succession and none stayed longer than a few weeks. The last boy, who had left us on the day Wilf called about Melissa, was as quiet as a mouse. He had been bullied at school and had some anger issues, but when he was at home with us he just wanted to be left in peace and spent most of his time reading comic books in his room, or playing snooker with one of the boys in our neighbourhood. As I've said, despite coming to us as specialist cases, the boys proved to be less trouble than some of the children we'd had staying with us previously – bar a couple of incidents involving cigarettes and alcohol and in one case a fist fight at school.

'I suspect we're about to discover we've had it easy so far,' Jonathan said as we finally approached the grounds of the children's centre and secure unit.

'I agree. This is where our specialist training is really going to kick in.'

I swallowed hard. Looking after a runaway girl was uncharted territory for us and I was filled with trepidation.

'Are you ready to take on the challenge?' Jonathan asked. He was trying to sound bold and upbeat but I could tell he was as nervous as I was.

'Ready as I'll ever be.'

3

'I hope you're going to get me out of here!'

A discreet black and white welcome sign saying Residential Children's Centre told us we were heading in the right direction, though the building itself was hidden behind a screen of trees beyond the car park. Wilf had told us to park up, head towards the main building and then carry on past it, following signs to the secure section of the centre beyond it, where Melissa was being kept.

I took a deep breath when the car stopped and Jonathan took the key from the ignition. I felt nervous but at the same time I was looking forward to finally meeting Melissa. It had been a long drive and we'd talked about nothing but fostering and training. Now it was time for action.

A wide, tree-lined path led us from the car park to a gravel driveway in front of what looked like a big, old house, and from there a signpost directed us down a narrow side passageway to the secure unit at the rear.

Jonathan and I exchanged glances when we saw it. In contrast to the main centre, which looked like it could have been a splendid country manor house in years gone by, the small, flat-roofed secure unit was built of drab concrete and steel and appeared more like a prison than part of any kind of children's centre. Detached from the main house, it was marooned in the centre of what looked like a piece of waste-land. In order to reach the entrance door we had to pass through a ring of security fencing topped with jagged razor wire. I started to feel quite daunted by what we were about to experience.

I pressed the door buzzer and took a deep breath. I was aware that my heart rate had increased and I wanted to calm myself. I stole a look at Jonathan. He was clenching his jaw, something he does when he's feeling anxious.

A very tall and stocky man in what looked like a prison guard's uniform appeared, bobbed his bald head in our direction by way of a greeting and took us silently into a small, stark reception room. We had our bags searched and had to show some ID, which Wilf had forewarned us about. Once the guard was happy that we were who we said we were, he instructed each of us to take a seat and wait while he fetched the duty manager. We did as we were told; it was not the sort of place where you felt inclined to do anything else.

The guard had a huge bunch of keys hanging from his belt. He unlocked a metal door leading out of the reception area, stepped through it purposefully on his heavy legs and locked it behind him, leaving Jonathan and me alone in what felt like a holding pen. I had an uneasy feeling, one that reminded me of how I sometimes feel when passing through customs or security at an airport. Uncomfortable and somewhat intimidated, I had a sense I might make a mistake and be reprimanded even though I knew I'd done nothing wrong.

It took five long minutes for the security guard to return with the duty manager, who was a slight man with a grey complexion, grey hair and wearing a grey suit.

'Pleased to meet you. I'm Mr Gray,' he said very seriously. I noticed he had an even larger bunch of keys hanging from his belt, some of which were so big they looked fake, like something you'd see in a Disney film when a princess is locked in a tower. I can remember being amused by the fact the duty manager's name matched his appearance and, unexpectedly, I found myself stifling a laugh. I think it was just nerves, because I'm not normally someone who gets the giggles. The atmosphere of the place had made me feel uncharacteristically edgy. I'd never been anywhere like this before. The closest I'd come to seeing the inside of any kind of secure institution was when I watched *One Flew Over the Cuckoo's Nest* and saw how the psychiatric ward was run, and my one and only insight into the prison system was from seeing every episode of *Porridge* on TV when it first came out, which I'd loved.

Mr Gray led us through one, two and then three locked doors into an oval-shaped hall area with a polished wooden block floor. Two members of staff in white tunics and black trousers were stationed at a central desk and Mr Gray went to speak to them.

'Melissa is in room four,' Mr Gray told us gravely. 'She

knows you're here. I understand that she may be going to live with you?'

'That's right,' Jonathan said, giving a friendly smile that was not reciprocated.

'I hope the meeting goes well. She's a pleasant girl, so I'm told.'

Mr Gray then introduced us to another colleague called Malcolm, who appeared from a corridor at the side. He had a spring in his step and a smile on his face, which I was relieved to see. Malcolm welcomed us enthusiastically and said he'd take us across to Melissa's room. Meanwhile, Mr Gray bade us goodbye and slipped off so quickly and quietly it felt as if he'd simply faded away.

About twenty secure single rooms surrounded the hall area and each had a large window in its door, giving a clear view into the room as you went by. We could see youths in jogging pants and sweatshirts stretched out on their beds as we walked past several rooms to reach number four. They all seemed to be around seventeen or eighteen. We sensed that some were watching us, no doubt more from boredom than curiosity, and we instinctively looked away, not wanting to invade their privacy.

'The unit is designed like this so we can see every aspect of the room from the outside,' Malcolm explained, no doubt realising this was an alien environment to us. 'It's a safety measure.'

'Of course.'

As we approached door number four I could see Melissa sitting on the floor, her back to the wall on the left-hand side of the room and her knees hugged to her chest. She had thick auburn hair that was bunched on one side in a loose ponytail. It dangled over her right shoulder and almost reached the floor, and she was chewing a strand of it absent-mindedly. I immediately thought she looked younger than twelve and my heart went out to her.

Melissa sprang to her feet when she spotted us approaching and she smiled as Malcolm opened the door.

'Hello,' I said. 'I'm Angela.' Jonathan introduced himself too.

'Hi! Nice to meet you,' Melissa grinned. 'I hope you're going to get me out of here!'

She then shot a look at Malcolm. 'No offence, but I can't wait to get out of this place.'

'None taken,' Malcolm said.

Melissa was a slim, long-legged and very pretty girl with dark green eyes and milky skin. She was wearing a pair of baggy white tracksuit bottoms and a pale pink sweatshirt with prints of white stars on it. Her features were fine and dainty, giving her an impish look. Her lips made a neat bow and I noticed her hands were tiny too, with slender fingers and the smallest fingernails painted with pink nail polish. But it was her hair that really stood out. When she was on her feet the rich, red ponytail reached her waist. It was such a striking feature I couldn't help complimenting her on it.

'Everyone goes on about my hair,' she said, rolling her eyes playfully, and quite proudly. 'The lads have nicknamed me Rapunzel but I've told them that if I was really Rapunzel

I wouldn't still be here, would I? A prince would have come to my rescue!'

We all laughed. Melissa intrigued me. If first impressions were anything to go by she seemed like a perfectly pleasant, happy-go-lucky young girl. It was hard to imagine her being a 'runner', as Wilf had called her, or the type of child a patient foster carer like Lynne would not be able to deal with any longer.

Malcolm suggested that as it was nearly lunchtime we could go to the canteen together.

'Sounds good to me,' Melissa said, pulling on a pair of trainers and fastening the Velcro. 'Do you know what's on the menu today, Malcolm?'

'I know there's chips on. I smelt them cooking. Not sure what else.'

She clapped her hands together. 'Good. That's all we need to know!'

'See him in the red shirt, he's a rapist,' Melissa said, moments after we'd sat at a Formica-topped table in the austere canteen. She nodded discreetly to the far end of the room. The boy looked no older than sixteen. He was rocking back in his chair, like he didn't have a care in the world. 'And that one – see him, there, with the skinhead? – he's due in court for assault and battery. Or was it grievous bodily harm? I'm not sure of the difference. Either way, he's a really bad lad. *Really* bad. Some are in here for drugs and stabbings. You'd never know it to look at them, would ya?'

She tucked into chips, sausage and beans while Jonathan

and I had jacket potatoes topped with tuna and cheese. Malcolm had brought his own packed lunch and he sat at the end of the bench, quietly doing a crossword while he ate, leaving us to chat and get to know each other.

Melissa told us that the wire fencing around the unit was specially designed to deter ram raiders, and that they had no wardrobes or closed cupboards in their rooms so that the staff could see into every nook and cranny from the window in the door, and nothing could be concealed. The only window was the one in the door and Melissa said that, in her opinion, the rooms might as well be called cells, as it was just like being in prison. 'Not that I've been in prison,' she added. 'I just don't get why anyone would be that stupid they'd end up in prison. I'm never going to prison, me. I'm never going to break the law. No chance. I can't imagine anything worse than being locked up somewhere even worse than this.'

A few lads came over and joined us at our table, nodding and saying 'all right' as they sat down with their trays of food.

'I'm just saying what people are in here for,' Melissa said confidently. 'What was it you did, Baz? It was a robbery, wasn't it?'

'Aye. Not just any robbery though, our kid. Armed robbery. We'd have fuckin' got away with it if it weren't for an off-duty copper. I'm a fuckin' bank robber, me! I don't do things by half!' He banged the table with his fist and the lad next to him slapped his back and whooped.

Melissa didn't seem intimidated or alarmed at all. She shrugged and looked at us slightly apologetically, as if embarrassed by the boy's language and misplaced pride in his criminal behaviour. How incongruous she looked. *A rose among thorns,* I thought. It was as if she read my mind.

'You see, I don't really think I fit in here,' she said, leading in to us conspiratorially so the boys couldn't hear. 'I don't think I should be here. Apart from anything else, I'm the only girl. I mean, I've got on all right with the lads, don't get me wrong, but I don't need to be locked up. I'm not a criminal.'

I caught Jonathan's eye and knew he was supportive of what I was about to say. Having seen this set-up and the types of boys she was living alongside, there was no way we were not going to offer her a home.

'We know you ran off from your last foster carer's and the police brought you here. It was a last resort and we know you aren't a criminal, we understand that. If you're happy to, you can come and stay with us, until Social Services finds you somewhere more permanent.'

She smiled and her eyes lit up. 'Yeah, thanks, I'd like to. You seem really nice people. I can't stay here. They're real bad lads, I mean *proper* bad boys. Fancy the police picking me up for hanging round with my mates and then putting me in here with this lot? They said my mates were bad, but they're not like these. You couldn't make it up really. "Oh here you go, we'll take care of you, Melissa, by locking you up with a load of violent lads. Aren't we doing a good service for the community, keeping you away from all those boys who are a bad influence on you!"'

She didn't really seem angry or bitter. If anything she was

poking fun at her situation. We didn't join in with this. We didn't know enough about her story to be able to make any comment, and we didn't want to encourage her to criticise the police or any of the authorities.

We spent another hour or so with Melissa after lunch, sitting in a lounge area just off the main hall. We'd taken along a scrapbook we'd made, to show her our home and some of our family photographs. She took her time looking through it, making polite remarks and asking questions. We told her we'd just said goodbye to a teenage boy we'd had staying with us for a short time and that the house was empty at the moment, which was unusual. She asked about my mother, who featured in several of the photographs, and I said her name was Thelma and she'd been passed by Social Services as a babysitter, and that she loved meeting all of the children who stayed with us.

There was a recent picture I'd taken of the shop and I explained how it had been a family business, on my side of the family, for many years. After my father died in the mid-eighties my mother ran it on her own for a while before passing it down to us, and now we lived in the attached town house, I told her.

Melissa asked why we didn't have children of our own and I told her it just hadn't happened for us yet, but we hoped one day we might be lucky. We were still in our thirties, and though it never actually did happen, at that point we still thought we might become parents. 'You'll be experts before you even have your own,' she laughed.

'We love fostering and we've looked after some smashing

children,' Jonathan told her. 'You might meet one or two of them as we do try to keep in touch. Vicky was with us for about three years. She's seventeen now and has her own flat, but she comes round for her tea quite often.'

'Cool. I wish I was old enough to live in my own flat. That would solve a lot of problems for everyone!'

She chuckled to herself. 'I think you're very kind people,' she said. 'Thanks for taking me in and getting me out of this place.' She smiled very sweetly and seemed genuinely appreciative.

Melissa moved in with us two days later. Jonathan and I still had our concerns about how the placement would work out, but she fundamentally seemed like a decent, pleasant girl who had strayed off the rails - maybe through no fault of her own - and needed all the help we could give her to set her on the right track again. Though her stay in the secure unit should never have happened, Jonathan and I both hoped that some good might have come of it. Maybe it had shown her how things can spiral downwards if you're not careful, and hopefully it would encourage her to stop running away. It had certainly put her off going to prison.

When she arrived at our door, having been picked up and driven to our home by a support worker, Melissa was wearing the same pair of tracksuit bottoms and sweatshirt we'd seen her in, and she was carrying a large duffel bag stuffed with belongings. I showed her up to her room on the top floor straight away.

'A window to look out of!' she exclaimed excitedly, admiring the view over the playing fields at the back of our house. 'That was one thing I really hated in the unit. Those spy windows. Gave me the creeps. I didn't sleep much in there.'

Melissa tested out the bed and declared it was 'bliss' compared to the metal-framed bunk she'd spent the last few nights in.

'Thanks for having me,' she said. 'It's very kind of you.'

'We're very pleased to have you here. Now then, is there anything you don't like to eat?'

'No, I like everything. What are we having for tea?'

'I've got some fish fillets.'

'Can we have them with chips?'

I smiled. Chips were obviously her favourite. I was planning to bake the fish and do mashed potato but I could just as easily fry the fish in batter, which I thought she'd prefer, and make some homemade chips.

'Why not? And do you like mushy peas?'

'I love them!'

We enjoyed eating with Melissa. The conversation flowed easily. She chatted about how she was hoping she could move in with one of her aunties – Auntie Cathy – when she left foster care for good and said she was looking forward to going back to school. It's always slightly awkward when a child has only just arrived and you don't have much background information on them. I wanted to ask Melissa what had happened to her mum and dad, and why she didn't live with them, but as always I had to stick to what I'd been trained to do and wait for Melissa to volunteer information. Even when she mentioned her auntie and school I had to watch how I replied, as I didn't want to pry or ask any leading questions, in case I opened a can of worms that she wasn't ready to deal with.

'Will it be OK if I see my friends while I'm staying here? I've stayed with some other foster families around here, you see. I've got quite a few friends in the neighbourhood.' We knew about her stay with Lynne, of course, but we knew nothing about her previous foster home or homes. All we knew was that she'd been with Lynne for about a month, and in foster care for approximately a year in total.

I told Melissa I knew Lynne, though I kept quiet about the fact we attended support meetings with her and had been privy to what had gone on during Melissa's placement. It was unusual to know so much about another carer's foster child. Lynne had done nothing wrong – everything that was said at the support meetings was in the strictest confidence and stayed within the group – but I didn't want Melissa to feel her privacy had been invaded in any way.

Melissa explained where her home town was, which was more than an hour away by car. I wondered if she'd been moved out of her own area for a specific reason, or simply because there was a shortage of foster carers, and particularly specialist carers, where she came from, given that Social Services generally try to keep children in their local area if possible.

Earlier on I'd seen Wilf and briefly met Melissa's social worker, Doreen. They did a routine handover shortly after Melissa arrived. We filled in all the usual paperwork, but neither social worker gave me any further information on Melissa's history. I got the impression they were both mightily relieved to have moved Melissa in with us, and who could blame them? Signing off the placement as swiftly as possible was uppermost in their minds.

The one thing Wilf did make time for was to discuss the fact that, despite Melissa's history of running off, we could not keep her in the house against her will. All we could do was talk to her about sticking to our rules, ask her to be respectful, try to get her on our side and hope for the best. If she was late coming back and we became worried about her whereabouts, we were to report her missing to Social Services. If it was daytime we were advised to wait two hours before calling the office. If it was after 5 p.m. we had to call the out-of-hours team – at night, when it was dark, we were only to wait an hour before phoning in if we became worried, and the emergency social worker would log it and most likely advise us to call the police straight away.

Doreen told us Melissa had a support worker called Elaine who would be in touch. I was given her number and told to expect a call. Her role was primarily to transport Melissa to and from her home town and family. She'd known Melissa throughout her time in care, and I said I was looking forward to speaking to her.

'I'm so grateful to you and Jonathan – this is a huge weight off my shoulders,' Wilf said, thanking me once again as I saw him out. When Melissa was out of earshot he whispered, 'I wanted to do a cartwheel in the office when

I heard you were happy to have her! Thank God she's out of that unit. Totally unsuitable for her. Thank you again. Must dash but I'll be in touch.'

Doreen rushed off too, talking about how busy she was and how ridiculously large her caseload was. 'Good luck. I hope she behaves,' were her parting words, spoken rather witheringly. I got the impression Doreen did not have a huge amount of confidence in Melissa's ability to stay on the straight and narrow.

I asked Melissa whereabouts her friends lived in the neighbourhood and she told me one of them was the daughter of one of her former carers. When she told me their names – the mother was called Anne-Marie and the daughter was Imogen – I realised I knew who they were. The family had been coming in the shop for years and I'd spoken to Anne-Marie about fostering several times when we discovered we were both carers. Her daughter, it turned out, was exactly the same age as Melissa and they'd been in the same class at school for a while, the previous year.

I agreed that Melissa could go and visit Imogen, who lived within walking distance of our house.

'Am I allowed to use your phone?'

'Of course. Help yourself. There's one just there, I'll show you how it works.'

Moments later I heard Melissa excitedly talking to her friend. 'Great, isn't it? Yes, I'm literally round the corner. See you soon!'

Before Melissa went out I asked her to pose for an instant photo.

'I hate having my picture taken. What d'you want one for?'

'We always like to have a photo of every child who stays with us. I keep them all in an album, a bit like the one I brought to show you at the unit.'

'I didn't see any pictures of other kids.'

'No, and I wouldn't show your picture to other children either. It's just for us.'

This was only partly true. In fact, Wilf had advised us to take a photo in case Melissa went missing and we needed to show it to the police.

She pulled a face but then agreed to smile for the camera. She had small dimples in her cheeks, I noticed, and as I pressed the button I told her she looked really great and it would make a lovely, happy picture.

'It'll be developed in a minute or two,' I said.

'Really? I've never seen one of those cameras before.'

The picture popped out and Melissa said she was surprised how good it was. 'I quite like that,' she said.

'You should. You look really lovely.'

As she was leaving the house I asked Melissa to pass on a little note and my phone number to Anne-Marie and ask her to give me a call, having explained that I knew her and we hadn't spoken in a while. In reality we rarely spoke and didn't know each other well, but I thought it would be wise to keep the channels of communication open. Most of all I wanted to make sure Melissa was doing as she'd said, and actually going to visit Imogen.

'No problem!' she said breezily.

Melissa went out at 7.20 p.m. and I asked her to be home by 9 p.m. and no later. It was a very dark night so I asked if she wanted Jonathan and me to walk with her. Not surprisingly she baulked at that suggestion, albeit politely.

'I'm not scared of the dark! It's only five minutes away anyhow. I'll be fine. See you later! I'll be on time, I promise.'

The route she would take was well lit with streetlights and I told myself not to worry. Allowing a twelve-year-old out alone at this time of night in the winter was not something I liked to do, but from experience I knew Social Services would endorse this, and Wilf had made clear that they would not support me keeping her in against her will.

Jonathan and I had both had a word with Melissa about our house rules, explaining they were there for her benefit. We asked for politeness and punctuality and told her firmly but kindly that she could see her friends provided she stuck to the times we agreed and always let us know where she was, and who she was seeing. I told her that 9 p.m. would always be the latest she was allowed out alone and she seemed perfectly accepting of this.

'Fair enough,' she said. 'Thanks!'

I wondered if we were being duped by her pleasant, amenable manner. We'd have been fools not to think that, despite her promise, which seemed genuine, she might come back late or even go missing. Nevertheless, we had to let her go and hope for the best.

Jonathan and I stood at the door together, watching Melissa walk away. She was whistling happily – I remembered how this whistling had grated on Lynne when she caught Melissa walking off into the night – and now there was a jaunty spring in her step. 'You've got our number,' I called after her. 'Ring if there's any problem. And don't forget to give my note to Anne-Marie!'

'OK! Bye! Have a good evening! Go in and shut the door, it's freezing!'

Jonathan and I sat in the lounge, warming ourselves in front of the gas fire. 'It's hard to believe she's the same girl Lynne described,' Jonathan said.

'I know. She seems absolutely lovely. Mind you, Lynne did say she was a nice girl . . .' I paused and Jonathan and I both said at the same time, 'when she wasn't running away.'

I wrung my hands and questioned how we were going to cope if, and most likely when, she got up to her old tricks.

'We can't think like that,' Jonathan said. 'We can only deal in the here and now. Our house is a home, not a detention centre. We can only do our best.'

4

'My stepdad was a scumbag'

'Angela? It's Anne-Marie. I got your note.'

My heart was in my mouth and I realised how tense I was.

'Thanks for calling. Is everything OK?'

There was a pause. 'There's nothing to worry about. The girls are together and they've gone to the corner shop. Melissa told me she's only just arrived at yours and I guess you'd like to hear how she got on when she was staying with us?'

'Yes, today's the first day of her placement. She's with us for five weeks, as far as we know. I've only just found out she lived with you before.'

Anne-Marie gave me a potted history of Melissa's stay. It was the previous year, when she was eleven going on twelve, and she stayed for about six months.

'Everything was fine until she got a boyfriend and wanted to be out with him all the time,' Anne-Marie said. 'She wasn't running away, but she started coming back later and later and she also began smoking and drinking, or at least experimenting with both.'

'I see.'

'We never met the boyfriend,' Anne-Marie went on. 'He wouldn't come to the house, she always went out to meet him. There was a gang of them who all hung around together, and I know some were a few years older. I wasn't happy about this, but you know what it's like. I couldn't stop her seeing her friends, or boyfriend. All I could do was try to talk sense into her, which mostly I did. She was never missing long enough for me to call the police and thankfully she didn't get Imogen involved, not for a long time, anyhow. Imogen was heavily into her dancing and was out every night rehearsing.'

Anne-Marie explained that the placement started to break down after Melissa was caught smuggling alcohol into her bedroom. She said she'd been given it by her boyfriend and then Imogen confessed she had had a drink of vodka with Melissa when they had walked to a youth club disco together one Friday night. Things quickly unravelled when Imogen started seeing a friend of Melissa's boyfriend. 'I said I wanted to meet Imogen's new boyfriend or they couldn't go out but the girls said it was "babyish" to do this. I grounded them both. Imogen accepted it but Melissa didn't. She complained to her social worker and after that the placement broke down completely and she asked to be moved. She was a good kid, but very easily influenced by that gang of friends she had. I didn't want her dragging Imogen into any more trouble and I agreed it was best for Melissa to move on.'

Anne-Marie said Melissa and Imogen had kept in touch on and off. She told me she wasn't very happy about this but she trusted her daughter not to get involved with Melissa's crowd of 'undesirables,' as she called them. Anne-Marie reassured me she had given the girls the 'witches' warning' to come straight home from the shop tonight.

'Imogen's got her head screwed on now. I know she won't do anything daft. She has a lovely new boyfriend and she's not interested in that gang, thank God. I hope Melissa isn't still in with them. Oh, I can hear the girls coming in. I'll get off the phone and I'll make sure I send Melissa back on time. Good luck, Angela.'

The line went dead. I sensed that Anne-Marie felt a bit sorry for me for having been landed with Melissa, but she was older now – just like Imogen – and hopefully a bit wiser too.

Jonathan and I had looked after kids who'd dabbled with cigarettes and alcohol before, and having boyfriends, pushing the boundaries and finding out who your friends were, and who to trust, was all part of growing up, wasn't it? *I'll just have to be extra vigilant,* I thought. At least I was forewarned; I'd never had access to so much information from previous foster carers before, and it was extremely useful.

Melissa returned home on the dot of 9 p.m. She was in a chatty mood and accepted my offer of a cup of tea. Jonathan was watching something on TV and Melissa and I sat in the kitchen together.

'Did you have a good time?'

'Yeah. I like Imogen, but I know her mum isn't keen on me.'

'Anne-Marie isn't keen on you?'

'No, I guess she must have told you about that stuff with the drink? I didn't want to get Imogen into trouble or anything. I didn't think Anne-Marie would go mental like she did. It was only a sip of vodka, it's not like we were drunk or anything.'

I gently made a point about the fact the girls were only twelve at the time of the incident. I didn't want to come across as too judgemental in case I put Melissa off talking, so I stuck to the facts and reminded her that it was illegal for children to drink alcohol.

'I know, but it's no big deal, is it? I've been having a drink and smoking since I was a lot younger.'

She held my gaze and I could tell Melissa wanted to get something off her chest. I stood up to put the kettle on again, as I've often noticed that children find it easier to talk when you are pottering around and not looking them in the eye.

'You've been having a drink and smoking since you were a lot younger?'

She nodded and let out a long, care-worn sigh.

'My stepdad was a scumbag. When Mum was at work he had his mates around all the time. I'd get in from school to find men passed out drunk on the floor. There'd be fag ends and empty cans and bottles all over the place. The whole flat stank of booze and smoke. He told me and my stepsister we could have a drink and a fag if we didn't tell Mum about his parties and helped him clear up.'

'Melissa, I'm sorry to hear that. It must have been difficult for you.' I kept my tone calm and was careful not to be drawn into passing comment on her stepfather. Even when children volunteer to talk frankly and make stinging criticisms of their family like this, it's never a good idea to join in, or even assume their story is true. You have to just listen and show support in an impartial way, and try to create an environment in which they feel able to disclose whatever they want to.

'Yeah, it wasn't a good situation. He abused one of my little cousins and after that we found out he'd been in prison for being in some weird sex gang. My mum had a breakdown. She totally lost the plot. She lives in Australia with my nan now. He's back in prison.'

'I really am very sorry to hear this.'

'It's all right. It's in the past now. He got a long sentence. It's over. I hope he never gets out.'

Though it's impossible to be sure, my gut instinct was that Melissa was telling the truth. She spoke calmly and quite dispassionately, whereas I've noticed that children who are inventing tales are more inclined to inject drama and outrage into their storytelling. That's a generalisation, of course, but more often than not I've found it to be an accurate observation.

Before Melissa went to bed, she asked if she could use the phone to call her boyfriend. I was concerned this might be the same boy she used to see when she lived with Anne-Marie, or another member of that gang, and I was worried she might be plotting a night-time flit. I suggested it was a bit late.

'I'll only be a few minutes, please can I? I promised him I would ring today.'

'I'd rather you left it until the morning.'

'But I promised I'd call today and let him know I was OK. Please?'

She gave the sweetest smile and I reluctantly agreed she could make a brief call. It was the days before mobile phones, and she slipped out of the kitchen to make the call from the landline in the hallway. True to her word, she was only on the phone for a few minutes.

'Everything OK?'

'Yeah. He's fed up in there so I think I cheered him up!'

'In where?'

'The unit.'

Without prompting, Melissa explained that she used to go out with this boy, Oz, several months earlier. It was a coincidence they'd ended up in the same children's unit, where she'd been locked up. She said he'd done nothing wrong and, like her, he would be out of there soon. Without pausing for breath she then went on to tell me she had another boyfriend in the unit, Degsy. This perplexed me as she'd only been in there for a few days. I didn't hide how I felt and I frowned to show my concern and confusion.

'It's OK, he's not really my boyfriend, but he sort of was in there. I like them both. Don't look so worried – it's nothing serious! I know how to handle myself. I'm off to bed now, night!'

She tripped up the stairs, whistling as she went, like she didn't have a care in the world.

*

After Melissa had gone up the stairs I put everything she'd said into my notes for Social Services, which I'd pass on to Wilf. He would then hand over any relevant information to Melissa's own social worker, Doreen, or I'd tell her myself if she phoned us first, or paid a visit. It was second nature to me by now to scribble out notes. Any information that may be important to Social Services in dealing with a child's case has to be shared, and I always wrote important conversations down as soon as possible afterwards, so I could remember as much detail as possible. I still do that to this day.

Jonathan joined me in the kitchen and I brought him up to speed. 'Poor girl,' he said. 'If all that's true about her childhood it's remarkable she's such an upbeat character.'

We spoke in whispers, even though Melissa's bedroom was on the top floor and we were on the ground level. This was instinctive, as we'd had instances where kids had appeared, as if by magic, at the door, having come down for a glass of water then started wandering around or, in some cases, because they were deliberately trying to eavesdrop. The layout of the house did generally work in our favour, however, with all the kids' bedrooms out of earshot at the top.

Jonathan read my mind, as he often does. 'How worried are you that she'll try to sneak out tonight?'

I knew it was not beyond the realms of possibility but I really couldn't imagine that she would try it, at least not on this first night. We'd sat together for about an hour in the kitchen, drinking tea, and I'd listened to her talk very frankly.

It was extremely hard to imagine she would suddenly turn from being a polite, open and apparently honest girl into a reckless runaway, even if she had just made contact with this boyfriend from the unit.

'No, I don't think she will run away tonight,' I said. 'But please don't quote me on that.'

I didn't sleep well. Melissa's bedroom was directly above ours and every creak and movement put me on my guard. After a restless night I woke with a jolt early the next morning when the heating started to come on. The sound of the pipes groaning into action made me jump. I felt like I'd barely slept a wink and my head was aching. Jonathan's generally a better sleeper than me but he'd also been awake several times in the night, sitting bolt upright in bed, straining his ears to work out if the sounds of the house might be Melissa's footsteps on the stairs or the turn of a key in the door.

I'd shown Melissa where we kept the keys to the front and back door. I had to do this so she knew how to get out in case of emergency. I could see how tempting it might be to hide them, to stop her getting up to her old habits, but of course we could never do that. It would be a fire hazard and we'd be opening ourselves up to accusations of safeguarding malpractice, or possibly even false imprisonment. We also had locks on all the windows, but again there were keys at hand and I had shown Melissa where we kept them, just as I did with every child when they first arrived, when I gave them a tour of the house. I'd also talked about the best escape route from the house in case of fire, as this was another part of our standard safety routine whenever a new child moved in.

I put on my dressing gown and slippers and headed downstairs to put the kettle on. It was too early to wake Melissa, though I desperately wanted to go up to her bedroom and check she was still there. When I reached the hallway I was relieved to see her trainers were where she had left them the night before, and the front and back doors were still locked.

We'd survived one night. I slumped into a chair at the kitchen table, feeling shattered and wondering how on earth we were going to cope like this for five weeks.

5

'She's not welcome here'

Once Melissa was up I offered to take her shopping in town and she jumped at the chance. She'd brought plenty of things with her, including her school uniform, but nothing was in great condition and she didn't own a pair of slippers, pyjamas or a dressing gown. She told me she always slept in her tracksuit bottoms and T-shirts. I wanted to question this, as I was certain her former foster carers would have made sure she had a nightie or pyjamas, but I didn't want to seem nosy, or critical of anybody. Also, as I'd learned on my training, children may do things that remind them of home. There may be a sensitive reason behind their behaviour or habits, and to question them may upset them unnecessarily. Not wearing night clothes could have stemmed back to when Melissa lived at home, so I kept quiet.

'I love shopping for tracksuits,' Melissa said enthusiastically as she crunched on a large bowl of cereal. 'I like Adidas and Puma, they're my favourite brands. I like shell suits too, in any colour.'

I told her she didn't have to stick with tracksuits and shell suits but she said she didn't feel comfortable in anything else, and the baggier the better. Again I didn't judge or question her and besides, whatever she wore, I noticed that Melissa managed to look good. Her mane of red hair looked stunning even when it hadn't been brushed and was hanging like a shawl around her shoulders, as it was now. *Oh to be young!* I thought.

She said she'd have a quick shower and be ready 'in a jiffy' and I laughed and told her I'd be a bit longer than that, as I needed to wash my hair and put a bit of make-up on in order to make myself look 'presentable'. She giggled and told me she thought I looked great as I was, which made my morning. I felt like I'd been dragged through a hedge backwards and was sure I must have huge bags under my eyes after such a disrupted night's sleep.

We drove the short distance into town, as it was bitterly cold. Melissa wore a large puffa jacket but refused to wear a hat or gloves. She didn't own either but I offered her some of mine, which horrified her. 'What if I saw one of my boyfriends and I was in one of your bobble hats!' she laughed. 'I'd never be able to live it down!'

'One of your boyfriends?'

From what Melissa had told me, I understood that the two boys she'd mentioned – Oz and Degsy – were still in the unit.

'Yeah, I've got a boyfriend called TJ. He's my *proper* boyfriend.'

'I see.' I raised my eyebrows expectantly, hoping she'd tell me more. She was a sharp and perceptive girl. It was obvious I was all ears but Melissa shrugged and said, 'I don't know what I can tell you about him really.'

'Is TJ his nickname? Does he have another name?'

She furrowed her brow and thought about this for a moment. 'I'm not sure. Everyone just calls him TJ. Anyway, can we go in that big sports shop at the top of the high street?'

'Yes we can.'

'Good. I love it in there. I'd like to get a job there when I'm fourteen. You get a staff discount.'

Melissa began telling me about some of the jobs her friends had. One worked in a sweet shop, another had a job at a riding school. An older boy worked in a local taxi rank and another in a kebab shop. 'They earn the most,' she said. 'You get more when you're older.'

'How old are they?'

'Fifteen or sixteen.'

Melissa was nearly thirteen – her birthday was in a couple of months – so I tried to reason that it wasn't surprising she hung around with boys who were a few years older. I wondered if they were part of the gang she ran off with, and I made a mental note to listen out for any more information I could get on the boys, or any other of her friends or boyfriends for that matter, in case Melissa went missing again.

*

When we got home from town there was a message on the answerphone from Anne-Marie. She sounded cross and asked me to call her back as soon as possible.

'Any idea what that's about?' I asked Melissa, as she was standing next to me when I played the message.

'No idea. I'm gonna try my new stuff on. Thanks for everything, it's really kind.'

I'd bought Melissa a couple of new tracksuits, some underwear and slippers and a man-size T-shirt to wear in bed. She picked that out when I gently nudged her towards the nightwear section, telling me she'd wear it with her tracksuit bottoms underneath.

Melissa scooted upstairs with her shopping bags and I dialled Anne-Marie's number.

'I'm afraid I can't have Melissa seeing Imogen again. She's not welcome here.'

'Whatever's happened?'

'Last night, she gave Imogen a packet of condoms. My daughter is twelve years old! I know Melissa hangs around with some older boys and I don't want Imogen mixing with that lot. I think you need to really watch her, Angela. She knows how to act all sweet and innocent, but God only knows what she gets up to with those kids from the estate. There's some bad pennies in amongst that lot. Imogen said they turned up at the corner shop last night. One of them was bragging about getting questioned by the police about something, and another one said he was on bail for a stabbing.'

My heart sank. It was one thing Melissa associating with

the law-breaking youths in the secure unit, but out on the streets was quite another. I thanked Anne-Marie for tipping me off and assured her I would explain to Melissa that she wasn't allowed to see Imogen. If she turned up at the house, Imogen would not be allowed to let her in or go out with her. Anne-Marie was very firm about this, and she said Melissa was not to phone either. I said I understood and we said goodbye amicably. Anne-Marie's parting words were, 'I'm glad you haven't got any other kids with you, Angela.'

I called up to Melissa, saying I wanted a word, and she bounded down the stairs like an excited puppy, all legs and elbows, sporting one of her new tracksuits.

'What do you think?'

She gave a twirl and I said she looked very good in it. Then I sat her down in the kitchen and told her straight what Anne-Marie had said.

'What's her problem?' Melissa scowled, looking genuinely perplexed. 'I mean, we were only *talking* to the boys.'

'So why the condoms?'

'Oh that, yeah, that was just a joke. One of the lads was mucking about with them. We were all chucking them at each other. Imogen ended up with them, that's all. I don't know why she took them home. She should have just thrown them away.'

'Melissa, are you involved with these older boys?'

'Involved? Do you mean having sex with them?'

I wouldn't have put it to her as bluntly as that, but I was glad she wasn't afraid to discuss things so frankly.

'Yes, I suppose that's what I do mean. Or doing anything else you shouldn't?'

'No. Absolutely not. I can't believe you've even asked me that. I'm only twelve! And they're dickheads anyway. Sorry, I mean idiots. Sorry to use bad language. I wouldn't touch them with a bargepole, not like that.'

She sounded like she was telling the truth.

'What about drinking and smoking? I know you've done both in the past, but what about now?'

'I sometimes drink a little bit of cider or have a drag on a fag. I won't lie to you. Everyone does it. I've tried a bit of pot too, but I don't like it. Drugs scare me. I'd never get mixed up in anything like that. Heroin *terrifies* me. They say you take it once and you're hooked for life. It's a loser's game. No, I'd never ever be daft enough to do that.'

I listened and didn't pass any judgement or show any shock. Instead, I talked matter-of-factly to Melissa, starting with our rules on smoking. We knew that some foster carers allowed kids to smoke in the house because they were addicted and were going to smoke anyhow, but we never did. Our way of handling this has always been to talk to them about the dangers of smoking and how addictive it is. We accepted we couldn't stop them smoking outside the house, but we hoped our stance discouraged their habit. Jonathan and I had both smoked when we were younger and found it very hard to give up, and the fact we had first-hand experience sometimes helped us get through to the kids, though not always.

Melissa's response was, 'I know you're right but it's hard

when you've been smoking since you were a kid.' I suspected Melissa was a regular smoker now, not just a girl who sometimes had a 'drag on a fag,' as she'd said.

I went on to talk about how alcohol was very damaging to health and could lead to inappropriate or dangerous behaviour, and how cannabis could be a 'gateway' drug, leading to harder substances.

'You don't have to worry about me, you know. I can handle myself.'

That evening Melissa asked if she could go and meet her boyfriend TJ.

'I'd like to meet him,' I said.

She laughed and asked me why.

'He's your boyfriend, and I always like to get to know the friends and boyfriends of anyone who stays here. Why don't you ask him to come here, and I can say hello?'

'You just want to check him over, see if he's all right, don't you?' she said cheekily.

'I have to be honest, that's part of it. I care about you, Melissa, and I want to know who you're with and make sure you are safe.'

'OK, I'll see what he says. Will that mean I can stay out later, if he's taking care of me?'

'No, it doesn't! You still have to be in by nine. But if you think about it, if he's collecting you and bringing you home, you'll get more time with him, won't you?'

She accepted this with a smile and asked me if she could ring him.

'Yes. Help yourself, you know where the phone is.'

Melissa picked it up in the kitchen, where we were both standing, and dialled a six-digit local number from memory.

'Is TJ there?'

There was a pause and she put her hand over the receiver and whispered, 'He's in the back of the shop.'

I nodded and then Melissa spoke down the phone again. 'TJ, listen, you know I'm in a new foster home? My foster mum wants to meet you, and if you come and pick me up we'll get a bit longer together, won't we? She's really lovely. Her name's Angela.'

There was a bit of a pause but he obviously agreed to this and she went on to give TJ our address.

'See ya later!' Melissa said excitedly, ending the call. She looked thrilled to bits. 'He's going to pick me up,' she said.

'Pick you up? You mean he can drive? How old is he?'

'Oh, he's seventeen. He's just passed his test. How cool is that?'

'Seventeen?' I said. 'But you are only twelve.'

'Yeah, but I'm nearly thirteen and he's only just turned seventeen, so it's not that much of a difference, is it? He passed his test first time. Some of my friends go out with even older boys. We can't help it if they like us, can we?'

Melissa looked proud of herself for being popular with the older boys. 'The lads our age are all nerds. I wouldn't be seen dead hanging around with most of them.'

Obviously, this information would go in my notes. I had never dealt with a scenario like this before and I wanted to be sure Social Services knew precisely what was going on. Again, I think Melissa read my mind.

'You don't need to worry,' she said. 'I don't *do* anything. I'm not like that.'

The way she spoke was quite childish and incongruous; the tone she used would have been more fitting had she been accused of stealing sweets from the tuck shop.

'Anyway, can I go to the toilet now please? I think I'm going to wee myself if I don't go now.'

'Yes, Melissa. You don't need to ask if you can go to the toilet.'

'Oh yeah, I forgot. Thanks!'

With that she bounded up the stairs two at a time, her shock of red hair flowing behind her.

Melissa ate a good meal that evening and once again Jonathan and I enjoyed her company around the dinner table. She talked about which bands she liked and said she wanted to work with children when she was older.

'I love babies and little children the best. They're so cute. I'd love to just cuddle them and play with them all day. It must be the best job in the world.'

She had a lot to learn, I thought, but now wasn't the best time to talk to her about the realities of a career in childcare. Instead I gently said, 'It's good you have an idea what you want to do. Lots of people haven't got a clue, even when they're a lot older than you. You're in a good position, and you've got plenty of time to find out more about the jobs available, and to make your mind up about exactly what you want to do.'

Melissa had missed quite a lot of schooling over the past few months. Social Services had arranged a meeting with the head teacher at the mixed comprehensive school she attended and we were hoping they would work out a 'reintegration strategy' for her return. Jonathan and I hadn't been provided with any further details at this stage and we didn't know exactly how much school Melissa had missed.

'I want to go to college and do a childcare course,' she went on. 'That's my plan. Mind you, that's if they ever let me back in school.'

I told Melissa I'd ask Wilf for an update on the school situation and asked her if she had been given any work to do at home. She said she had some projects from her history and geography teachers to be getting on with, and I told her I'd help her to get organised and set aside some study hours in the day. She happily agreed, telling me she enjoyed history the best.

After dinner Melissa helped us to clear up and went to her room until 7 p.m., the time TJ was collecting her. When the doorbell rang she raced down the stairs at breakneck speed. Jonathan and I arrived in the hallway just as she threw the door open.

'All right!' TJ said, giving her a wink. He was dressed in jeans, a black bomber jacket and a back-to-front baseball cap. In one ear he had a diamond stud earring and he was wearing several large, gold sovereign rings. His complexion was spotty and he had the faintest moustache of baby-fine hair. My overall impression was that TJ looked young for his age – more like fifteen than a boy who had just turned seventeen.

'Step in a minute, it's cold,' Melissa told him. She was beaming and clearly excited to see him. 'This is Angela, and this is Jonathan. They are my foster carers.'

'Very nice to meet ya both,' he said, shaking our hands.

'And you.'

Jonathan, being interested in anything to do with cars, congratulated TJ on passing his test and asked what he was driving. TJ explained he was using a van that belonged to his boss at the takeaway he worked at and dismissed it as 'just an old Ford.'

'Oh well,' Jonathan said. 'You've got to start somewhere. The only thing I got to drive at your age was a tractor on my parents' farm.'

'That sounds wicked.'

'Not really, I used to crash into things all the time as my eyesight was terrible. I hope you're a better driver than I used to be.'

'You don't need to worry on that score. I'll take good care of Melissa. I'm no boy racer or anything.'

TJ took Melissa's hand in his and she grinned from ear to ear. She was still in her new tracksuit and had brushed her hair, tied it in a high ponytail and put on a pair of hooped earrings. I imagined she felt very grown up, although she still looked incredibly young to me.

'Right, we'll be off then,' she said. 'See you at nine thirty.'

'Nice try,' Jonathan smiled. 'Nine. On the dot. See you later.'

I closed the door and Jonathan and I gave each other a look of resignation. This was not ideal, but what could we do? Our job was to offer Melissa a home and do our best to prevent her from running away and going missing with unidentified 'undesirables'. We were bound by Social Services guidelines. We couldn't keep her in the house all the time, but perhaps if we gave her a certain amount of freedom and treated her and her boyfriend with respect, she'd be more likely to respect us, and less likely to do a runner. At least TJ seemed to be a young seventeen, I reasoned, but I still felt very uncomfortable about the situation.

'I'm going to call Wilf first thing tomorrow and tell him how old TJ is,' I told Jonathan.

I wanted to tell Social Services immediately, but I wasn't sure the social worker manning the out-of-hours phone line would appreciate me calling with this information. It wasn't an emergency, or at least I sincerely hoped it wasn't. What could the duty social worker do about it at a time like this? I desperately wanted to pass this information on, but I was resigned to the fact it was best to wait until I could speak to Wilf the next day.

6

'It's nice of you to care so much'

Melissa returned at the stroke of nine. I heard the car door slam and her cry of 'See ya!' and when I opened the front door she bounced into the hallway, complaining about the biting cold night.

'Brrrr, I'm frozen to the bone,' she said. 'Can I have a cup of tea? I need warming up.'

I already had the kettle on and she went and stood next to the radiator in the kitchen while I made the tea. I noticed she looked a bit dishevelled, as her ponytail had come loose and she'd spilt something down the front of her tracksuit top. It looked like food.

'How was it?'

'Great. We went to meet TJ's brother and his mate, and a couple of my friends were at the takeaway. We got free food, how cool is that? I was allowed whatever I wanted. I had burger and chips and it was lovely.'

I wondered where she put it all, as she'd eaten a good

meal earlier on. She suddenly hiccupped, and at that point I detected the smell of alcohol on her breath.

'I can see you've had some food – have you spilt something on your top?'

She looked down and said it was ketchup. 'I thought I'd got it off.'

'And have you had anything to drink?'

'A coke.'

'Just a coke?' I raised my eyebrows expectantly.

'And a teeny-weeny vodka. Only one.'

I told her I appreciated the fact she was being honest with me but disappointed she had done this. Once again I spoke about the health dangers of alcohol, and especially of drinking something as strong as vodka at her age. She listened politely, said sorry and helped me finish making the tea. 'I didn't think you'd be bothered. It's nice of you to care so much.'

'Of course I'm bothered and of course I care. You're a lovely girl and I want you to be safe and healthy. I care very much about you.'

'Thanks. I'm going to ask for a new Care Bear for my birthday and I'm going to give it the nickname Angela.'

She sat at the kitchen table drinking her tea and telling me about the collection of Care Bears she used to own when she was a much younger girl. She had Friend Bear – 'my all-time favourite because it was orange, my favourite colour when I was little,' Love-a-Lot Bear – 'the first one I owned and I hugged it so much it got squished,' Wish Bear – 'my mum bought me that when I had to go in hospital' and Bedtime Bear – 'I refused to go to sleep without him – ha ha!' Her eyes shone as she described her collection. 'Friend Bear had flowers for her symbol. I love flowers. You're so lucky to have a flower shop.'

'Do you know what sort of flowers they were?' I was familiar with the Care Bear characters as they were incredibly popular in the eighties and nineties, and we'd had quite a few children staying with us who owned Care Bears. I knew that each bear had particular characteristics and that they were made in a range of bright colours, each with different symbols emblazoned on their tummies, like flowers, a four-leaf clover or a rainbow.

'I think they were sunflowers,' Melissa said, looking thoughtful.

'Sunflowers? I love those. We sell them in the summer and I usually try to grow some in the garden too.'

'See, you're a nice person. I'd still have my collection of Care Bears if everyone was as nice as you.'

'You are a nice person too, Melissa,' I said. I wanted to ask what had happened to her bears but I didn't want to intrude; I felt she would have elaborated if she'd wanted to.

'No, I'm bad.'

'No, you're a nice person who sometimes behaves badly, and that's a very different thing. It's the behaviour you need to change, not who you are.'

Melissa shrugged, put sugar in her tea and asked me if anything was planned over the next few days. I told her that her support worker, Elaine, was due to visit in the next day or two.

'Do I have to tell her everything, like about the vodka?'

'It's up to you what you want to discuss with Elaine, but I think it's a good idea to be as open and honest with her as you can. She's here to help and support you, and she can only do that if she knows what's going on in your life.'

I hoped that hearing good advice about alcohol and peer pressure from someone she had known throughout her time in care might encourage Melissa to think twice next time. I'd be letting Wilf know about the vodka as well as going over the condom incident when I called him about TJ, though I didn't spell this out to Melissa.

'Sorry again,' she said. 'Everyone was having some and I didn't really want it, but I'd have felt like a nerd if I said no. Really I'd rather have a cup of tea.'

She slurped from her mug and asked if she could have more sugar. The bowl was right in front of her and she'd already helped herself to one sugar.

'Yes, you can have one more,' I said, thinking how very young she seemed, and feeling confused by the fact a girl who asked permission to have extra sugar in her tea was drinking vodka outside of the house when she knew it was wrong.

Jonathan came into the kitchen, and he told Melissa a story about a time when his big brother offered to take him to the pub when he was underage. Jonathan didn't want to go and said no, and his brother took the mickey and called him a scaredy cat. The following day one of his brother's friends got a call from the police and was charged with underage drinking, as he was a few days short of his eighteenth birthday. The boy had to appear in court and pay a small fine out of the wages he got from his part-time job.

'Obviously I was relieved I'd said no,' Jonathan told Melissa. 'And afterwards my brother apologised and told me he admired me for sticking to my guns. Growing up and finding your way in the world isn't easy, but sometimes you can make life even more difficult than it needs to be. You should listen to your gut feeling and do what you think is right.'

Melissa seemed to be receptive to Jonathan's words of wisdom and so he went on. 'I can see you're a smart girl. You don't have to follow the crowd if you don't want to, and if people judge you for being your own person, then I'm afraid they're not good friends.'

'Fair play,' she said, looking thoughtful once more. 'I'll remember that. Thanks Jonathan.'

I had a lot of paperwork to write up that night and the next day I called Wilf first thing to pass on all the information I'd picked up. My instincts were telling me that despite the many good qualities Melissa displayed, and the fact she seemed receptive to our advice and support, this was not going to be a quick fix. It was obvious she could very easily go down the wrong path again, and I voiced my concerns to Wilf.

'You're doing brilliantly, by the sounds of it,' he said. 'I'm told Melissa is usually very secretive about who she sees and where she goes. Do you know the boyfriend's full name?'

'It's TJ, that's all I know. We've met him and I know the takeaway he works at, and the vehicle he drives.'

'That's good to know. At least if she does go missing again he might be able to help us track her down.'

'So you don't think she goes missing with him?'

'I don't know. I'll pass all this on to Doreen. She would be the one who might know more. The more information we have the better.'

Doreen, Melissa's social worker, visited the following afternoon. Melissa seemed happy to see her, even though I'd explained that I'd had to pass on a few things to Social Services, notably the incident with the condoms and also her drinking vodka.

Melissa didn't flinch when Doreen brought the issues up, and asked her directly if she was having sex with her boyfriend. I'd offered to leave them to talk privately, but Melissa said she didn't mind me staying, and Doreen said it might be helpful if I did.

'Why would you even ask me that?' Melissa said, sounding mildly agitated. 'Angela asked me the same thing. And the answer's still no.'

I thought back to when I was twelve, going on thirteen. I'd have been incredibly embarrassed if the word sex was mentioned to my face by an adult, and absolutely mortified if I were ever questioned about having sex with a boy. Though she was irritated, Melissa was taking it in her stride. I wasn't sure how to interpret this. Was it because she really was as innocent as she claimed and therefore the questioning didn't threaten her? I hoped so: the alternative didn't bear thinking about.

'The reason I'm asking,' Doreen sighed, 'is because TJ is seventeen.' She was a down-to-earth, matronly type of woman with a kind, friendly face.

'So! I'm not like that. I wouldn't ask *you* about your sex life, so why are you talking about him like this?'

'Because you are twelve,' Doreen replied, unruffled.

Her tone was gentle yet unapologetic; it clearly wasn't the first time Doreen had been asked such an impertinent question and she dealt with it with impressive ease.

'Exactly – I'm twelve years old. I'm way too young to be having sex. TJ's my boyfriend, that's all. We just hang out with our mates and eat chips and have a laugh. It's not a crime, is it?'

Doreen said she was asking the question because if Melissa was having sex, she needed to know, to protect her.

'I'm not, so no. No is the answer. I don't need protecting. I'd tell you if I did. Unless you think I need protecting from eating chips?'

Doreen reminded her not to be cheeky and Melissa sighed and said sorry. Even though she'd spoken in a rude manner, I'd formed the opinion that Melissa was at heart a good-natured girl who didn't enjoy confrontation.

Doreen went on to discuss underage drinking and, amongst other things, she told Melissa it was unfair on Jonathan and me if she came home drunk or having had a drink, and that it might jeopardise her placement with us.

'We don't want you having another placement breakdown, do we?' Doreen said, somewhat ominously.

'No,' Melissa whispered. She now looked a bit lost and I wanted to throw my arms around her. It seemed so sad that a girl her age was in such a situation. She wasn't a bad girl; she'd just got in with a bad crowd. I didn't want her to worry that she might end up back in the secure unit. I found myself wishing that Doreen would stick to explaining the health risks of underage drinking, and the dangers Melissa might be putting herself in with the lifestyle choices she was making. Any inconvenience that may be caused to Jonathan and me was the last thing I was concerned about, but I trusted Doreen's methods. She'd been Melissa's social worker for many months and knew her better than we did, and I imagined she thought the threat of another placement breakdown or a return to the secure unit might be the trump card she needed to play in order to get Melissa to behave herself.

Next, Doreen moved on to the subject of school. She was still trying to fix up a date to meet Melissa's head teacher and agree on the strategy for her return. I learned that Melissa had been going missing from school and, after multiple suspensions, had finally been excluded for her truancy, and because the school felt unable to keep her safe on account of her numerous 'breakouts' and 'unauthorised absences.'

The head teacher was currently away at a conference but Doreen was expecting a call the following week. I felt frustrated when I heard this, wondering why another member of staff couldn't step in while the head was away. A child's education is so precious and Melissa was in secondary school; it wouldn't be long before she started to think about her GCSE options and I didn't want her to be at a disadvantage before she even started the courses. I held my tongue, however, and reassured Doreen we'd discussed Melissa doing some history and geography work while she was off, and that she seemed happy to do it.

'Good,' Doreen said, getting to her feet. 'Everything seems to be going well. So no more running off, young lady!'

Melissa smiled at her social worker and mischievously stuck out her tongue.

'And you can put that away, cheeky madam!' Doreen scolded, wagging her finger playfully.

I was pleased to see Melissa had this kind of relationship with her social worker. Between us, I felt Doreen, Jonathan and I might be able to get through to Melissa, and hopefully keep her on the straight and narrow. Jonathan and I had a very good support worker in Wilf too, and there was also Melissa's support worker, Elaine. She had phoned me and was coming to visit in the next few days. All in all, it seemed Social Services could not be doing any more to help Melissa.

'You seem quite happy,' Jonathan commented when I popped into the shop to take him a cup of tea later on. He was making a list of things we needed to order from the wholesaler.

'I suppose I'm feeling *fairly* optimistic,' I said. 'For a girl who's caused havoc by sneaking out and running away goodness knows where, Melissa's a remarkably open book. That can only be a good thing, can't it?'

Jonathan said he supposed so, though I could tell he was thinking I was maybe clutching at straws. He probably also wondered if we could believe anything Melissa said. I knew this, of course, but I was only going with my gut instinct.

'Anyway, the other thing I'm happy about,' I went on, 'is that I feel we have a lot of support from Social Services and the channels of communication are open with their social workers. That's so important, isn't it?'

He nodded wisely. 'You're absolutely right. Good communication is key.'

At that moment a very grumpy-looking customer slapped some coins on the counter, startling us. 'That's for these,' he said, waving a bunch of carnations under our noses.

'Thank you. Would you like them wrapped?'

'Nah!' he said rudely, sniffing and rushing out of the door before we'd even had a chance to pick up the money, let alone put it in the till.

'As I was saying,' Jonathan smirked. 'Good communication is *so* important!'

Melissa sat down for a couple of hours, reading and making notes from one of the history books she'd brought with her. She complained that she was finding it hard to concentrate and also said her right hand was sore. I noticed her notebook was decorated with doodles of hearts and stars and flowers, and when I looked at her little hand I could see it was swollen.

'How long's it been like that?'

'Dunno. I've only just noticed it, when I started writing.'

I fetched some ice wrapped in a tea towel and told her to hold it over the swelling to see if it brought it down, or at least soothed it. After a while she said it didn't make any difference. I checked to see if she'd been bitten by something but thought this was unlikely, deep in the middle of winter. There was no bite mark, but I did notice some very faint grazing on her knuckles.

'Did you scrape your hand or hit something?'

'No, not that I remember.'

'Odd. OK, I'd better make a doctor's appointment.'

'Thanks. Can I go and see my friend Sonia after tea?'

'Sonia? Which friend is she?'

I hadn't heard this girl's name mentioned before and, once again, I was keen to glean as much detail as possible about who she was seeing, and where. Wilf had told me this was all I could do in the circumstances. He'd reiterated that we could not keep Melissa in the house or stop her from seeing her friends; all we could do was arm ourselves with as much information as possible about her whereabouts and the company she was keeping.

Melissa told me Sonia was a girl she'd met at school when she was living at Anne-Marie's. Sonia didn't go to school any more as she had a baby. She'd also just got a new flat of her own. Melissa told me the address and I knew the block; it was on a large council estate in town.

'I want to catch up and see the baby,' Melissa said. 'I haven't seen them for a while.'

'Right. Does Sonia have a phone number, in case I need to get hold of you?'

'I don't think so but I can find out. Anyway, I'll only be an hour there. But after that, can I meet Rosie?'

Rosie was another old school friend, it seemed, and apparently she was going out with TJ's best mate.

'What's he called?' I asked, after Melissa had volunteered the information about Rosie.

'Des. And before you ask, I don't know his full name, sorry!'

Melissa did tell me Rosie's surname, however, and she said her friend's father was a solicitor who ran a well-known local practice. Though I didn't know him personally, I knew Rosie's father by reputation; he had lived in the town for many years, sat on various committees and did a lot of work for the Round Table, or was it Variety? Either way, this gave me some comfort. I imagined Rosie would be well cared for and living by similar rules to those we were putting in place for Melissa, or at least I hoped that was the case. Melissa volunteered Rosie's home phone number too, which also helped put my mind at rest.

We came to an agreement that Melissa could walk to Sonia's flat then come home for quarter past seven at the latest. After that Rosie was going to meet Melissa at the top of our road – at quarter to eight – and from there they were going to walk together to meet TJ and Des in town at eight, which was in the opposite direction to Sonia's flat. TJ was to bring Melissa home, or she was to walk with Rosie.

'So that's the deal – you come back from Sonia's by

quarter past seven, then you can go back out and meet Rosie at quarter to eight.'

'Then how late can I stay out?'

'Nine as usual,' I said, reminding her that she was not to drink anything. She agreed, rolling her eyes and telling me again she didn't even like vodka. 'Am I allowed to eat chips or do I need to ask your permission for that? What about ketchup? Shall I ring you and ask how many squirts I'm allowed on my chips?' She shrugged her shoulders playfully and turned her palms to the ceiling as she looked at me quizzically.

'Cheeky!' I said. 'It's very simple. Be good and come home at nine, not a minute later.'

As Melissa was in an upbeat and receptive mood I took the opportunity to ask her not to smoke either, although I'd detected the smell of cigarettes on many of her clothes by now and suspected she was a regular smoker. 'I'll be good,' she said. 'You can trust me. Don't worry, I won't get addicted.'

7

'All we have is words'

Melissa didn't return on time from visiting Sonia. I watched the clock like a hawk and from quarter past seven onwards, as every minute ticked past, I felt more anxious. Jonathan was ready to walk to the top of the road for quarter to eight, and if Melissa didn't turn up to meet Rosie we would have to think about calling Social Services and reporting her missing.

'We can do that at eight fifteen,' I calculated, as it was dark and that was when she would officially be an hour late home.

There was a news programme on TV but I couldn't concentrate on anything the presenter was saying.

'I wish we could just stop her going out,' I said to Jonathan.

'I know, but we can't.'

'I know, I know. It's so frustrating.'

To our great relief, Melissa burst in the door just after half past seven. 'Really sorry I'm late,' she said, sounding genuinely apologetic.

'What happened?'

'Nothing, I just walked the long way round. Oh is that the time? I'll have to go straight back out to meet Rosie.'

She smelt of cigarettes and I thought her eyes looked a bit glazed, but she was perfectly alert.

'Have you drunk or smoked anything?'

'What? No! Why?'

'I thought your eyes look different to normal and I thought I could smell cigarettes, that's why. Are you OK?'

'Well, my hand's still swollen and it was hurting, so I took some painkillers. Sonia gave them to me. They did make me feel a bit funny. You don't need to worry about me though. I'm fine, honestly. Sorry to dash off again.'

Melissa had only taken one pace through the door and now she stepped swiftly out again. She turned and walked away quickly, shouting 'Bye!' over her shoulder.

'Don't forget you need to be home at nine, no later.'

'I know. Have no fear, Melissa will be here!'

I watched her walk jauntily away. I sighed, and just before I closed the front door I caught the sound of what was becoming her trademark whistling. Melissa sounded happy, which was a good sign, I figured. At least she had made the effort to pop back and let us know she was OK before she met Rosie. Nevertheless, I was still worried about what she was up to. I knew I would now be spending the next hour and a half watching the clock all over again. Despite Melissa's demeanour and the reassurances she gave me I was filled with an uneasy feeling from the moment she disappeared from view. I didn't trust her to come back on time and I was annoyed that I couldn't follow my instincts and keep her in, safe from harm.

'Do you think it's her personality?' I found myself saying.

'How do you mean?' Jonathan asked.

'I mean, is the real problem that she's one of those people who finds it difficult to say no?'

'It could be. That would certainly explain how she is such a nice girl, as well as being such a worry.'

'Precisely. I don't think she goes out of her way to deliberately defy us or cause upset, do you? I think she genuinely has good intentions, but things seem to go wrong when she's with her friends.'

Jonathan frowned. 'Easily influenced? Gullible? Naive? I guess she may be all of those things.'

'Yes, and I wonder if she's like that because of what's happened to her in the past. Maybe her self-esteem was damaged and that's dented the confidence she has in herself? So she looks to others for guidance and follows their lead?'

'Sounds very plausible. The trouble is, the people she looks to aren't helping. She needs friends who are the same age and aren't going to lead her astray. Maybe Rosie's a good influence.'

I thought about this but then started to worry that Rosie was in exactly the same boat as Melissa, going out with TJ's friend who I imagined was also sixteen or seventeen.

*

Jonathan encouraged me to watch a film to try to relax. We had the video of *Pretty Woman* and I chose that. The film had come out a few years earlier and was one of my favourites. Normally I was gripped by it, even though I knew the story well, but this time I couldn't concentrate. I was thinking about Melissa, wondering what she was doing, if she'd come in on time, and whether she was being talked into doing something she didn't want to do.

There was no sign of her at nine. We had a grandfather clock in the lounge that chimed loudly, making me catch my breath. I usually felt soothed by its steady, predictable rhythm, but tonight it was a countdown timer, an emergency alarm. Each tick-tock taunted me, plucking at my nerves. I was becoming more anxious and irritated as each second passed.

'I knew this was going to happen. Why did we even let her go out? I wish we had more power. It seems so ridiculous sitting here. I can't bear it. It's like waiting for an accident to happen.'

Jonathan said all the right things, reminding me that attempting to keep Melissa in the house might make her rebel and run away, and then we'd be in a worse position. He also said we couldn't do anything differently, because if we kept her in then Melissa might put in a complaint to Social Services about us restricting her freedom.

'I know all this, of course I do. And I can see how frustrating it was for Lynne. Remember she said it's harder to keep a foster child in the house than one of your own? I can totally see that. The rules we have to follow to safeguard the kids are all well intentioned, but the reality is that in respecting Melissa's right to freedom we're potentially allowing her to walk into danger. Sometimes I wonder about Social Services. The rules we have to follow are so rigid, when really we need to be able to follow our instincts, like a parent would.'

Jonathan was frowning again and looking exasperated. We were both finding this placement difficult already, and it was still very early days. He admitted that it felt like our hands were tied and agreed with my point about feeling like we were waiting for an accident to happen. It was such an unpalatable thought and it made me shudder.

'The fact is, we're not parents,' I said ruefully. 'If we were, I imagine we wouldn't be letting her out, but who knows? Kids are kids. And as we've said before, when you start restraining and restricting a wilful child, their instinct is to rebel. We need to work *with* Melissa. If she sees us as the enemy we could lose her, and then what? Five weeks is a long time in the life of a vulnerable twelve-year-old.'

We switched the video off when it was less than halfway through. Neither of us was interested. At 9 p.m. we put on the TV news instead. In those days there were no 24-hour, rolling news channels. Tuning in to the BBC and hearing the familiar 9 o'clock theme tune was something we did all the time. It was part of our everyday life, but that night the programme only served to push us even further out of our comfort zone. There was a story about a child killed in a hit-and-run and this sparked a whole new wave of worry in my head.

I resisted the temptation to stand at the window, looking out for Melissa. The grandfather clock chimed at quarter past nine, half past the hour and again at quarter to ten. We switched over to another channel but nothing caught our attention. Jonathan flicked through the paper and I tried to read a magazine.

'I can't stand this,' I said. 'I'm going to put the kettle on.'

Jonathan put the paper down and immediately got to his feet. 'I'll come with you. If she's not in at ten we'll call out-of-hours.'

On the way to the kitchen I stopped, unlocked the front door and stepped outside, looking out into the black night and willing Melissa to appear. Everything was still and quiet and I wondered if it might snow. I instinctively looked up at the sky to see if I was able to see any stars. I always do this when I'm out in the dark, whatever the weather. It reminds me of childhood camping trips, when my parents used to point out the constellations and encourage me to make a wish. Thanks to them I grew up associating the stars with hope and possibility, and to this day starry nights always lift my spirits as they remind me never to stop wishing and dreaming.

On this night there was nothing but darkness above, which somehow didn't surprise me. I stared into it, searching for any glimmer of light, but the sky was a dense black canopy. It didn't feel like a good omen.

When I came back inside I closed the door but left it unlocked. I'm not normally a superstitious person, but it felt wrong to lock the door when all I wanted was for Melissa to walk through it. Jonathan gave me a hug and rubbed the cold away from my arms and I put the kettle on the hob to boil. When it whistled I thought of Melissa, whistling contentedly to herself. How could such a happy-go-lucky child create so much havoc? Why didn't she just come in on time? I made the tea but didn't drink it. I realised I'd only made it for something to do, and not because I was thirsty. I watched the steam disappear slowly as the brown liquid went cold in the cup.

At five to ten we heard footsteps outside and then, finally, we heard the front door opening. Jonathan and I jumped to our feet and rushed to greet Melissa. As we did so, the hallway was flooded with bright light spilling from the kitchen. Melissa looked like a rabbit caught in the headlights as she stepped through the door, and she immediately tried to sidestep us and make for the stairs.

'Just a minute, Melissa. You're late. Are you OK?'

'Yeah, sorry. I'll go straight to bed. I'm really sorry.'

I hadn't heard a car outside and I asked her how she'd got home. 'TJ dropped me off at the top of the road. I'm going to bed now. Sorry. I'm tired. What time's the doctor's? Have you been waiting up?'

'It's nearly ten o'clock,' I said, 'and, yes, we've been watching the clock for nearly an hour, Melissa. You really need to come home at the agreed time, or we're going to have to have a rethink about the rules. You were meant to be in at nine and you told us you would be.'

'OK, I understand. It won't happen again. See you tomorrow. Sorry again. Lost track of time.'

I noticed her hand was still a little swollen and she looked generally dishevelled again, with her hair messed up and dirty marks on her tracksuit bottoms. Her eyes were still a bit strange-looking, as they had been earlier, but she didn't appear to be drunk or high. I found myself feeling very glad we were going to see the doctor and that Melissa herself had asked about the appointment. I hoped that meant she had nothing to hide, and I thought it would be reassuring for the GP to cast his professional eye over her, as maybe he would pick up on anything I may have missed.

I told her what time she needed to be ready for the doctor's the next day and we let her go to bed. Then I wrote down yet more notes for Social Services.

'I wish we could do more than write notes and tell the professionals what's happening,' I said to Jonathan. 'Just because everyone knows what's going on doesn't make it right, does it?'

Jonathan shook his head. He looked really tired and he had to get up very early in the morning to go to the wholesaler. We had a part-time worker coming in to help us in the shop, as we had done ever since we'd become specialist carers, but even so Jonathan was going to have his work cut out tomorrow.

'You get to bed and I'll lock up and switch everything off down here,' I told him.

By the time I got up to the bedroom Jonathan was already falling asleep, and when I finally put my head on the pillow he was sleeping soundly. I lay silently beside him, my brain whirring. I wanted to help Melissa make the right choices in her life but I felt powerless.

I was drowsy but unable to sleep. Yet the next thing I knew I was waking up from a fitful sleep, remembering a dream. In it Melissa had gone missing in the dead of night. There was a major police search launched and I saw Jonathan and me on the TV news, talking to police officers and telling people she had long red hair and was good at whistling. We gave a news conference and then the whole world started looking for Melissa.

I sat bolt upright in bed, staring into the darkness. What would happen if Melissa really did go missing, perhaps the very next time she went out with TJ, or Sonia, or Rosie? What if she disappeared and was never found? What if something terrible happened to her? I started to imagine what people would think if Melissa really was in the news because the police were looking for her. Would they point the finger at us, and at Social Services, and ask why we couldn't collectively have done more to keep her safe?

What more can we all do? I thought. *How can we protect her better?* I'm not sure if I spoke the words out loud, but Jonathan stirred.

'What?'

'It's OK,' I whispered. 'Go back to sleep.'

'Are you sure you're OK?'

'Yes. I was just thinking about Melissa.'

'There's nothing more we can do,' he said, yawning. 'We have to sleep.'

'But what if we hear her running off?' I hissed, feeling a sudden stab of fear.

'We'll do our best to stop her, but . . .'

Jonathan stopped talking and let out a long, dejected sigh.

'But what?'

'But the fact is we have no power. All we have is words.'

'Is that enough?'

'Maybe. Hopefully. Get some sleep, Angela.'

At about three in the morning I got up to go to the toilet. I'd drifted in and out of sleep again and felt exhausted. As I padded across the bedroom carpet I heard a noise upstairs so I crept onto our landing. Straining my ears, I tried to work out what it was. I could see a light was on upstairs and I slowly headed towards it. Of course, the light was coming from Melissa's room, as was the sound of her whistling quietly to herself, and the hairdryer going on and off.

I reached the landing on the top floor of the house. Melissa's bedroom door was wide open and as I approached I could see that she was sitting at the dressing table, wearing one of her tracksuits, blow-drying her hair as if she didn't have a care in the world.

'What are you doing? It's three o'clock.'

She didn't seem at all bothered that I'd found her like this.

'I know. Mad, isn't it? I couldn't sleep. I decided to wash my hair, because it takes ages to do and I thought I could have a lie-in in the morning, before we go to see the doctor.'

'Aren't you tired?'

'Yes, but I couldn't sleep.'

I told her I knew the feeling, and we ended up going down to the kitchen and each having a mug of warm milk. Melissa dunked malted milk biscuits in her drink and started telling me all about her friend Sonia and the baby.

'He's absolutely gorgeous. She's called him Kazim. He's got lovely light brown eyes. I told her they look like Maltesers! He's so adorable.'

'Kazim? That's a Muslim name. Is she Muslim?'

'No, but her fella was.'

'She's not with him now?'

'No. It's a real shame. He broke her heart. She thought naming the baby after him might make him stay but it didn't.'

Sonia sounded very young and naive. I asked Melissa exactly how old she was and she said she was sixteen.

'She was lucky to get a council flat as soon as she turned sixteen. She wasn't on the list for long.'

'I suppose she was. How old is the baby?'

'He's nearly two.'

I was shocked, though I tried not to show it. I'd expected the baby to be much younger than that, given Sonia's age.

'So Kazim is a toddler, and Sonia must have been fourteen when she had her son?' I said evenly.

'Yeah. She'd had an abortion before that too. She always said she wanted her own family when she was young but her family made her get rid of the first one. They didn't like her boyfriend and thought he'd clear off after that, but he didn't – not then, anyhow. She loved him and thought they'd get married, but when Sonia got pregnant again he didn't want to know.'

Melissa then started telling me that Sonia came from a 'crappy family'. It seemed her stepbrother had once said to her, 'I'd shag you if you weren't family' and Sonia's dad was in prison for raping a teenager. I could hardly believe what I was hearing. It sounded so extreme I wondered if it could be true, but who would lie about such things? I considered whether Sonia had been truthful in what she'd told Melissa, or whether Melissa was exaggerating or trying to shock me, though what purpose that might serve I had no idea.

When Melissa finished talking and I felt she had no more to say, at least not then, I started to tell her a bit more about my own family, and Jonathan's. I wanted her to realise that the things she was describing, and the worlds she was involved in, were unusual and that she should aspire for the best life possible. I spoke about how I met Jonathan at a local dance when we were both seventeen. I was the younger of two children but grew up feeling like an only child, as my brother was fourteen years my senior. I felt loved and cherished as a child, despite the fact things were not perfect: my father had a drink problem when I was young, and I mentioned this to make the point that my childhood had not been completely charmed.

For Jonathan's part, he was the youngest of four

brothers, raised on a farm. He was a small, short-sighted boy and unfortunately his father gave him a hard time, treating him like the runt of the family. Melissa looked genuinely saddened when I told her that, and said how mean it was. Jonathan rose above it, I reassured her. He worked hard and moved away to the city after doing his A levels at eighteen. I explained how he went on to carve out a great career for himself, working in logistics, while I also left home after my A levels and went to work in a bank in the same city. We thoroughly enjoyed spreading our wings and lived life to the full.

'My mother always told me that the world was my oyster,' I said to Melissa. 'Life was not always perfect and I certainly wasn't born with a silver spoon in my mouth. Nor was Jonathan. But we both made the best of everything, always worked hard and took opportunities. It doesn't matter who you are or where you come from, we can all be what we want to be and we can all change our lives for the better. There is something great out there that everybody can do. What are your dreams for the future, Melissa?'

'Like I said, I want to work with kids, that's it really. I think I'd be good at it.' She paused and looked thoughtful. 'Also, I want to be a mum myself one day, but not yet. I want to be a great mum and have a lovely big family.'

At this point she started to cry.

'Can I give you a hug?'

'No. I'm all right.'

I let the silence linger, hoping she would be the one to fill it. I imagined she was crying over her own family. Her mum was on the other side of the world and her stepfather was in prison, at least that's what she had told me. I'd heard nothing about her real father.

She quickly wiped her eyes, stood up abruptly and took a deep breath in. 'Sorry to cry. I'm going to try to get some sleep now. I'm fine, don't worry.'

I told Melissa there was no need to apologise for crying and that she could talk to me about anything, any time she liked. We climbed the stairs together, and I walked up to the top landing and said goodnight to her as she closed her bedroom door.

Jonathan was awake again when I got back into bed and I told him what had gone on. We both lay there for a while, listening. Melissa was clearly not in bed as we could still hear her shuffling around. Her door creaked open and I heard the sound of the toilet flushing. Then there was more padding about, and I realised her footsteps were getting closer.

'What's she doing?' Jonathan hissed.

'I don't know.'

It sounded like she'd gone into the living room, which was along from our bedroom, on the middle floor of the house.

'I'm going to see,' I told him.

I pulled on my dressing gown and tiptoed along the landing. I could hear Melissa talking quietly and urgently, and realised she was on the phone.

'Yeah, I'll be there. Yeah, I'll bring her. Why does he have to come? OK.'

I pushed open the door.

'Hang on,' she said. 'My foster carer is here. I'll see you then. Bye.' She hung up and immediately apologised for using the phone without permission.

'It's the fact you're using it at this time in the morning I'm bothered about,' I said. 'Who on earth were you talking to at this time?'

'Just my boyfriend.'

'TJ?'

'No, not TJ. It's Degsy.'

'Degsy?'

'You know, I've told you about him before. He's one of the boys from the unit.'

'I'm surprised you got through to him at this hour. Surely you can't phone the unit in the middle of the night?'

'Oh no, he's not in there any more. He's out, I know the number where he stays. He's always awake in the night. I said I'll see him tomorrow. Is that OK? Sorry, I should have checked first.'

'I don't want to interfere, Melissa, but it sounds like you might be getting yourself into a tricky situation.'

'Why? Will Jonathan be annoyed about this?'

'No, what I mean is, seeing more than one boy at the same time. Are you sure it's a good idea? I thought TJ was your boyfriend?'

'I'm OK. I know what I'm doing, honest. I'm gonna go and have a coffee with Degsy tomorrow afternoon, that's all.'

I steered her back to bed and said we'd talk about it in the morning.

I already didn't like the sound of this Degsy boy. What had he been in the unit for and why was he always awake in the night?

Melissa got up at ten the next day and seemed anxious and distracted as she got herself ready for the appointment with the GP.

The surgery was close by and I walked there with her. The swelling and pain in her hand had almost disappeared now. I hoped we wouldn't be wasting the GP's time over it, although I was still grateful he was seeing her, from a more general point of view. With longer-term placements we're obliged to take children for routine medical and dental check-ups, plus eye tests and any other health appointments the children may need. I always find it reassuring to have the children seen by a range of medical professionals, as I don't think you can ever be too vigilant when it comes to a child's health. With such a short placement we were not required by Social Services to take Melissa for any routine check-ups, so I was going to make the most of this opportunity. I'd decided I was going to ask the doctor what advice he could give about the dangers to teenagers of smoking, alcohol and drugs. I wasn't going to divulge anything personal about Melissa, but I hoped she'd take notice of whatever advice the experienced GP might offer.

Melissa had shown herself to be quite unfazed when talking about topics many teenagers would have blushed at or hidden from, and so I wasn't concerned about her reaction if the doctor decided to ask her direct questions. I'd known Dr Peters for many years, and he understood my role as a foster carer and was always helpful and supportive.

'So what seems to be the problem?' the smiling GP asked.

Melissa explained about the swelling she'd experienced on her hand. Dr Peters looked at it and manipulated each of her dainty fingers in turn, then her thumb, asking if she felt any pain.

'No, but I have got stomach-ache,' she volunteered.

'Stomach-ache?'

'Yeah. I thought it was because I took painkillers for my hand and they didn't agree with me, but I think I might be pregnant.'

She said this without flinching, in a surprisingly confident voice. I looked at her in alarm and the doctor raised his bushy eyebrows. I imagined he must have been as taken aback as I was, though we both managed to keep our composure very well in the circumstances.

Melissa was dressed in a jumper with candy stripes on it and had a shiny ribbon in her hair, tied in a pretty bow. With her soft skin and pink lips she looked like a little doll that day; I could hardly believe what I'd just heard.

'Well if that's the case, we'll need to do a urine sample,' the GP said calmly. 'How pregnant do you suspect you may be? Have you done a test?'

He looked at me and I looked at her, letting the doctor know this was all news to me.

'I've only missed two periods.'

I felt nauseous myself now. Surely this wasn't happening? What if Melissa was pregnant? Who had she been sleeping with? And what other secrets was she keeping?

8

'I'm only doing my job'

To my huge relief it turned out Melissa wasn't pregnant after all. When Dr Peters told us the result of the urine test he was kind and sensitive and started to give Melissa a gentle talk about reproduction and contraception. He used very basic language – so basic I wondered if he doubted whether she'd had sex at all. Perhaps he thought she might be an incredibly naive twelve-year-old, maybe one who thought you could get pregnant simply by kissing her boyfriend?

It did seem unbelievable that Melissa had had sex at her age, particularly as she looked younger than ever on the day we went to the doctors. Unfortunately, my gut feeling was that she had had sex, and that her pregnancy scare was genuine.

In the circumstances we didn't get on to talking about the perils of drugs, smoking and alcohol with the GP as I'd planned to do. Dr Peters wished us both the best of luck and said he'd leave Melissa in my 'capable hands'. Of course, I'd be reporting everything to Social Services. It's possible the doctor himself would flag up to the authorities that a twelve-year-old girl had been in his surgery saying she might be pregnant, but I got the feeling he was leaving it to me to deal with Social Services, as he knew I would. Dr Peters didn't ask who the father might be, or the age of Melissa's boyfriend. She was not in need of any medical attention and she was in my care, which automatically meant she was under the Social Services radar. Therefore, I suspect that that was the end of the matter for the pleasant but somewhat apathetic GP; I noticed that he was already opening the next patient's file before we'd left the room.

'I'm sorry for causing a fuss,' Melissa said afterwards. 'And for not telling you what I was worried about, before we went to the doctor.'

She looked genuinely apologetic, as she had done on previous occasions, and she said she'd decided not to meet Degsy for a coffee that afternoon as planned.

'I don't feel like it now. I'll let him know. Can I phone him?'

'Yes, of course.'

I told her I was very glad she'd let me accompany her to the GP and reiterated that she could talk to me about anything she wanted.

'Thanks, but I don't want to talk about it any more. It was a mistake, sleeping with that boy. I feel stupid now. I didn't really want to do it but all my mates are having sex and I would have felt daft to say no.'

I talked to her about being her own person and looking

after herself emotionally, as well as from a sexual health point of view. I mentioned sexually transmitted diseases and talked about HIV and AIDS. I didn't want to frighten Melissa, but if she was sexually active I had to make sure she was well aware of all the risks she was taking. I was very grateful for the HIV and AIDS training we'd undergone on our specialist foster care course. In the wake of the Government's hard-hitting 'Don't die of ignorance' campaign in the eighties, training, education and raising awareness of HIV and AIDS were still a high priority. I felt very well informed and able to speak with some authority about the risks of unprotected sex, and I hoped that if all else failed this might just be the thing to make Melissa sit up and take notice.

She seemed to listen to me, and so I took the opportunity to say as much as I could about the choices she was making. 'You're a lovely girl, Melissa. You don't have to do anything you don't want to do with a boy. You are worth more than that. Be proud of who you are and believe in yourself. You never, ever have to put yourself in a compromising position. You're far too young to be having sex. Nice boys will respect you for saying no. Good friends won't judge you either.'

I realised I couldn't assume TJ was the boy she might have had sex with. In fact, I was wondering if it might be Degsy, as she'd originally arranged to see him after the doctor's appointment. I made it clear to Melissa that she could tell me anything she wanted to about which boy it was, but she was looking at her feet by the time I broached this subject, and I was worried I was starting to sound like

I was delivering a monologue. My instinct was that Melissa wouldn't tell me who it might be, and that she would possibly become defensive and shut me out if I probed too much, but I did make sure I talked to her about the fact it was illegal for a boy over sixteen to have sex with an underage girl.

'I know that, but it's the boy who'd get done for it,' she said flatly.

I reiterated that the most important thing was that she was safe and protected and not doing anything against her will.

'I'm on your side,' I told her. 'I'm here to help you.'

I needed to continue to encourage her to trust me and talk to me about whatever she wanted, or whatever was worrying her.

Elaine, Melissa's support worker, tapped quietly on the front door. 'Hello,' she said in a thin voice, not much louder than a whisper. 'I'm Elaine. I hope it's still a good time for me to pop in?'

I thought this was an odd thing to say, as we'd spoken on the phone just a short time earlier.

Though her main role was to transport Melissa to supervised visits to family and friends, she had suggested she pop in as she had another appointment close to where we lived. When she phoned in advance to confirm the arrangements I told her I was looking forward to meeting her and was very glad she was coming to see Melissa.

'I think she needs all the support she can get,' I said.

It would be up to Melissa what she told her support worker and whether she mentioned the pregnancy scare, but I hoped she would, and I encouraged her to do so.

'We're all here to support you, Melissa. Of course, Elaine can only help you with things she knows about, so I'd make the most of her visit if I were you.'

'Yes, of course,' I said to Elaine now, 'we've been expecting you. Come on in, it's freezing out there.'

She was a wiry and pasty-skinned woman who looked to be in her fifties. I noticed her nose was very red and her lips were chapped. She stepped into the house apologising for dripping rain from her long woollen coat onto the wooden floor in our hallway. She immediately began taking off her sensible flat, black shoes, which looked soaked through.

'Sorry about this. I used a car park that was full of potholes this morning and I stepped straight in a puddle. I'm already full of cold and that was all I needed!'

I took Elaine up to the lounge and called Melissa down from her bedroom. She came immediately.

'Hi,' Melissa said, giving a slightly half-hearted wave of her hand as she entered the lounge and saw Elaine perched rather uncomfortably on the edge of the sofa.

'Hello, Melissa. How are things?'

'Er, fine. How are you?'

'Well I was just saying I stepped in a puddle this morning and I've got a cold. What terrible weather we're having, but we mustn't complain, must we?'

Melissa smiled politely, shuffled her feet and asked if

she could get anyone a drink. I wasn't sure if she was putting off talking to Elaine, was already bored by the meeting or genuinely wanted to make herself useful.

'Thanks, Melissa, but I can do the drinks while you talk to Elaine,' I said. 'Tea or coffee?'

They both asked for a cup of tea and I went to the kitchen. When I returned with a pot on a tray shortly afterwards they were sitting in silence. Elaine was reading some paperwork and Melissa was studiously examining her fingernails, which looked like tiny seashells, baby pink and uneven. I wanted to give her a big cuddle and tell her everything was going to be all right. I wanted to tell her she just had to listen to the adults, stop trying to grow up too fast and stay away from people who were a bad influence on her.

'Would you like me to leave you two to talk privately?' I volunteered. 'I can leave the tea here for you to help yourselves, if you like?'

'Pardon?' Elaine said. 'Oh no, no bother. We're nearly done here. If only I could find a pen that works!'

Elaine shook the biro she was trying to use then gave up on it and started fishing in her cavernous handbag. She pulled out old tissues, a glasses case and a blunt pencil, complaining that she went through pens 'like nobody's business.'

'Here, you can use this one,' I said, handing her the reliable pen I always kept beside the telephone in the lounge.

Melissa looked at me and, after checking that Elaine was engrossed in her paperwork once more, rolled her eyes in an exaggerated way and gave a little smirk. It was clear she wasn't particularly impressed with Elaine, which was a shame. Not every child gets a support worker, and a good one can have a hugely positive influence on a child. Typically, support workers are people who work on a part-time, ad-hoc basis and are perhaps semi-retired and matched to just a few children. When a child moves from one foster care placement to another, as Melissa had, their role can be vital. Along with the child's social worker, the support worker may be one of the few adults with whom the child has had consistent, long-term contact. This means they can be an invaluable source of support, offering wisdom, kindness and steady guidance. I was therefore disappointed Melissa didn't seem to have a great bond with her.

I poured the tea and told Elaine to help herself to milk and sugar. She did so, slopping milk and sprinkling sugar across the tray.

'Oops sorry, I've made a bit of a mess, silly me. I really should give up sugar in my tea in any case . . .' She fished in her bag again and pulled out a crumpled tissue, which she used to dab the base of her mug.

Melissa excused herself politely, saying she needed the toilet. She did another discreet eye-roll in my direction on her way out, as if to say, 'What is she like?'

I was concerned that Elaine might drink her tea and disappear. I thought she wasn't here to talk about potholes, old biros or spilt milk and I sensed I had to swiftly steer the conversation back to Melissa in order to make the most of this visit. After all, Melissa needed every ounce of support and backup we could get for her, and I wanted Elaine to help in any way she could.

I told Elaine how much Jonathan and I liked Melissa's company, that we thought she was a lovely girl and we wanted to do all we could to protect her. Then I explained that Jonathan and I felt conflicted.

'What do you mean, conflicted?'

'I mean, we're doing everything by the book, in terms of following Social Services guidelines. We're letting her go out and we're doing our best to impose reasonable rules and boundaries, but is that enough?'

Annoyingly, Elaine looked distracted and began scrabbling around in her handbag yet again. She pulled out another crumpled tissue and blew her nose loudly.

'I don't think you've got anything to worry about. You're doing a good job and you and your husband are both specialist carers. I'd say Melissa's landed on her feet. She's lucky to be here, and very fortunate that you're willing and able to have her. As we've seen, other carers have not been able to deal with her.'

'Thank you; it's kind of you to say that. But it's very early days for us, and I'm not sure I agree that we haven't got anything to worry about.'

Elaine conceded that I was right. She said Melissa had just told her – clearly very briefly – about the pregnancy scare but said she didn't want to talk about 'any of her boyfriends'. Elaine said she was aware some of the boys she went out with were older than her.

'I'm glad you know that,' I said. 'What I want to know is

this. Now she's saying she's had sex – presumably unprotected sex – surely there is something more that can be done? She is still only twelve years old. I know we can't lock her in the house, but is it right for me to let her go out with boys over sixteen? She's only a child and they are over the age of consent.'

Elaine considered this for a moment. 'Yes, I hear what you're saying,' she said cautiously, 'but the issue we have is that she is not admitting she slept with a boy over sixteen, is she? The pregnancy scare could have been the result of her sleeping with a boy the same age, or at least a boy who is under sixteen. We have no proof that anything illegal is going on, and she is consenting, after all. I've been doing this job long enough to know that you have to take everything you hear with a pinch of salt. Are the boys she hangs around with even the age they say they are? They could just be trying to impress her. If she's not saying any more, we can't do much more, can we? Girls like Melissa are clever. When push comes to shove they will always say they had sex with a boy who was the same age, or at least under sixteen, or they'll say nothing. They're craftier than you might think, and they know all about the age of consent. You've made fantastic progress in the short time Melissa's been with you. She's talking to you and she made sure you were there at the GP's with her when she thought she was pregnant. I know I'm not *your* support social worker, but from where I'm looking I'd say you just need to keep up the good work. The placement is only for five weeks, in any case.'

I could see that Elaine meant well and was an experienced support worker. I was grateful for her counsel and encouragement, although some of what she said sounded quite defeatist to me, as if Jonathan and I didn't need to trouble ourselves too much as Melissa would be off our hands in no time, given that she was only with us for five weeks. Also, I didn't like the way Elaine used the phrase 'girls like Melissa', as if her actions completely defined her. I was riled by Elaine, to tell the truth. I felt like saying to her, 'So shall we just sit back, writing reports and following the Social Services guidelines until Melissa actually does get pregnant? Is that all we can do with "girls like Melissa"?' I held my tongue, of course. I didn't want to be rude or antagonistic and I knew Elaine was only trying to help.

Instead, I took a deep breath. Then I spelled out my fears as baldly as possible. 'I know Melissa's placement here is only for five weeks, but I worry she could get herself into trouble in that time. Potentially life-changing trouble.'

Elaine acknowledged this and advised me to voice my concerns to Wilf. He could then talk to his manager if he felt more needed to be done. I wondered if the manager would then speak to his or her superior and if, at any point, any of these people would decide action rather than words and written reports was required.

'Do you know anything about her longer-term plans?' I asked.

'I don't know any more than you, I expect. I believe there's one relative who might have her. That's the hope, as this person lives out of the area and it would be a fresh start.'

Elaine began putting her notepad in her bag – and my pen, absent-mindedly – and she got to her feet as soon as Melissa returned from the bathroom.

'I'd better get going,' she said. 'The weather's caused havoc on the roads and I expect I'll be running late all day. Thanks for the tea.'

As we made our way downstairs she explained once again that she had another child to see who didn't live very far away from us. I already knew this was what had prompted her visit to us today. *She must have forgotten she told us that,* I thought. Elaine then said she would return the next day, to take Melissa back to her home town to visit one of her aunties and to call in on her previous foster carers, if that was OK with me and we had nothing else planned. I assumed the two of them must have discussed this when I was making the tea: it was news to me that Melissa had been in foster care in the area where she grew up or that Elaine was planning this visit back to her home town.

'Oh, I thought all your foster carers were in this area,' I commented, looking at Melissa.

'No. I stayed with Dawn and Patrick to start with, near where I grew up. I wasn't there for that long but we got on well. I liked them a lot, they were really cool. Then it was Anne-Marie, then it was Lynne and what's his name?'

'Nick,' I said.

'That's it. Lynne and Nick. He was OK, but I like Jonathan better, he's much nicer.'

Elaine smiled. 'Well that's a good note on which to end

things. I'll see you tomorrow afternoon. I'll be here at one thirty?'

Melissa and I agreed to this. We were at the front door now and Melissa swung it wide open, letting in a gust of ice-cold air that made us all shudder.

'Bye then!' Melissa chirped. 'Thanks for coming to see me. It's very kind of you. See you tomorrow afternoon.' She looked like she couldn't wait to get rid of her support worker.

'Don't thank me, dear,' Elaine said with a withering smile. 'I'm only doing my job.'

When I told Jonathan about the meeting later I repeated that phrase, 'only doing my job'. 'I'm afraid that's the trouble. *She's* only doing her job. Why put yourself in that role if you're *only doing your job*? *We* are only doing our job. *Social Services* are only doing their job. The *police* who took Melissa to the unit were only doing their job. Even the *GP* was only doing his job when he tested her urine and told her she wasn't pregnant. But are any of us really doing all we can for Melissa?'

Jonathan nodded sombrely. 'I know exactly what you're saying. It's very difficult to know what else to do. I guess we have to hope this pregnancy scare will make Melissa think twice about what she gets up to and who she's mixing with.'

'Let's hope so. I could see she didn't enjoy the visit from her support worker and I can't imagine she wants to have any more intervention from Social Services than she already has.'

Melissa was tired that evening and went to bed at half past eight. I didn't hear a sound from her room and by the time I went to bed myself I was confident she was sleeping soundly. Nevertheless, I woke several times in the night, and at around three o'clock I even went downstairs to check her trainers were in the hall and the house was still locked up.

It crossed my mind, but I didn't want to open Melissa's bedroom door to check on her. For one thing, I didn't want to wake her up by accident. Most importantly, I didn't want her to feel I was invading her privacy or that I didn't have any confidence in her. I was sure the only way I could get through to her was by letting her know I was on her side and that she could trust me. If she didn't have faith in me, then I knew I'd have less chance of making a connection with her, and making a much-needed difference to her life.

9

'Is there something you want to tell me?'

I was very pleased to see that Melissa was in a sunny mood when she got up for breakfast the next day.

'I'm going to the park with Sonia this morning,' she said. 'Is that OK?'

I glanced out of the window. The weather had cleared up a bit and even though it was still very cold it was the brightest day we'd had for a while.

'What time were you thinking?'

'Not sure yet. She's got a toddler group later. She's gonna ring me in a bit, if that's OK? I gave her your number the other day – she hasn't got a phone but she can go to the call box. Is that all right? Sorry, I should have checked.'

'It's fine, that was a good idea. Why don't you do a bit of schoolwork while you wait for her to call? We should be hearing any day about getting you back to school.'

'OK,' she smiled. 'I'll have a shower first. Thanks.'

The phone rang while Melissa was in the bathroom.

'Mrs Hart? Hello, it's Sonia, Melissa's friend. Is she there?'

I explained that she was in the shower.

'OK, in that case can you tell her I'm going to the park at about half eleven so she can meet me somewhere there, maybe by the duck pond?'

'I can, but would you prefer to call here for her on the way?'

Knowing where Sonia's flat was, I realised she would almost have to walk past our house to reach the park. I thought that might be a better plan for the girls, and I also thought it was a good idea for me to meet as many of Melissa's friends as possible.

'OK, if you don't mind,' Sonia said brightly. 'I know where you are. You've got the flower shop, haven't you? I used to love going in there with my mum when I was a little girl.'

'Did you? You would probably have been served by *my* mum in those days,' I said.

'Really? Oh, I'll have to go as my money's running out.'

'Bye Sonia, see you soon.'

When she came back downstairs, Melissa was happy with the fact Sonia was calling for her and thanked me for taking the call. 'It must be a right pain having to go out to the phone box with the baby,' she commented.

'Yes, I can't imagine anything is very easy for Sonia, looking after a two-year-old on her own.'

'No, I don't envy her. I'm glad I'm not having a baby. I don't think I'd be able to deal with it half as well as she does.'

'I don't think any twelve-year-old would,' I said definitively, thinking to myself that Melissa really had no idea at all what she might have been letting herself in for, if she had a baby at her age.

She sat at the dining table for an hour or so, reading a history book and writing some notes from it. I was impressed with how well she was applying herself to her schoolwork considering she'd been out of the classroom for what I now knew to be four weeks.

Sonia knocked on the door at twenty past eleven. Melissa was upstairs putting her schoolwork away so I answered the door and invited Sonia to step inside.

'It's OK, Kazim's all cosy in his buggy and I don't want to get him out. I'll just wait out here.'

I said hello to the little boy and he waved at me, kicked his legs and said, 'Quack quacks.'

'I *heard* you're going to see the ducks. Have you got some bread for them?'

Kazim looked at me blankly and said, 'Bwead.'

'I never thought of that,' Sonia said.

I told her I'd fetch her a few crusts if she liked.

'That's really kind, thank you. I tell you what, I'll just pull your door closed to keep your heat in.'

'I don't mind if you bring the buggy in the hallway.'

'No, honestly. We're fine out here.'

As I bagged up some bread I thought what a pleasant, well-mannered girl Sonia was. Melissa was downstairs by the time I returned with the bag of bread and I was glad to see she was sensibly dressed in a thick sweatshirt, warm coat and her sturdiest pair of trainers.

'Enjoy yourselves,' I said. 'I'm sure the ducks will be glad of some food on a winter's morning.'

Melissa and I had agreed that she would be back for twelve thirty. That would give her time to have lunch before Elaine came to collect her at one thirty, to take her to visit her home town.

'We will!' Sonia said. 'Cheers for the bread. We'll have a lovely time, won't we, Kazim?'

'Bwead, bwead. Quack, quack.'

Melissa laughed and pulled a funny face at the little boy, making him giggle. The two girls said goodbye to me and I watched as they turned the corner, chatting happily and walking along energetically. I was pleased to see Melissa enjoying spending time with her friend and getting out for some fresh air, even though it was very cold outside.

I had some housework to do and I also decided to make a big pan of soup, ready for when Melissa came home for lunch. It was ready and simmering on the hob at twelve thirty but unfortunately there was no sign of Melissa. I reasoned that the girls might have got held up because of Kazim. Maybe he needed changing just as they were setting off home? I was sure there was a reasonable explanation and I told myself not to fret. Melissa knew Elaine was coming at one thirty, and I was sure she wouldn't be late for her trip out. Besides, an hour in the park was plenty long enough at this time of year; Kazim would be getting cold and would need his lunch before his toddler group in the afternoon. Surely Melissa would turn up any minute now?

When the clock ticked past one o'clock I couldn't help but worry. I turned the pan of soup off and stood looking out of the window. I was wondering whether to walk up to Sonia's flats or to the park.

'I feel a bit silly,' I said to Jonathan, when I popped into the shop to tell him what was going on.

'Why?'

'Because I didn't think for one minute she'd go missing today, like this. I mean, she was with Sonia and her little boy. What on earth can they be doing? It's cold and they can't be feeding the ducks for this length of time, can they?'

'I wouldn't have thought so. But maybe they went to have a drink in the cafe and lost track of time? You know what youngsters are like. If I were you I'd go and have some lunch and I'm sure they'll appear just as you're enjoying your soup. That's usually how it works, isn't it?'

I knew Jonathan was probably just as worried as me; ever since Melissa moved in we had both been doing our best to carry on as normal, but the truth was we were living in a perpetual state of anxiety about her running away. However, Jonathan did his best not to show it and instead put his energy into trying to keep me calm.

I told him he was probably right about the soup but I wasn't hungry and didn't want to eat yet. Instead, I offered to take over in the shop so he could have a quick lunch break. He agreed to this, and I told him the soup might need reheating and that there was a fresh loaf in the bread bin and some Camembert in the fridge, which is his favourite cheese.

'It's my lucky day,' he said jovially, rubbing his hands together and taking off his apron.

*

There was a steady flow of customers and I enjoyed helping some of them select the right flowers for the occasion, and gift-wrapping their chosen bouquets with cellophane and ribbons. I was just finishing a conversation with a gentleman who had bought flowers for his elderly mother when Melissa and Sonia clattered into the shop, chattering nineteen to the dozen as they manoeuvred the pushchair through the door.

'It's years since I've been in here,' Sonia said, looking around in wonderment, like a child in a grotto. Kazim pointed excitedly at a display of helium balloons that danced when the door opened and the chill air blew in.

'Hi Angela,' Melissa said breezily as soon as I'd stopped chatting to the customer and he left the shop. Her cheeks were pink and her eyes looked greener than ever.

'Hello girls. You've been longer than I thought you'd be. I was getting worried.'

I glanced at my watch: it was quarter past one.

'Sorry,' Melissa said. 'We lost track of time. What time is it? We've been on every piece of play equipment in the park, haven't we?' She leaned into Kazim in the buggy and he kicked his legs and chuckled. Melissa then started telling me how cool the climbing frame was, and how she would have easily completed the monkey bars if her hands weren't so cold.

'I can't believe you!' Sonia laughed. 'You're a bigger kid than Kazim. Right, I need to get going.'

I asked Sonia if she was in time for the toddler group and she said she wasn't going to bother now, as Kazim was tired out and needed a nap.

She grinned at Melissa. 'Good to see you, and see you soon, yeah?'

'You bet,' Melissa beamed.

'And good luck with you-know-who!' Sonia winked cheekily at Melissa as she waved goodbye and left the shop.

I glanced at the clock. It was now twenty past one.

'Jonathan's in the kitchen getting some lunch. Elaine will be here shortly. Why don't you quickly go and get yourself a sandwich or a bowl of the tomato soup I made today? There's plenty of fresh bread and cheese too.'

'OK,' Melissa said, but it didn't look like she'd listened to a word I'd said. She had a dreamy look in her eye and was batting the helium balloons absent-mindedly, making them bob up and down.

'Is there something you want to tell me?'

'No, well, yeah. Oh, you heard what Sonia said? Ha ha! I've got a crush on this guy and I just saw him up the park, that's all.'

'So I guess we're not talking about TJ or Degsy? This is another boy?'

'No, not TJ or Degsy! This is a different one. He's mates with Oz, but he's well nicer looking than Oz, and TJ and Degsy, come to think of it. He wears gorgeous clothes too and he's got great taste in music. He's a proper sophisticated guy and he's got a really good car. We like the same stuff. It's amazing. Our taste in music is *exactly* the same. What are the chances of that?'

'Does he have a name, "you-know-who"?' I said.

'You don't miss anything, do you?' she laughed. 'I'll kill

Sonia for calling him that! His name's Tommy. And no, before you ask, I don't know his last name.'

She said she was going to grab some lunch, and before I let her go I told her again that I'd been worried. I hadn't wanted to tell her off or embarrass her in front of her friend, but I quickly took the opportunity to remind her that she needed to come in on time, every time, even if she was just going to the park in daylight.

'I know, I'm sorry. I won't do it again. When I get my pocket money, can I have it in change, so then I'll always be able to use the phone box if I need to let you know where I am?'

We gave every child who stayed with us weekly pocket money and I always gave it out on the same day of the week. I didn't make exceptions to this, as I wanted to teach the kids to do a little bit of budgeting and only spend what they had. Melissa was getting £4 on Saturday and she was very happy with this. She promised me that she wouldn't be late on purpose and would only call and tell me she was late if she really couldn't help it.

'That's good,' I said. 'But you need to learn to stick to the times we've agreed. I don't want you to be late back again, whatever you're doing.'

'OK, that's fair,' she shrugged. 'Anyway, I hope Elaine is late because I'm starving and I've hardly got time to eat!'

Melissa was in luck because Elaine was running twenty minutes late – she'd had a problem with her car – and they eventually set off for the afternoon at about 2 p.m. Before they left I'd told Melissa to put any washing she had in the laundry bin in her room, and after I'd finally had my lunch and Jonathan was back in the shop I went up to fetch it. In the summer and on dry days I always do the washing in the morning so I can hang it out on the line to dry, but in winter I do it whenever it's convenient and dry it in the tumble dryer. In those days I also used the laundrette from time to time, particularly when I had a lot of bed linen to do. I liked to support our local precinct shops (sadly the laundrette has closed down now) and it also made life easier, as the bedding came back not only washed and dried, but ironed too.

I glanced at the clock and saw it was two thirty. I didn't fancy trudging out in the cold that day and decided there was plenty of time to get Melissa's washing done at home before she returned. I climbed the stairs and went into Melissa's bedroom, where I immediately noticed a handwritten list of names. It had fallen on the floor beside her laundry bin and I couldn't avoid seeing it. The list was on a piece of brightly coloured paper, with stars and hearts drawn alongside the different names. At a glance I could see about twenty names on the list, and they all seemed to be boys' names. Oz and Degsy leaped out as they were highlighted with fluorescent yellow pen. I noticed Tommy's name, which had a heart and a kiss beside it, and TJ was there too. It looked like the sort of list any young girl might make, maybe when she ranked boys she fancied. There were also some names of pop stars like Michael Jackson, David Bowie and Gary Barlow. I'd heard her listening to Take That music and I assumed all the singers she'd listed must be her favourite artists.

I felt like I was prying when I allowed my eyes to sweep down the list, but at the same time I told myself I needed to know as much as possible about Melissa and the company she was keeping. I had to be very vigilant, particularly after the pregnancy drama. I needed to keep encouraging Melissa to talk openly with me, and I also needed to keep my eyes and ears peeled for any signs that she might be getting herself into trouble or putting herself at risk, and if so who she was mixing with. I saw that at the bottom of the page it said Ozzy Osbourne and Tom Jones. I was surprised she had those two names on the list; they were not the singing idols you'd expect a young girl to be interested in.

Vicky, the girl who'd lived with us long-term until the previous year, called round later in the afternoon, while Melissa was still out. I invited her to stay for dinner that evening, as I did as often as I could. She accepted and said she'd like to meet Melissa.

'What's it like having a girl of that age living with you?' Vicky said. 'I thought I might have put you off forever!'

Vicky had been slightly older – thirteen going on fourteen – when she first arrived with us. She would turn eighteen later this year and was blossoming into a lovely young woman.

'We survived!' I smiled. 'Although there were days when you lived with us when I thought "never again!"'

Vicky laughed. 'I don't know how you and Jonathan

coped. I was a nightmare, wasn't I? How do you start all over again with another girl? It must be like Groundhog Day.'

I cast my mind back. Vicky had been neglected and abused by her mother and it was the memories of her traumatic childhood that made her freeze in terror, turning her from a seemingly self-assured teenager into a silent, white-faced statue.

'You weren't that bad,' I smiled. 'You'd had a tough time. I don't see fostering as being like Groundhog Day at all, because each child is so very different. I think you'll like Melissa, she's a nice girl.'

Of course, I never discuss the details of any child's life with anybody else. Vicky knew this and didn't ask me anything about Melissa's history.

'I look forward to meeting her,' she said.

Vicky was helping me in the kitchen when Elaine dropped Melissa home. The support worker said the two visits they'd made that day had been successful but she didn't elaborate and didn't stop to chat, even though I offered her a cup of tea. 'I'd love to but I've been running late all day and I've got to dash. I'll be in touch. Have a good evening.'

I introduced the girls to one another and left them chatting while I took a phone call in the hall. When I walked back into the kitchen Melissa was telling Vicky about the people she'd been to see that day.

'I get on OK with my auntie but I couldn't live with her. She's a proper nag, and her stepson is a weirdo.'

'What's up with him?' Vicky asked.

I kept quiet and busied myself at the sink. It was obvious I could hear every word she was saying but my presence didn't appear to affect how Melissa spoke. She carried on talking, seemingly unguarded.

'He looks at me in a funny way and says things about wanting to "do it" with me. It's disgusting. He's my fucking cousin!'

I had to interject now. I reminded her not to swear and made a mental note of what she'd said.

'Sorry, Angela. Sometimes I just forget where I am. I'm really sorry.'

Vicky offered to lay the table. She looked a bit shocked and embarrassed at what Melissa had said and she changed the subject, asking her if she played netball or went to the local youth club like she did when she was younger.

'No. I'm not really into sports. I used to go to the youth club disco at the community centre with my mate Imogen, but I got bored of it. I think we outgrew it.'

'Oh,' Vicky said. I could tell she was thinking twelve was a young age at which to outgrow the youth club, which was for kids up to the age of sixteen.

The two of them went into the dining room with the cutlery and the salt and pepper. Meanwhile I thought back to what Melissa had told me about Sonia, because this latest conversation reminded me of it.

Her stepbrother had once said to her, 'I'd shag you if you weren't family.' That's what she'd told me. I could remember Melissa saying those words, very clearly, and now she was accusing her cousin of making similarly inappropriate remarks about having sex with her. I had no idea if this was an odd coincidence or not. What I did know was that I was alarmed that such a young girl spoke about sex in this way. If you added to this the fact Melissa had had a pregnancy scare and appeared to have a collection of 'boyfriends', it was highly concerning. I wondered if she was truly as sexually precocious as it appeared, and if so, why?

I was becoming increasingly puzzled by Melissa, and felt I couldn't really work her out. On the face of it she seemed like a very normal, pleasant young girl. If you didn't know her background you'd have said she was very young for her age. For one thing, she had some very childish traits, like the way she enjoyed playing in the park and drawing hearts and stars in bright-coloured pens. Even the way she dressed seemed to highlight how young she was. Though she favoured sweatshirts and tracksuit bottoms, she never looked streetwise. In fact, it was the opposite. Most of her clothes had some kind of childish design on them, whether it was a picture of a butterfly, a print of a pretty flower or a cute Disney character. Her collection of hair accessories also belied her age: she had glittery bobbles, fluorescent bows and some hairgrips embellished with little painted daisies, toadstools and shooting stars.

I went up to my bedroom and quickly scribbled down some notes for Social Services while everything was fresh in my mind. I did this because I had a strong feeling that something was off about the way Melissa spoke so casually about shocking sexual remarks. A girl her age should not be discussing such things in such a seemingly blasé manner. I also had alarm bells ringing about that list of names, though I wasn't sure why. It could have been totally innocent, but maybe this was something the police needed to know about, if and when Melissa ran away again. I had to let Social Services know the list existed, just in case.

We are always told to stick to facts only and not express personal opinion in our notes for Social Services. However, on this occasion I couldn't help noting down that what Melissa said felt wrong and worried me, and that I had concerns about the list and who might be on it, though I wasn't sure if this was relevant to her case. Maybe I was running the risk of appearing to have an overactive imagination? I didn't care. I felt I owed it to Melissa to do everything in my power to safeguard her. That was what mattered, above all else.

10

'Who's Melissa?'

When Jonathan joined us around the dinner table the conversation turned to snooker and pool. Vicky had been a dab hand when she lived with us, and Jonathan reminded her about how she used to beat the boys at the youth club. Melissa looked impressed and said she'd never played, but she'd like to.

'We've got a table stored in the garage,' Jonathan told her. 'We could get it out if you like. I'd love to have a game myself.'

'That sounds great,' Melissa said. 'Although, thinking about it, my friend Sam has got a pool table already set up in her mum's conservatory. I've just remembered. I think I'll ask her if we can have a game. I never thought it would be much fun.'

Vicky encouraged this. 'Yes you should. I used to love it so much, especially when I thrashed the boys!'

Immediately after dinner Melissa asked if she could use the phone, to call her friend Sam.

'It'll be great if I can go round there and have a game,' she said. 'And it'll save you having to get your table out.'

'It's no trouble,' Jonathan said. 'As I said, I'd enjoy a game myself, and I know Vicky would love to join in too. Mind you,' he joked, 'we don't want to be thrashed, do we?'

'No we don't! Can I call Sam?'

We agreed that she could, and minutes later Melissa bounced into the kitchen looking like the cat who'd got the cream.

'Guess what? Sam said I can go over tonight! Is that OK?'

Jonathan and I gave each other a look.

Here we go again, I thought, and I knew Jonathan was thinking the same thing. It was difficult to tell if Melissa was genuinely enthralled by the idea of playing pool, or whether this had simply given her a good excuse to go out. Nevertheless, we said she could go to her friend's house, as long as she told us where Sam lived, didn't go anywhere else and was home by nine.

'Nine? But she lives on the other side of town. It's quite a long walk so can I come home a bit later?'

'No, if that's the case we'll drop you off and pick you up.'

Before Melissa had a chance to reply Vicky interjected.

'Do you remember that time you grounded me?' she said, bursting out laughing.

We remembered it well. We were very new to fostering when Vicky first came to live with us. After she got into trouble one time – for being rude in front of a customer in the shop, as I recall – we told her she was grounded for a whole month. Within days we realised it was a big mistake as she drove us mad, moping around the house bored to tears, getting under our feet.

'How could I forget?' I smiled. 'And do you remember that top you wore?'

'Oh my God, yes I do!'

I explained to Melissa that Vicky wore an old maternity sweatshirt of her sister's that had the words 'Let Me Out!' emblazoned on the front. She walked around in it when her social worker visited, saying how 'very appropriate' the slogan was for someone who was grounded.

After that experience, Jonathan and I learned that grounding children is not the best way of disciplining them, and in subsequent years it was not something that Social Services encouraged in any case. The thinking now is that stopping kids from doing a club or activity, or going on a trip, is probably only going to have a negative outcome. The children lose out on exercise, socialising with friends and learning new skills, which of course are all very important parts of life for healthy, growing kids. I agree with this in principle, and it's what we are still taught in training and practise to this day. However, in Melissa's case, the fact we could not stop her leaving the house seemed only to create problems, given that she was going out and mixing with the wrong crowd rather than taking part in enriching activities with her friends.

The word 'punishment' was becoming outdated in the nineties too. Jonathan and I have never liked the word and have never used it, and 'penalising' or 'punishing' a child by sending them to their room or docking stars off a chart, for example, are no longer acceptable ways of disciplining a child who has suffered trauma. Modern experts say these tactics can make already vulnerable children feel unloved, unwanted or ashamed. Foster carers are instead taught to use 'natural consequences' that don't have a detrimental effect on a child's wellbeing or self-esteem. A good example is that if a child calls you 'stupid' and subsequently asks you for a lift, then you may want to say, 'I'm terribly sorry, but I'd be concerned for your safety if a stupid person, as you feel I am, were to drive you around.' Next time, hopefully, the child will think twice about insulting you, having faced the consequences of their rudeness.

With Melissa, it was difficult to know what to do to encourage her to stick to the boundaries we put in place. Previous foster carers had tried everything they could think of to keep her safe and nothing had worked. I was concerned that if she was late again and we said she had to stay in, or asked her to come home earlier than nine, then she might rebel and run away. There wasn't a lot we could do, given the fact Social Services would not let us keep her in against her will. Driving her to and from her friend's house seemed like the best idea in the circumstances.

Thankfully, Melissa agreed to us taking her and collecting her from Sam's house. She made no fuss about this at all and we were pleased. It seemed like the best way of keeping Melissa safe and making sure she didn't go missing.

After we'd all eaten, we dropped Vicky off at her flat on the way to take Melissa to Sam's house.

'Good luck at pool,' Vicky called as she got out of the car. 'I look forward to hearing all about it next time!'

Melissa gave her a thumbs-up. I was pleased the girls had

got on, and also that Melissa had seen we'd stayed in touch with Vicky and got on well with her. I wanted Melissa to know we cared very deeply about the children who came to live with us, and that even after they'd moved on they were all welcome in our home. Some children don't have a family to go back to after a spell in care, or they don't ever manage to reconnect with their parents or other relatives. It means that sometimes Jonathan and I end up being the closest they have to any kind of stable family base, and we make sure every child knows we will always be there for them, come what may.

'You can drop me at the top of the road if you like,' Melissa said casually as we approached Sam's address. 'Here's perfect. It's a narrow street and it's fine just here.'

She sounded insistent, which didn't go unnoticed and made us feel wary.

'It's no bother at all,' Jonathan said, carrying on and pulling up right outside the house, even though the road actually was extremely narrow and pitted with potholes. 'There you are, Melissa. And I'll park up right here at nine o'clock when we come back to collect you.'

'OK, thanks!'

She jumped out of the car and tried to wave us off before she knocked on the door.

'Bye!' we said. Jonathan started the engine but didn't move an inch until we saw her go inside the house.

There were thin net curtains in the front room and from the dark street we could see silhouettes of several people milling around. They looked like a group of teenagers mucking about, but we couldn't be sure of that. There was a television on: we could see a bright but blurred glare spilling through the curtains, and when the car door had opened we caught the sound of a dull bass beat punching through the dank evening air.

'Do you think this is a good idea?' I said as Sam's front door opened and Melissa disappeared inside.

Seconds later – before we'd pulled away – the door opened again and a woman came out. She was wearing fluffy boots and was puffing on a cigarette. She walked to the gate at the side of the house and pulled out the bin, dragging it down the drive.

Instinctively, I darted out of the car.

'Are you Sam's mum?'

'Yes,' she said brightly. 'And you must be . . .'

'We've just dropped Melissa off.'

I didn't want to say we were her foster carers in case Melissa had chosen to keep quiet about the fact she was in care.

'Right, of course. Our Sam's got a few mates round.'

'Thanks for having her.'

I explained that we were coming back to collect Melissa at nine, and Sam's mum nodded in a vague way and said that was absolutely fine by her.

'Thanks,' I said. 'Nice to have met you. I'm Angela.'

'Nice to meet you too, love. I'm Carol.'

Jonathan and I enjoyed a couple of hours to ourselves. Having met Sam's mum and knowing Melissa was at her friend's house, we didn't fret about her. It was only when we felt free of worry that we realised how stressed we'd been every time Melissa had gone out. She'd only been staying with us for just over a week but it felt like much longer. Neither of us had slept well since she'd arrived and we both admitted we felt exhausted.

We arrived back at Sam's house at five to nine. It looked like the TV was still on in the front room but there was no sign of anybody, and no noise coming from the house. We didn't want to cramp Melissa's style by knocking on the door and bringing her out early, so we waited patiently until nine o'clock. When she still hadn't emerged a few minutes later I went and tapped on the door. A scruffy-looking youth in a black T-shirt and black skinny jeans answered. He looked about eighteen and I imagined he was Sam's big brother.

'Hello. I've come to pick up Melissa.'

'Who's Melissa?' The teenager laughed and then another lad came to the door. He looked slightly younger than the first boy – perhaps fifteen – and he was smoking and holding a can of lager.

'Melissa is Sam's friend.'

'Oh, I'm with you now. Our Sam's not in.'

My heart sank.

'Do you know where she is?'

'No idea. Sorry.' The older boy shrugged apologetically and went to shut the door.

'Hang on. Is your mum in? I take it Carol's your mum?'

'Yeah, she is. I mean, she's my mum but she's not in. She's gone to the club.'

'OK. Do you know what time Sam went out, or if Melissa was with her?'

'Sorry, I haven't got a clue. Our Sam did go out with a couple of mates, that's all I know.'

'Melissa has long red hair. Was she with Sam?'

'Yeah, I think she was with her. There were a couple of them I think. They went out ages ago though. Our Sam never said where they were going.'

I explained that I'd arranged to collect Melissa at the house at nine.

'If she comes back here, please can someone let me know or get her to ring me so I can collect her?'

I scribbled down my phone number and passed it to the boy. He took it reluctantly and shoved it in his back pocket, saying, 'I will. I'll tell Mum if she gets in.'

'If she gets in?'

'Yeah, when she goes to the club she doesn't always come home. She never said what she was doing tonight.' The boy sniggered and went to close the door. My stomach turned over. Though it was obvious the boy was trying to get rid of me, I stood my ground. I told him my name was Angela and asked him if he could give me any clues at all as to where the girls had gone.

'Like I said, I've got no idea. Sorry. Good luck.'

He was already shutting the door.

Jonathan had got out of the car now and was striding up the path, realising I was having trouble. I shook my head and we both walked back to the car.

'What do we do now?' I asked.

'Only one thing we can do. We'll have to call the out-of-hours number if she doesn't show up by ten.'

I put my head in my hands and groaned, asking how we could have been so foolish. Jonathan put his arm round me. 'Look, it's not our fault. We gave her boundaries and she's broken out of them. We've done our best.'

We sat outside the house for a short time in case Melissa turned up there, before Jonathan drove us home. He then spent the next forty minutes driving back up to Sam's house and searching around the town before returning home at around ten.

I called Social Services, and as expected they told me that because Melissa had been missing for over an hour and it was dark, we needed to tell the police. The officer who took my call at our local station sounded very sympathetic and concerned at first. I began to give him all the information I thought might be useful, including a detailed physical description of her, the names of her friends and boyfriends, plus Sam's address. He patiently logged the details, but once I'd explained that Melissa was in foster care and had a history or going missing I detected a shift in his attitude. 'I take my hat off to you,' he said, letting out a despondent sigh. 'I don't know how you do it, taking in a kid like that. I know I couldn't do it.'

He was trying to pay me a compliment I guess, but I didn't like the way he described Melissa as a 'kid like that'. It sounded dismissive, and I thought to myself that, at this moment in time, what kind of kid she might be was irrelevant. She was a missing twelve-year-old girl, and we needed to find her, fast, whatever she was like.

The officer said someone would call if there was any news. I asked him if any other children – and specifically Sam – had been reported missing. He said he couldn't discuss any other child's disappearance with me, but he could confirm Melissa was the only child reported missing that night.

'Great,' I said sarcastically when I put the phone down. 'It looks like Sam's mum hasn't even noticed she's gone.'

Despite Jonathan's reassurances that we'd done nothing wrong I did feel an idiot for assuming Carol was going to stay in and supervise the girls; it simply hadn't occurred to me that she would go out like this, giving the girls free rein to come and go as they pleased. In hindsight it seemed obvious we shouldn't have made any assumptions about what Carol may or may not do. It had looked like her front room was full of young people and we should not have taken it for granted that Carol was going to keep an eye on them. 'Maybe Sam is allowed out later than ten?' Jonathan said. 'Maybe they'll turn up back at Sam's house soon and we'll get a phone call from Melissa instead of from the police?'

I told him I admired his optimism, but it seemed very unlikely. We waited up for hours, watching the clock and willing the phone to ring. Eventually, when there was still no sign of Melissa at almost one o'clock, we reluctantly tried to get some rest, but sleep didn't come easily. Subconsciously we were on red alert, and it was impossible to think of anything but Melissa.

I woke at two in the morning. It felt like I'd only been asleep for a few minutes and perhaps I had; my eyes were heavy and my head was buzzing and aching. There was a noise in the garden. I immediately woke Jonathan, which wasn't difficult; he must have also been in a very light sleep.

'I'll go and see what's going on,' he said straight away. 'You stay here.' He got up and looked out of the window. 'I can't see anything, but I'll go down and put the lights on. You stay warm. Don't get up.'

I felt sick with worry and was annoyed and frustrated that we were in this situation. We had fully expected to collect Melissa from Sam's house. Why had she done this? It seemed so unnecessary and selfish. What on earth was she thinking?

Melissa had no key – we wouldn't give out a house key to a child on such a short-term placement, and particularly not to a girl of twelve with a history of running away. Maybe Melissa was trying to break into the house somehow? Or had she been knocking on the back door? I really wasn't sure what I'd heard.

I stayed wrapped up in our thick duvet, listening intently as Jonathan went outside. The bedroom curtains illuminated slightly as he switched on the patio and garden lights. Then I heard his footsteps as he explored the garden and side passageway, and a few minutes later I heard him re-locking the back door and padding up the stairs.

'Nothing there. No sign. Maybe it was wishful thinking? Or maybe it was just next door's cat?'

'I'm going to check her bedroom,' I said, unwrapping

myself from the warm duvet. Jonathan didn't stop me, even though we both knew I wasn't going to find her there.

When I walked into Melissa's room and turned on the light I saw the list of names I'd seen before. It was on her pillow now, with the top of her duvet partly covering it. I sat on her bed and my weight pulled the duvet down the bed slightly, revealing the note in its entirety. I studied it without touching it. I didn't want Melissa to think I'd been rooting around in her room and snooping on her, but I did want to read this list again, in case it gave me any clues about where Melissa was and who she was with.

The name Sam was on the list, which I hadn't noticed before. Beside that name was an equals sign, and next to that it said Sadie. Under that was written Melissa = Maz. Buzz was also there – the name Sonia had told me Kazim's dad went by.

'Do you think I should call the police and tell them Melissa might be using another name?'

Jonathan rubbed his eyes.

'What are you talking about?'

I explained about the list. 'Why not?' he said. 'The more information they have the better.'

Another officer eventually took my call; it had taken a while to get through. He told me there was no news and politely listened as I explained about the list I'd found in Melissa's bedroom. I told him she could be using the name Maz, making it clear this was guesswork on my part. He thanked me, though I had no idea if he was going to act on the information in any way or if he thought I was just a desperate foster carer, clutching at straws.

I woke again at three, then four thirty and finally six o'clock. It was still dark and the house was cold, as the heating had not yet clicked on. I checked the phone for messages but already knew there were none before the digital voice told me, 'You have no new messages.'

Jonathan had slept just as badly as I had. We both tried to get another hour's sleep but didn't succeed.

Jonathan got up and said he was going to make a cup of tea while I lay in bed, my mind wandering to places I didn't want it to go. What if Melissa was hurt? What if she and Sam had got themselves into a dangerous situation? What if she went missing for days or even weeks, and what if she was never found? I thought I would never be able to live with myself.

11

'Melissa knows a lot of people'

At 8 a.m. Jonathan drove over to Sam's house. There was no reply at the door and he put a note through the letterbox giving our phone number again, explaining who we were and asking Carol, or any other member of the family, to give us a call.

Meanwhile I rang the police once more, only to be told they had no news on Melissa. Sam had still not been reported missing: the police confirmed Melissa was still the only missing child on their records over the last twenty-four hours.

This didn't tell us anything and only served to raise more questions. If Carol had stayed out overnight and the girls had gone off together, it was possible Sam had still not been missed. Or maybe Carol had got back home from her night out, gone to bed and was none the wiser and still sound asleep? Hopefully a member of the family would call soon and we'd get more information.

Having never dealt with a situation like this before, I wasn't sure exactly how the police would be handling

Melissa's disappearance. Would they be following up on every piece of information I'd given them, making contact with Sam's family and Melissa's friends, in an effort to track her down? I doubted it; I realised they hadn't even asked if we had a photograph of her. I later found out my instincts were correct. With many more years of experience under my belt, I now know that overstretched police forces do not have the resources to actively go looking for missing children. In reality, it's a question of alerting officers to the disappearance and hoping one of them might spot the child or pick up some useful information when they are out on duty, at least in the very early stages.

At 9 a.m. I began to call Wilf, Doreen and Elaine in turn. They each offered reassurances and said we had done nothing wrong.

'She'll turn up,' Doreen said rather wearily. She didn't sound overly concerned. 'She always has in the past. I'm afraid you'll just have to try to carry on as normal until she does. There really isn't much point in losing sleep. You need to look after yourselves so you're fit to care for her when she's back.'

I guess it was sensible advice, but it felt wrong. Melissa was a little girl. She was missing and we had no idea where she was. She could be lying in a ditch somewhere. She could be drunk or drugged or . . . I had to keep calm. I knew that panicking wasn't going to help, but even so I couldn't stop fretting about Melissa and fearing all kinds of terrible things. I could picture her pretty face and her hair tied up with one of the colourful scrunchies she used to secure her ponytail.

Her face was sad and frightened and there were no dimples in her cheeks because she wasn't smiling; that's the only way I could picture her.

I told Elaine how very worried I was. 'You shouldn't think like that,' she said. 'She's choosing to run away and she'll come back when she's had her fun.'

'Fun?' Jonathan commented when I passed on what Elaine had said. 'It's baffling how running away, going missing, having the police called and frightening the living daylights out of your foster carers could be described as fun. I just don't get it. It seems so strange that a girl like Melissa could do this. How is this fun for anyone?'

Sam's mother didn't call, not ever, and we didn't understand that either. Surely she'd got the message eventually and would realise how worried we were? Wasn't it obvious that any little piece of information she had might be helpful? We didn't even know if Sam was home or not, and all kinds of other questions went round and round in my head. I wondered if maybe Sam was missing too, but had not been reported missing to the police. Perhaps, for some reason, Carol didn't want any involvement with the police?

Whatever the truth, we never heard a thing from the family.

When I spoke to Wilf he listened and sympathised, then sounded me out about taking in another child. Ryan was a ten-year-old boy whose twenty-three-year-old brother had taken his own life, leaving Ryan on his own. I was taken aback at Wilf's suggestion, given the situation we were in.

'I don't know, Wilf. I feel we've already got a lot on our plate with Melissa.'

'I understand completely, but it should only be for a week, until we can move Ryan in with a relative. The poor little lad has already lost both his parents, and now this. The alternative is to put him in a children's home.'

Of course we said yes. It would be wrong not to take this boy in while we were here and had the space. Besides helping Jonathan run the shop, I wasn't planning on doing anything or going anywhere while Melissa was missing. When she came back – if she came back – I'd be keeping a very close eye on her. I imagined I'd be staying in as much as possible, to supervise her and be on hand to drop her off and pick her up whenever I could.

Ryan arrived later that morning. He was very small for his age and my first impression was that he seemed like a quiet and thoughtful boy. His social worker dropped him off and did a routine handover, providing me with some contact numbers and basic information about Ryan, such as his date of birth, but little else. It wasn't until he'd already moved in that I learned an investigation had begun into alleged neglect in his family home. It seemed Ryan's brother had left a suicide note and had made accusations about their now deceased father and mother.

Ryan was a pupil at one of the local primary schools. We were told he should be encouraged to attend but that the school was aware of his situation, and if he wanted to stay at home for the time being, that was fine. A new school place was being found for him near the relative who was going to take him in when he left our care. Ryan was due to be interviewed by the police and was having counselling, and his social worker said she would be in touch and let me know if Ryan had any appointments during the week he was with us.

'What would you like to do?' I asked him when the social worker left.

'Dunno. Are there any other children living here?'

I explained that we had Melissa living with us, but she was not here at the moment. My mum was due to call in for a cup of tea later on and I told Ryan I was going to bake some scones.

'Would you like to help me in the kitchen?'

A big smile spread across his face. 'I'd like that.'

Much to my surprise, I soon discovered that Ryan was quite the little entertainer. He picked up a couple of satsumas from the fruit bowl, covered his eyes with them and swivelled them around in opposite directions.

'What am I?'

'I don't know.'

'A chameleon!'

I laughed and Ryan looked really pleased. He was easy company and enjoyed helping me bake, and when my mum turned up he told her some jokes.

'What do you call a guy with a bald head who loves to eat raisins and biscuits?'

'I've no idea!' Mum said.

'Gary Baldy.'

Mum looked bemused and I had to explain the play on the word Garibaldi. Then she laughed a lot, telling Ryan he was very funny.

He beamed when she said that.

Jonathan came into the kitchen for a break from the shop, and I wish I'd taken a photo because his expression was priceless. He looked surprised and delighted that there was such a good atmosphere and we were all having fun. The kitchen was warm and cosy, the smell of baking filled the air, and Ryan was in stitches as he tried, and failed, to get my mum to recite a silly tongue twister.

'Now look here, young man,' Jonathan smiled. 'I'm the one who does the jokes around here.'

'Go on then!' Ryan challenged, and Jonathan gamely rattled out some of his old favourites. Ryan groaned at every punchline, which delighted my mum. 'I've been telling Jonathan for years he needs some new jokes,' she said. 'We've heard them all a million times.'

'You know what they say – the old ones are the best, Thelma.'

'No. The old ones are just old and need replacing!'

When Mum was leaving she said what a smashing boy she thought Ryan was. I would never divulge any child's private details, not even to my mum, and I think she'd have been absolutely flabbergasted at the tragic chain of events that had led Ryan to our door. Looking back, I can see that humour was Ryan's coping mechanism – to this day, whenever I hear the expression 'if I didn't laugh I'd cry,' I think of little Ryan.

*

After three nights Melissa was still missing. We were in regular contact with the police and Social Services and there had been no sighting of her. We eventually discovered that Sam had also been reported missing, though still nobody from her family had been in contact with us. Wilf advised me to leave the search to the police and not return to Sam's home or get involved with any of Melissa's friends. Though this went against my instincts, I agreed to follow his advice.

By day four of Melissa's disappearance we'd taken in another boy. He was a very sad-faced eleven-year-old who had been sexually abused. The boy was called Marty, he was in his first year of secondary school and would also be with us for a week, coming to us as an emergency placement.

After Marty arrived we learned he had touched a younger child inappropriately. He'd since had therapy and now knew it was wrong to touch another child as he had done. His social worker said they had no reason to believe Marty would repeat his behaviour; he had only been doing something that had unfortunately been normalised in his home environment. Now he'd received therapy and was having ongoing counselling, he was not considered to be a threat or danger to any other child.

It's fair to say that Jonathan and I were put under some pressure from Wilf to take in first Ryan and then Marty. We wanted to help and didn't want to say no. However, I knew that one of the major factors in the breakdown of Melissa's placement with Lynne and Nick had been that they had their own children to consider. Melissa had left their house unlocked when she broke out and ran away at night, and I reminded Wilf that this had been the final straw for Lynne.

'It's a valid point,' Wilf had said, when he first approached me about Ryan. 'But when we're faced with a choice between a foster home and a children's home, I'd always prefer to place a child with carers like you and Jonathan. Boys like this need to be in a loving environment, and you and Jonathan can provide that. You're wonderful foster carers. I wouldn't ask you if I didn't think you could cope. And it's only for a week.' He said more or less the same thing when we discussed Marty.

I'd told Wilf I appreciated the compliments, especially in the circumstances, with Melissa still missing. He reiterated that her disappearance had absolutely nothing to do with us and that we'd done nothing wrong. 'You mustn't blame yourselves in any way. You're fantastic carers. You're taking on kids who would otherwise be in children's homes and you should give yourselves a pat on the back. Girls like Melissa will always find a way to run off if that's what they want to do. You can only do your best, and your best is extremely good.'

Ryan and Marty seemed to get along OK, and the social workers were clearly happy to place the boys together. We hadn't been told to keep an extra close eye on Marty as a result of his history of inappropriate touching, but because of our specialist training we did. We'd learned about how deeply a child is affected by child abuse, and how there can be repercussions for many years, if not throughout a person's lifetime. I supervised the boys whenever they were together and made a point of regularly checking with Ryan that everything was OK.

The boys both liked the same computer game, so much so that I had to set limits on their screen time. With neither boy in school – Ryan chose to have the week off and Marty was between school places – we made an effort to keep them as active and entertained as possible. During the day I encouraged them to do some educational CD-ROMs on the computer, as well as playing their favourite computer game, and even though it was cold and drizzly we went on a couple of bike rides and the boys managed to have a good kick-about in the park with Jonathan. Our shop assistant put in some extra hours for us in the florist and I think the bracing, fresh air and change of scene was as refreshing for Jonathan and me as it was for the two boys. In fact, it was at this point that we started to think about taking on even more help in the shop. Though we'd only recently started working as specialist carers, we could already see that it was going to put more demands on our time than mainstream fostering, particularly if we were going to continue to take in children of all ages too.

As Jonathan and I had always worked so well as a team, both in the shop and with our fostering work, we wanted this to continue. However, with such demanding children, and the fact the kids who were now coming to us were often out of school, it was becoming obvious we'd need extra help in order to do so.

It wouldn't be long before an old friend of ours, Barbara, started to help out in the shop too. She was extremely flexible and was available most days of the week if we needed her, freeing us to devote more time to the children. The arrangement worked so well that Barbara eventually replaced our original assistant, who had other commitments and was happy to move on. I don't think we realised quite how much of a godsend Barbara was; looking back, I can't see how we'd have managed over the years without her.

In the evenings Jonathan and I took Ryan and Marty out to the cinema and the local swimming pool, which was also a tonic for us all. When Melissa first went missing I'd anticipated staying at home as much as I possibly could, in case she returned of her own free will. However, Wilf continued to urge us to carry on as normal, pointing out that when she'd been missing overnight in the past Melissa was typically picked up and returned by the police. He reminded us that the police or Social Services would deal with Melissa in the first instance and so there was no need for us to sit by the phone, as she would be perfectly safe with them until she was returned to us. Still, we always made sure we left the answerphone switched on, and if Jonathan and I were both out during the day we left instructions for whoever was working in the shop to pick up the phone and take a message, and we also checked in regularly. In retrospect I wonder how on earth we managed without mobile phones!

Sonia phoned on day six of Melissa's disappearance. She had no idea she was missing and was ringing to see if she wanted to go to the park, so I explained the situation and asked if she had any idea where Melissa might be. In accordance with Wilf's instructions, I hadn't gone round to Sonia's to look for Melissa, though I had let the police and Social Services know that Sonia was one of her friends and I'd passed on her address, as I'd done with everyone I could think of who Melissa might contact, including TJ and the handful of other local friends I knew of.

'No, I haven't seen her at all,' she said. 'I've got no idea where she could be or who—'

Sonia stopped talking for a moment, and then she said, 'Oh, maybe . . .'

'Maybe?'

'Well, I'm not sure but I know she was hoping to meet up with a guy, so maybe she's just with him and has lost track of time or something.'

Sonia said this as if it was not an unusual thing for a young girl to do, even though Melissa had been gone for six days.

'Was this the one you described as "you-know-who"?'

'Yes, that's who I'm thinking of.'

'His name's Tommy, isn't it?'

Sonia seemed surprised that I was so well informed.

'Er, yes, that's right. I wasn't sure if she'd have mentioned him to you. Anyway, I know she likes him. She asked me for some change for the phone, because she wanted to call him. That's what she said, but I don't know any more. Like I say, I haven't seen her since we went to the park that morning so I can't tell you anything else. And I might be completely wrong. She might just be with other mates. Melissa knows a lot of people. Lots of people I don't know.'

'I don't suppose you know where Tommy lives or what his full name is, or where he works?'

'No. My ex would know, but I'm not speaking to him and anyway I don't know where he is either.'

I heard Kazim grizzle. 'Tommy's Asian, like his dad – Kazim's dad, I mean.' I pictured Sonia looking at her son in his buggy. 'That's about as much as I can tell you about Tommy. He's a bit of a bad lad, but not in a really bad way. I mean, he's not been in prison or anything like that. One of my other mates used to go out with him.'

I told her Tommy didn't sound like an Asian name.

'I don't think Tommy's his real name. They like to have nicknames, don't they?'

At first I thought the 'they' referred to a gang Tommy and her ex were in, but Sonia elaborated, making me realise that wasn't what she was talking about at all.

'Yeah, all of them do it, don't they? It makes it easier.' She listed a few ethnic minorities, using slang words to describe particular ethnic groups. I'd heard most of the terms before but I was uncomfortable with Sonia's choice of language. The words she used sounded derogatory and racist, but now wasn't the time to dwell on this.

'What do you mean, it makes it easier?'

'What? Hang on.'

I heard Sonia feed another couple of coins into the pay phone.

'What do you mean about the nicknames "making it easier".'

'Oh, just easier for us to pronounce their names. That's

what my ex said anyway. I always called him by his nickname because he said I'd never be able to pronounce his real name. He always was a cheeky beggar. I think he must have thought I was thick or something.'

'What was his nickname, if you don't mind me asking?'

'Buzz,' she said.

I could hear Kazim starting to whine and Sonia said she had to go.

'I wouldn't worry too much,' she said. 'Melissa can handle herself. She'll be back. Can you tell her to come round to the flat and let me know when she's home? She's probably just having a good time, if I know Melissa. I used to be exactly like her. I think that's why we get on so well.'

I jotted everything down to tell Wilf later. He'd advised me to do this in the first instance, rather than calling the police every time I picked up a titbit of information that may be useful. I wondered if he was concerned the police might think I was wasting their time. Nobody said it and I have no proof of this, but I had a feeling Melissa's history had set a precedent for how the police were treating her disappearance; she was a known runaway, and I felt sure that affected how the police were handling her case.

I said this to Jonathan and he thought I made a good point. 'You'd think that all missing girls of her age would be treated the same,' he said thoughtfully. 'But once you're labelled a "runner" and have been locked up, it seems to change things. The urgency to find her doesn't seem to be there, not how you'd expect, anyhow.'

'Yes, unfortunately I think that's the case. I get the impression the police just see her as a bad girl who's out of control. It doesn't seem right to me though. She's a typical twelve-year-old when she's at home with us. If anything she seems quite sweet and childish for her age, but I think the authorities have her down as some kind of juvenile delinquent.'

Jonathan could see how upset and frustrated I was. He gave me a hug and reminded me to take Wilf's advice and not worry about what I couldn't control.

We took the two boys out for a pizza that night. I think we all needed a treat, and the evening ended on a high when Ryan won a colouring competition in the restaurant, walking away with a giant bar of chocolate.

12

'I'm not staying here'

Lynne phoned first thing in the morning, when I was making breakfast for Ryan and Marty. Both boys had an appointment that day and we were all up early, getting organised.

'I've had a message from Melissa,' Lynne said.

My heart leaped. 'Is she OK?'

I'd contacted Lynne when Melissa first went missing, and she knew she'd been gone for a week by now.

'I hope so. It was only on the answerphone. She left the message at 2.45 a.m., saying she was in another town and was "fine". She said she'd come back home soon.'

Lynne had not heard the call come in and had phoned me as soon as she played the message back that morning. She said she would call the police and Social Services and let them know and I thanked her and said I would also phone my support social worker.

'I wonder why she called you and not me?'

'She sounded a bit vacant, Angela. I wondered if she'd

been drinking and got muddled up. She also called herself by a different name, but it was definitely her.'

'What name?'

'Maz.'

I called Wilf at the office and left a message for him to call me as soon as possible. Ryan and Marty asked if they could play on the computer and I suggested I set them up with an educational game first, and once they'd done that they could play the battle game they both loved. Marty groaned. 'What's the point of life?' he asked. 'It's all work, work, work and then you're DEAD.'

I glanced at Ryan. His little face was a picture as he no doubt thought about the loss of his brother.

My mind went back to that wall of shoeboxes we'd been shown on our specialist training course. Though Ryan and Marty were not teenagers with complex needs, the training we'd had was still relevant and very useful. If you were a fly on the wall, looking at these two boys eating their Weetabix and talking about playing their favourite computer game, you would never have guessed at how they'd both suffered in their young lives. Each boy had several shoeboxes missing. I thought it was a miracle they were coping with things as well as they were, able to play, joke and get along with one another with such ease, in such testing circumstances and in unfamiliar surroundings too.

Marty's question about the point of life, and why we all have to work, is one I've heard in many guises, from various children. I normally respond by talking about how satisfying it is to enjoy the benefits of working hard and building a good life for yourself. I give examples from my own life, or from Jonathan's. We were both brought up to be grafters, and it's thanks to the effort we put in to keeping the business going that we were able to follow our hearts and become full-time foster carers.

'What's the point of life?' Ryan suddenly repeated back at Marty, screwing up his face. I think he was a bit shocked and wanted to lighten the atmosphere. 'That's a pointless question!'

'It's not!' Marty retorted. Ryan responded again before I had chance to say anything.

'It *is* pointless. Listen, I've got a better question.'

Ryan grinned cheekily and I realised he was going to tell one of his jokes.

'What's your question?' Marty said, groaning and rolling his eyes.

'Why shouldn't you write with a broken pencil?'

'Dunno.'

'Because it's pointless!'

Marty groaned again, even louder this time, and then the boys went on to chat about something that came on the radio about football.

Life goes on, I thought.

As I listened to the two boys chattering away I was struck by how sad it was that they had not had the best start in life. Ryan and Marty would need help and support for years – maybe throughout their lives – and it would not be easy, because many people they encountered would have no idea how difficult their childhoods had been. They may be misunderstood or judged unfairly, and this may undermine their already fragile sense of self and standing in the world.

It was Jonathan who answered the phone when Wilf called back, returning my call from earlier. I'd gone to have a shower and Jonathan updated me about Melissa as soon as I stepped out of the bathroom.

'The police found her last night, hours before Lynne had listened to the message on her answerphone and contacted them,' Jonathan said. 'She's OK, thank God.'

He went on to tell me the name of the town where Melissa was picked up. I was shocked. It was a large town in a fairly deprived area many miles away from us. I wondered how she'd got there and why she'd gone so far away. I didn't know a great deal about the town but I did know it had a large Asian population, which made me think that Sonia's theory about Melissa hooking up with Tommy might be correct.

Wilf didn't have much more information. Everything he knew had been taken down overnight by the out-of-hours social worker and passed on to him when he arrived at work that morning. He'd told Jonathan that the police had picked Melissa up very late at night and she was taken to a relative's home. She had told the police she 'used to be in foster care' but hadn't mentioned us. The relative she was staying with now lived fairly close to the town Melissa had been picked up in. We could only assume that the reason she'd called Lynne was because the police must have asked her who she used to be in care with. At this stage we had no more details about the relative.

Wilf said he'd call back as soon as he had any more details. I felt very relieved that Melissa was safe and with a relative, but I can't say I felt at ease in any way. There were so many unanswered questions.

A few hours later we heard that Melissa's aunt and uncle had collected her from the police station, rather than her being taken to their house by the police as we'd first thought. They took a call and drove to pick her up. It was not feasible for Melissa to stay with them, it seemed, and arrangements were being made to bring her back to our house as soon as possible.

As Ryan and Marty were still with us – both had had their week-long placements extended by several days due to hold-ups with their permanent moves – we couldn't go and collect Melissa ourselves, as we'd have liked. My mum would usually be happy to babysit for us in situations like this. However, the round trip to collect Melissa was going to take several hours and Mum would have to cancel a long-standing arrangement, which wasn't fair. Therefore, we agreed that a support worker would collect Melissa from her aunt and uncle's house and drive her back to us that afternoon.

Melissa arrived at our door at 4 p.m. Ryan was watching TV upstairs in the lounge and Marty was out with his social worker, due home within the hour. Melissa looked very pale and seemed tired out. She didn't give me any eye contact and stared at the floor when the support worker accompanied her into our kitchen.

'How are you?' I asked gently.

'I'm not staying here,' she said, without peeling her eyes off the kitchen floor.

I didn't recognise the tracksuit she was wearing and it looked too big for her. I turned to the support worker.

'I've explained to Melissa that she has to stay here, at least for the time being,' he said.

It turned out that the 'aunt and uncle' who had collected her from the police station were, in fact, family friends. There was no question she could stay there, but she said she didn't want to, in any case.

'I hate it where they live, it's worse than here! I'm not staying here. I'm going to pack my stuff.'

She ran out of the kitchen and up the stairs.

'Melissa . . .' the support worker started.

'Come back, Melissa, we can talk this through . . .' I said.

Jonathan appeared and also implored her not to run off upstairs, but she ignored all three of us.

'She has told me she wants to live near her friends,' the support worker said. 'But from what I can gather, these friends are not a good influence on her. She'd been drinking when she was picked up by the police and was with a gang who were making a nuisance of themselves, hanging around on the streets outside a takeaway in the town centre.' The support worker had been given these latter details by the family friends who'd collected Melissa. The couple had also described Melissa as 'boy mad.' They said she had been found with a boy, and that she had told them he was her boyfriend and she couldn't live so far away from him.

'Did she give a name?'

'Not that I know of.'

Melissa's social worker, Doreen, turned up just after the support worker left. I told her that Melissa had stomped upstairs, and I filled her in on what I'd just heard.

'I don't know,' Doreen said, rolling her eyes. 'I'm sorry she's done this again. It looks like she's got in with yet another bad crowd.'

Doreen explained that Melissa had never been picked up in this particular town before, at least not to her knowledge. The police at the station she had been taken to knew nothing about her history, which explains why they didn't know straight away that Melissa was in care with Jonathan and me. This was not unusual in the early nineties, before police databases were as efficiently computerised and centralised as they are today. I can remember that there'd been a story in the news around that time, about how an eagle-eyed journalist had helped return a missing child to his parents. The young boy had accidentally got on a train and ended up in another county. As soon as he was reported missing to the police by his family their local radio station ran appeals for information. Meanwhile, when the frightened boy got off the train alone, miles from home, the police force across the border also put out an appeal for information. They were struggling to identify him, as he was very young and couldn't remember the name of his home town. Meanwhile, a journalist who was reading the national news wires in London put two and two together and realised the missing child and the found child were one and the same. Thanks to her, the boy was reunited with his extremely relieved and grateful family, while the police were left to question how communication could be so poor between neighbouring forces.

Doreen had no information about who the new crowd of people Melissa was associating with may be, and she had not heard the name Tommy. 'It's always to do with the latest boyfriend, from what I can see,' she sighed.

I asked how things were progressing with Melissa's permanent move when her placement with us ended, and whether there was any update on her school place. Doreen said progress had been made and if everything went to plan Melissa would be moving in with her Auntie Cathy in roughly four weeks' time. She gave us the proposed date and said there were 'a few bits and bobs still to sort out.' I wondered if it would be possible to move her any sooner, given the circumstances.

'It's not possible,' Doreen said. 'Believe me, I've tried. But the good news is that Melissa can start back at her old school again next week, so that will keep her out of trouble for the rest of the time she's with you. Everything's in place. She's going to have a special timetable to follow, to help ease her back in, and the teachers will treat her as if she's on report. By that I mean she'll have to sign in to each lesson, to help keep tabs on her.'

I took down the details, and for the first time in days and days I felt there was some light at the end of the tunnel. I thought Melissa could be a good student. She was interested in several subjects and I'd been impressed that she'd done some schoolwork independently when she first arrived. I dared to hope that returning to school might be a turning point and that Melissa might follow a better path once she was back in the education system and had other things besides boys to occupy her mind.

I knew the coming weeks weren't going to be easy, given the fact Melissa didn't even want to stay with us. Nevertheless, I hoped she'd see sense and things would improve once she'd had chance to calm down and settle back into our house. We'd still have to be vigilant and she might run away again, but at least if she was at school there would be fewer hours in the day we had to worry about – that's what I thought, anyway.

I went upstairs and knocked on Melissa's bedroom door. I could hear her stomping around.

'Go away!'

'Melissa, Doreen is here now. She'd like to talk to you.'

'I don't want to speak to her.'

It sounded like Melissa had calmed down slightly.

'Can I come in?'

There was a pause.

'I'll come out.'

Melissa edged out of her room looking sheepish. She apologised for being rude and I told her Doreen had some news for her.

'Is it good news? Can I move in with Auntie Cathy?'

I explained that yes she could but not just yet, and that in the meantime she could return to her old school.

'If you come downstairs, Doreen will be able to tell you more.'

She shuffled down the stairs behind me, not saying a word.

When we reached the first floor landing, Ryan popped his head out of the lounge.

'Oh my God!' Melissa said. 'That freaked me out! I didn't think anyone was in there.'

I introduced her to Ryan, explaining that he was staying with us for the rest of the week. She politely asked him which school he went to and said she had once attended the same primary.

'It sucks, doesn't it?' she said jokily.

'Yeah!' he said, grinning.

'Is Mr Mace still there?'

'Ha ha, yeah he is!'

'Unlucky!'

I was pleased that Melissa had reverted to being her old self, but at the same time it was disconcerting to see how easily she could change. It was almost like she was controlled by a switch – and I was well aware that she could just as rapidly switch back to being the girl who wanted to run away.

'Now what did I tell you last time I saw you?' Doreen chastised.

Melissa shrugged and looked at the floor. I could see her shrinking back to the uncommunicative girl the support worker had brought home a short while earlier.

'I said no more running off, young lady!' Doreen went on. 'Now, do you want to tell me why you've done this again? I mean, you could have ended up back in the secure unit, and we don't want that, do we?'

She sounded like a nag and I could tell Melissa was not going to respond well to this veiled threat.

'But I didn't, did I?' Melissa said. 'And they won't put me in there again, will they? Not when I can come here, even if I don't want to be here!' She looked angry, but was just about keeping herself in check.

'No, you were very lucky your aunt and uncle were prepared to fetch you. It's lucky they were close enough to where the police found you.'

'They are not my aunt and uncle, actually. They are family friends.'

Melissa looked smug to have corrected Doreen's minor error.

Jonathan and I were sitting quietly at the opposite end of the kitchen table while this was going on. I wondered if Melissa had deliberately gone to a town in the opposite direction to the secure unit. Had she planned it that way, to avoid ending up there again? I doubted she was that cunning. It seemed far more likely that it was the company she kept that drove her disappearances and, as she said herself, it was unlikely she would be put in the unit while Jonathan and I were prepared to give her a home.

Melissa was now playing with her hair and refusing to give Doreen eye contact. I studied her, and her appearance and body language worried me. Her clothes were dirty, her hair was messy and when she wasn't fiddling with it she was wrapping her arms defensively around herself. How had she got herself so dishevelled? Whose clothes was she wearing? And what was she so defensive about?

Doreen was off again, quizzing Melissa about her school uniform and reeling off all kinds of instructions for her imminent return to the classroom.

'Whatever,' Melissa shrugged.

By the time Doreen left I think she'd done more to alienate Melissa than to get her back onside. She meant well, but I think she left Melissa feeling irritated and scolded, which wasn't going to get us anywhere. What we really needed, I thought, was to put Melissa at ease, tell her we were here to support her and somehow get her to open up. It was easier said than done, of course, but it was what I was going to try to do.

Jonathan went back to the shop to help close up and Melissa complained of having a headache and asked if she could go for a walk around the neighbourhood, which of course put me on my guard.

'I'd rather you stayed in,' I said. 'I'm going to start making the dinner soon. Are you hungry?'

'Yes, I'm starving. What are we having?'

I told her I was making a chicken curry and she said it was her favourite. 'Brilliant. I won't be out for long, honest. I'll just get some air. I'm sorry about what I said earlier. I didn't mean it. I like it here.'

'Thanks for saying that. I'd still prefer it if you stayed in. It's good to have you back. Why don't you help me cook? I'm a bit behind and could do with some help. Or, if your headache is really bad, you could go and have a lie down while I make the dinner?'

'OK,' she said reluctantly. 'I'll help you cook if you like. Can you do white rice? I don't like that yellow one they give you in the takeaway.'

'Yes, I can do white rice. Jonathan and I prefer plain anyhow and I'm sure the boys won't mind not having pilau.'

I explained about Marty staying with us, as well as Ryan, and told her he was eleven years old, in his first year of secondary school and due home soon. She said she looked forward to meeting him and went to the sink to wash her hands. As she did so she started singing the words 'chicken tikka' to the tune of ABBA's 'Chiquitita,' which made me smile. Her voice was very childish and high-pitched, but she could really sing. I complimented her and she said she'd love to be in a show and sing on a stage.

'Well if that's what you want to do, you should join a choir or a drama group.'

'Me? Really, do you think I could do it?'

'Melissa, you can do anything you want to do if you put your mind to it and work hard enough.'

She helped me prepare some ingredients for a few minutes and then said she needed to go to the toilet. She went to use the bathroom upstairs, and while she was gone Marty came home from his appointment. He was sitting at the kitchen table, drinking a mug of tea and telling me about his favourite football player, when Jonathan came running in. I could tell instantly there was a problem.

'What's going on?'

'It's Melissa. Did you say she could go out with TJ?'

'What? No I did not.'

'Well, he's just picked her up in his van. I was taking in the displays outside the shop when he pulled up in the street. She darted in the van, quick as a flash. I shouted after them, but it was no good. She's gone again.'

Marty looked confused and I gave him a very short but honest explanation. 'Melissa came back earlier and has gone out when we asked her not to,' I said.

'Why?' he said, looking puzzled.

Jonathan and I looked at each other, the words 'we wish we knew' hanging in the air between us.

13

'Fostering is a world of worry!'

It was already dark when Melissa disappeared in TJ's van and so we only waited an hour before calling the social services out-of-hours number to report her missing. They told us to call our local police station.

'I can give you the nickname of the boy she's with and I know where he works and what vehicle he was driving,' I said to the sergeant on the desk. Jonathan had managed to see the registration number of TJ's van and had scribbled it down on a pad he kept in his apron pocket. We already knew it was a small white Ford, and Jonathan even knew the name of the model, being the avid reader of *Auto Trader* he's always been.

The police officer took down the information and assured me that patrols would be alerted and we'd get a call as soon as there was any news. Then he asked me if I had any concerns that TJ had taken Melissa against her will.

'No, I have no reason to think that,' I said. 'He's her boyfriend, and she's run away before.'

'Gotcha,' the officer said casually, as if that explained everything.

I told him that even though this was not Melissa's first disappearance, I was as concerned as any parent or guardian of a missing twelve-year-old would be in the circumstances. I also mentioned we had a recent photograph of her.

'What's her date of birth?'

I gave it to him and he commented cheerfully that she was nearly thirteen, as if that made the situation somehow less serious or pressing. Then I heard a colleague in the background ask him if he wanted a cuppa.

'OK, love. I've got all this. Leave it with us. Thanks for phoning. If you could bring in the photo to copy that would be helpful.'

The line went dead.

I know now that police usually come out to the house to collect a photo in the case of a missing child. At the same time they sometimes check the child is not hiding in the house, as this is not unusual. But, just like the first time Melissa had gone missing, the police did not volunteer to come to the house, and it was up to us to take the photo in to the station to be copied. I didn't question this as I didn't have experience of dealing with a missing child and had no idea what the normal police routine was. In hindsight, I wonder if the officer who took my call knew there would already be a file on her, because of her history? However, if that were the case, nobody spelled this out to me and I was left feeling that Melissa's disappearance was not being taken as seriously as it would have been if she'd had no history of going missing.

I tried to eat some chicken curry with the boys but I didn't have much of an appetite. I couldn't compute how Melissa had been merrily singing 'chicken tikka' to an ABBA tune one minute, and then disappearing in TJ's van like that the next. As I'd thought before, it was almost like she'd been put under a spell, one that instantly transformed her from a sweet young girl into a reckless rebel, and all at the click of a boy's fingers.

Meanwhile, Jonathan drove up to the takeaway where TJ worked. 'I know Wilf's advice is to leave it to the police,' he said. 'But I don't think this is going to do any harm. I'll be able to see straight away if the van's there.'

I agreed. Jonathan always thinks before he acts and I trusted him to handle the situation in the right way, whether he saw the van and found Melissa there or not. As soon as he left I called Lynne. Unfortunately she had heard nothing. She knew we had Ryan and Marty staying with us and she told me plainly that she wasn't impressed with Social Services for putting us in this situation.

'I thought the whole idea of placing Melissa with you was that there were no other kids in the house. What if she comes back then sneaks out in the middle of the night again, while you're all in your beds? It's not a pleasant experience, I can tell you, knowing the house has been left wide open with kids asleep in their rooms. It's not on, Angela.'

Lynne was angry and I wanted to reassure her. I told her Jonathan and I weren't sleeping well, and if Melissa did return then break out in the night, I was sure we would wake up. 'We may not be able to stop her running off, but we'd be able to lock up and keep the boys safe in the house,' I said. 'Don't worry about us, Lynne. We're quite happy having the boys. They're both good lads and no trouble really. We're doing fine.'

Lynne sighed and said she admired my positive attitude but was still cross with Social Services. 'It's all about money. That's what annoys me. Social Services is always stretched to breaking point. If only the government would invest in recruiting more social workers and foster carers – not to mention training more specialist carers and increasing the budget for mental health services for kids. That would solve a lot of problems, and a lot of money in the long term.'

'I can't argue with any of that,' I said. I admitted that I didn't feel I had much choice in taking the boys in, but told Lynne I didn't regret it and felt it was the right thing to do. 'Don't worry, I would have said no if I thought for any moment I couldn't keep them, or us, safe.'

'OK, Angela. We must be mad, you know. Fostering is a world of worry! I'll call if I get any news.'

'Thanks Lynne, and I don't care what time it is. If you hear anything at all from Melissa, phone me straight away. I'll pick up the phone any time, day or night.'

I was playing cards with the boys when Jonathan returned. He'd been gone for about half an hour and the boys were beating me hands down. I'm not bad at cards normally, but that evening I couldn't concentrate.

'Any luck?'

'Nothing,' he shrugged. He'd driven round the town after

going past the takeaway but there was no sign of Melissa or the van anywhere.

'Can I join in?'

The boys shuffled up and made room for Jonathan on the sofa while I dealt a new hand.

It was Ryan's turn now to ask about Melissa.

'She seemed, like, *normal*,' he said. 'She seemed all right. Why did she run away?'

We simply said we didn't know, which was the truth.

Marty, who was yet to meet Melissa, said if he was going to run away he'd do it after his tea, especially if it was a curry. Ryan laughed. 'Yeah, I'd do the same. Girls just don't have good survival skills, do they?'

Marty shook his head and said very seriously, 'It's the way of the world. Girls are dumb. Boys rule. That's just how it is, I'm afraid.'

He spoke slowly and deliberately, as if he were delivering some grave news about world events. Ryan laughed and I could see how Marty's manner and tone could come across as amusing to another young boy. However, I couldn't really let this go; clearly Marty had picked up some sexist views from somewhere.

I talked to both boys in simple terms about equality, and about not judging another person because of their sex. The two of them sat there looking rather nonplussed, just wanting to get on with the next round of rummy.

I had no luck at all with my hand, and Marty made a comment about cards being a 'man's game', which set me off on another attempt to educate him about equality and sexism. This time I gave a personal example, in the hope of getting my point across effectively. 'Look at it like this,' I said. 'Ryan, how would you have liked it if I'd said you couldn't help me make scones the other day? What if I'd said boys couldn't bake and only girls were good at making scones?'

'I'd have proved you wrong!' Ryan retorted proudly.

'There you go. We all deserve the same opportunities and you don't know what a person is capable of when all you know is whether they're a boy or a girl. Therefore you must never judge a person because of their sex.'

Ryan looked a bit embarrassed, although I think that was possibly at the mention of the word sex, which made his eyes temporarily widen. Nevertheless he seemed to take my point and gave a little nod of acceptance. For a moment Marty seemed less accepting of my view. He was still looking very serious and thoughtful, but then he said, 'I do get what you're saying. And I think I've kinda changed my mind about something.'

'You have?'

'Yes. You see, there's a five-a-side football tournament at the leisure centre. A lady mentioned it to me and I said I didn't want to go, but maybe I'd like to go now.'

I imagined it was Marty's social worker who'd mentioned it, or one of the other professionals he came into contact with, but it's very common for children not to talk about these people in front of other children. Even though the kids staying in our house know they are all fostered, it's often like there's an unwritten rule that nobody mentions it, unless strictly necessary. It's very rare for foster children to discuss their family backgrounds and the reasons they are in care with each other, and more often than not a foster child will not correct a member of the public who assumes Jonathan and I are their parents, and so we don't either.

I think this is all very understandable; it's not that they are necessarily ashamed of being in care and try to cover it up, but they don't want to be defined or judged negatively by their status, which can happen. For instance, on one occasion Jonathan and I attended a swimming gala with a foster child. A swimming instructor referred to us as 'Mum and Dad,' to which the child replied, 'They're not my parents, they're my foster carers.' The instructor's ill-judged response was, 'I'd never have guessed it – you're very well behaved *and* you've got a nice new swimsuit.'

Jonathan looked at Marty and considered what he'd said about the football tournament. 'Why the change of heart? What was it that put you off going before?'

Marty reluctantly admitted that the lady had told him her daughter was participating.

'My dad always said girls shouldn't be allowed to play football, see,' he said. 'But, er, that's not right, is it?'

'Well,' Jonathan said, 'that's your dad's opinion; it's not a fact. In my opinion, girls should definitely be allowed to play football. Everyone should have an equal chance.'

Marty looked lost in thought. 'Like boys are allowed to do ballet,' he said. 'Yeah, I get it.' He didn't say any more.

I looked at Marty and wondered if he was only just starting to work out that so many things he'd been brought up to believe, and mimic, were questionable. Sadly, having a sexist role model was only the tip of the iceberg. I thought about what had happened in his past. It was so sad, and I hoped his ongoing counselling would help him understand why he had behaved inappropriately with the younger child. I also hoped it would shine a spotlight on other aspects of his childhood, teaching him that not everything he'd been told in his formative years by the people he loved and trusted was necessarily correct and true.

When the boys were on their way up to bed I asked them if they would like me to get some information about the football tournament that weekend, and maybe try to book them both in for it. They said they would like that.

'Maybe Melissa could come too?' Ryan said. 'I mean, she'll be back then, right?'

'That's a good idea,' I said, giving him a smile. 'We can ask her. Hopefully she will come too.'

Marty thanked me for getting the information and said it would be good if Melissa could come, as he still hadn't managed to meet her. Ryan had told him she was 'sound,' which made me smile as he'd only spoken to her for a minute or two about the fact she'd attended his primary school and said 'it sucks.'

Both boys went to bed without any fuss. Their lights were out and the house was quiet within ten minutes of them going upstairs. I sincerely hoped Melissa would be home and in her own bed by the time they woke the next day.

Jonathan observed that we normally loved it when the house fell silent in the evening and we got to enjoy some peace and quiet together. Now, of course, we were willing Melissa to come back, or at least for the phone to ring. We didn't really know what to do with ourselves. We weren't relaxed yet, neither of us was in the mood to concentrate on anything or just do nothing. It was a horrible kind of limbo.

The phone did ring, twice. The first time it was a wrong number and the next time it was one of Jonathan's brothers calling about a family party. We both sprang out of our chairs each time the shrill ring cut through the silence, our heartbeats speeding up, only to feel a stab of disappointment when there was no news of Melissa.

We finally went to bed at midnight, feeling tired out but knowing we probably wouldn't sleep. Rain was lashing on our bedroom window and the wind was whistling around the house. It was an absolutely filthy night. Melissa had gone out in the tracksuit she'd had on that looked too big for her, and she hadn't taken a coat. I dreaded to think where she was and what she was doing. All we ever heard about her disappearances was that she was mixing with the wrong crowd. Each time the police found her she seemed to get picked up from 'the streets,' where she was found hanging around with other young people. That was about all the detail we had amassed. I figured that if she was with TJ at least she might be in his van, or maybe at his house. Maybe they even went back to the takeaway, after it closed? It would be shut by now – not much stayed open in our small town after eleven or maybe eleven thirty.

I started to think about why Melissa would run away to be with TJ when we had given her permission to see him. Granted, she had to be in at nine and she considered that too early, but at least she could see him for a short time. Why had she run away like this?

I eventually drifted in and out of sleep, thinking about all kinds of possibilities. Did TJ take her somewhere out of town, to be with another crowd? Was she at a party, drinking or even taking drugs, trying to be cool and impress older boys?

At quarter past three I woke with a start. I'd heard the sound of breaking glass in the back garden.

'It's her!' I said, sitting up. I'd been in a fitful sleep and felt instantly alert.

'I'll go,' Jonathan murmured. I could see he was still half asleep, yet he suddenly began pushing himself up onto his elbows. He knocked his head on the headboard as he did so and winced as he reached out and switched on the bedside light. We both blinked, dazzled by the sudden brightness radiating from the lamp.

I got up and looked out of the window, across the back garden and then at the playing fields beyond. I couldn't see Melissa, though the rain was still lashing and it was incredibly dark outside. I noticed there wasn't a star in the sky. The wind was wild now; its whistles had become howls in the dark.

Jonathan put on his dressing gown and went downstairs. I listened as he unbolted the door and I watched from the window as he emerged into the garden. He put the patio lights on, and then the dim security light we had on the wall of the house flickered on. It was triggered by Jonathan's movement and I had a dismal thought, *If Melissa is out there, that light would already have come on.* I could see that Jonathan had a pair of wellingtons pulled up over his pyjama bottoms, a raincoat zipped up to his chin and a large torch in his hand. He scoured the garden and the side passage, shining his torch all around the garage, the old pet hutch we had propped up against the back wall, the rockery and shrubs, and even behind the bins. Melissa wasn't anywhere to be seen.

We had a greenhouse tucked in the far corner of the garden and I watched Jonathan walk up to it, bracing himself against the wind as he did so. It was in darkness, as the yellow glow of the security light didn't reach that far, and nor did the patio lights. Jonathan searched all around the greenhouse, torchlight bouncing back at him as he illuminated the panes of glass. I saw him crouch down, pick something up and examine it. I guessed this must be the broken glass: it glinted brightly under the beam of the torch. For a desperate moment I dared to believe he was going to find Melissa hiding in the greenhouse, but that was just my sleep-deprived head giving me false hope. I was so tired I could hear a dull buzz all around my brain, like the sound of a beehive in a distant place.

Jonathan turned and trudged dejectedly back to the house. I heard him come back in and lock the door, at which point I exhaled deeply and climbed back into bed.

'Must have been the wind blew one of the door panes

out,' he said flatly as he came back to bed. He squeezed my hand; he was freezing cold and I shuddered.

'That's dangerous,' I said. 'It could have fallen out on one of the kids. We'll have to get it repaired.'

'I know. We'd better have the whole greenhouse checked. This wind has given it a real battering. There was a plant pot on its side and it looks like one of those diamond-shaped panels of glass had fallen out and landed on top of it. You know the type I mean? It was only a small piece of glass - I can't believe we heard it break from here.'

'I can,' I said wearily. 'I feel like I've developed super-sensitive hearing since Melissa came to stay with us.'

'You've *always* had radar ears,' Jonathan joked.

'You can talk - so have you!'

Several of the kids we'd fostered had complained about our 'radar ears,' saying we never missed a trick. One child even jokingly called Jonathan Mr Spock after he'd overheard a 'secret plot' that was being whispered about very quietly, but not quietly enough. The child could not believe Jonathan had heard anything at all, but I think you get used to tuning in even more than usual whenever you hear a child whisper, in case they are up to no good. Quite a lot of kids asked us if we were telepathic. This usually happened after I said they couldn't do something or have something, and gave the reason. They then chanced their luck with Jonathan, only to be given exactly the same response despite the fact we hadn't had time to speak to one another. 'How do you do that?' they'd ask, incredulous that we'd stuck to the same script without having chance to confer. 'Are you magic? Are you psychic? You *must* be telepathic!'

Jonathan and I were certainly on the same wavelength tonight; we were both feeling too fraught and anxious to sleep but agreed we had to try our best to get a few more hours or we'd be feeling wretched the next day.

I woke again soon after six.

'Tea?' Jonathan said the moment I opened my eyes.

'How long have you been awake?'

'Not long, ten minutes at the most.'

'How d'you feel?'

'Not too bad considering.'

'Me neither. We must be running on adrenaline.'

'I think you're right. I'll go and put the kettle on.'

Jonathan got up and as he did so I said, 'I'll check the answerphone.' He said the same thing at exactly the same time, which made us smile.

'The kids are right, we *are* telepathic.'

There were no new messages on the answerphone, and neither of us was surprised. There was no way we had slept soundly enough to miss a phone call in the middle of the night.

Wilf called me shortly after breakfast. There was still no news of Melissa but he said he wanted to come over to discuss Ryan and Marty. I assumed he wanted to talk about the arrangements for them both moving on from our care, which Jonathan and I were expecting to happen very shortly.

*

The boys were busy swapping football cards in the lounge when Wilf arrived. Jonathan was in the shop, after driving over to the police station first thing that morning to give them Melissa's photo, which they copied as promised and told us to keep hold of.

I invited Wilf into the kitchen and we chatted as I made us both a coffee.

'I never used to drink coffee before I did this job,' Wilf mused. 'I didn't even like it. Now I don't know how I'd get through the day without it!'

'I've always drunk coffee, but never in such large quantities as I do now. But I guess that's what happens when you have broken sleep and you need something to keep you going.'

I'd told Wilf about the night we'd had, with me hearing the sound of broken glass and Jonathan searching the garden in the small hours. 'Nobody ever told us social work and foster care was so stressful, did they?' he said ruefully.

When I gave him his coffee he wrapped his hands around the mug, as if he was taking comfort from it.

'They didn't, but would you have listened if they had?'

Wilf shook his head. 'Probably not. I always felt it was my vocation. I have no regrets, none whatsoever. We get our rewards, don't we?'

'Yes,' I said, immediately thinking of Vicky, and several other children who'd lived with us over the past few years. Seeing their self-esteem grow, watching them smile and helping them learn about the world, and make progress at school and with their friends, were all priceless gifts.

I shared with Wilf that Jonathan and I were incredibly naive when we first became foster carers. 'We thought the job would simply entail giving kids a warm, comfortable home, putting good food on the table and showing them they were loved and cared for. A bit like looking after flowers in the shop – you know, provide the right environment, love and nourish them and they'll all bloom perfectly!'

Wilf let out a hoot of laughter. 'There's a bit more to it than that, isn't there?'

'Just a bit.'

'I've probably said this before,' Wilf went on. 'But I don't think I could be a foster carer. In fact, I know I couldn't, as you never get a chance to switch off, do you? Even if I'm working until well after eight o'clock trying to place a child, at least once I'm home I don't have to think about anything until the following morning.'

As we drank our coffee and treated ourselves to a chocolate biscuit Wilf explained there had been another delay with the subsequent moves for both Ryan and Marty. He wanted to know if it would be possible to extend their placements with us further, by another week, or two at the most.

After checking with Jonathan I agreed to this. The boys were no trouble, and we were enjoying looking after them. A school place had now been found for Marty in the area he would ultimately be moving to full time, and Wilf said a taxi would be provided to take him and collect him while he was still living with us.

Jonathan and I always tried to do the school runs ourselves whenever possible, but Marty's school was quite a distance away and it wasn't feasible for us to take on this responsibility, having Ryan and Melissa to consider too.

Ryan's primary school continued to be very understanding about his situation and Wilf said it was up to Ryan if he wanted to return the following week.

'Maybe if Marty is back in school Ryan might want to go back too,' I suggested. 'It might encourage him, especially if Marty is going to be out for long days?'

Wilf said he thought I could be right and that he'd have a word with Ryan's social worker to perhaps nudge him in this direction, if the social worker was in agreement. We then talked about how I thought the boys were coping.

'Very well, I think. Neither of them has disclosed anything to us, although I wouldn't have expected them to at this early stage. You wouldn't guess they've both suffered as they have. They appear to be fine.'

I explained about Ryan being a little joker and that he and Marty got along well: there had been no arguments and in fact there was a pleasant atmosphere whenever they were together. We agreed it was a good thing they both had counselling and therapy available to them. In my experience children – and particularly boys – rarely open up at the start of a placement. It's not unheard of, but usually children who've been traumatised don't feel settled enough to disclose the details of their past experiences for weeks, if not months. In some cases it's many, many years, or never at all.

I told Wilf I was taking the boys to play five-a-side football, as I'd managed to book them both into the tournament we'd talked about, the one at the local leisure centre at the weekend. He said this sounded ideal and that it looked like we had everything under control.

'How are you and Jonathan coping generally?'

'We're doing OK. I really think we are, even though it's incredibly stressful caring for a runner.'

When I heard that word coming back off the walls my heart sank. I didn't like to use it as it sounded a bit cold, and I don't like to define any child by their actions. However, that was the word the social workers and other childcare professionals used to describe boys and girls like Melissa, and it was the word Wilf himself used.

I sighed and went on. 'I never could have imagined how difficult it is to look after a child who randomly runs away. You simply can't rest, at any time. When she's in I'm on pins. When she's out I'm afraid she won't come back. When she's run off and actually gone missing I'm afraid for her safety, imagining all the terrible things that could happen to her. I know waking up in the night isn't going to bring her back here any quicker, but we can't help the way we are. It's instinctive to be on alert, isn't it?'

Wilf nodded wisely and said he could see how much we cared about Melissa and that he understood how hard it must be for us. He acknowledged that he'd undeniably put us under a bit of pressure to take on Melissa, and then the boys so soon afterwards. I told him we understood he'd done what he thought was best for the children, and we had done the same thing, as looking after kids was our priority.

'You're good people,' Wilf said, finishing his coffee. 'I'm

not surprised you can't sleep properly. I'm sure I'd be awake all night if I were in your shoes. It's tough, but you're doing a fantastic job.'

Whenever he had the time to chat like this – which wasn't as often as either of us would have liked – Wilf was always very complimentary and made us feel highly valued. It never fails to brighten my day whenever a social worker praises us, and I told him I appreciated his kind words. 'I'm only speaking the truth. And I have to say, I really respect you for doing the specialist training. It's a big ask, and I have nothing but admiration for any foster carer who stays the course.'

The social workers who ran our specialist course had emphasised that we were professional foster carers now, due to the extensive training we'd received. Additionally, the social workers who supervised our ongoing, regular support meetings often reminded us how important our role was too, telling us we were on the front line, we knew the children best and should therefore be listened to.

Over the years we've heard foster carers complaining that some social workers don't treat them with respect and don't seem to listen to them, or value their judgement or opinions. Some felt they were treated even worse after doing the specialist course, saying they thought the social workers somehow felt threatened when confronted with a highly qualified foster carer. One carer told me she believed social workers went out of their way to ignore her views and assert their authority. Thankfully, that was never our experience; it was the opposite, in fact.

The saying 'foster carers are like mushrooms – keep them in the dark and feed them shit' is one we were made aware of very early on in our careers. We've had moments when we could identify with that but, by and large, once we'd done the specialist course, Jonathan and I felt very much more appreciated and respected than before, not least by Wilf.

'You'll both be as grey as me,' he joked before he left. 'It's not that many years since people used to say I looked like Tom Cruise, you know. Puts years on you, this job!'

This made me smile: I'd recently watched the film *A Few Good Men* and an image of Tom Cruise as a dashing, young Navy lawyer with a fine head of dark hair flashed into my mind. Wilf was bald on top and had a rim of silver hair forming a thin semi-circle around the back of his head. I quipped that I'd be straight round to the hairdresser if I got any grey hairs so nobody would ever know, but the truth was this was no laughing matter. I felt I'd aged five years already since Melissa arrived.

14

'I didn't know anyone was in trouble with the police'

Lynne came over to see me. Melissa had been gone for two nights by now and we'd heard nothing at all from the police.

'I thought this might be useful,' she said kindly.

Lynne had cut out from an old fostering magazine, a long article about kids who abscond and she pushed it across the kitchen table.

'I know how hopeless it makes you feel when the police and Social Services tell you to sit tight and do nothing. I'm not sure anything you do will stop Melissa running away, but I always say you can't have too much information.'

I thanked her and scanned the article. It looked really interesting and Lynne could tell I couldn't tear my eyes away from it, even though the kettle had started to whistle on the hob and I wanted to make a pot of tea.

'Go ahead,' she said. 'You have a read of that and I'll finish making the tea if you like.'

The article gave many reasons a child may abscond. These included the need to feel in charge of their own life; random recklessness; having feelings of antagonism or anger towards parents or carers; a failure to think about consequences; and a strong desire to join in with whatever their friends are doing, otherwise known as peer pressure. With Melissa, I felt sure it was all about her friends, and the fact she wanted to be accepted by the older kids who she looked up to, and who probably made her feel more grown up.

Lynne agreed with my view. 'She's definitely heavily influenced by her friends. Do you want milk and sugar?'

'Just milk, thanks. Skimmed please.'

Lynne opened the fridge and reached to the bottom shelf. We'd had many cups of tea together in my kitchen and she knew where everything was. While she poured the milk I stood up and fetched a packet of oat biscuits from the cupboard. 'I'm sure that with Melissa it's all about getting out to see her friends or boyfriends,' I said. 'I don't think it has anything to do with getting away from her carers, although maybe it is? Maybe she had a bad experience in the past and simply wants to run away because she's hostile to the whole idea of being in care?'

Lynne was stirring two sugars into her tea, looking thoughtful. She took a biscuit and dangled it over her mug, ready to dunk. Before she did so she said, 'Maybe. Who knows?'

I went on to read a section entitled 'Strategies to stop a child absconding and what to do while they are gone.'

This talked about considering the layout of your house and how easy it was for the child to leave without you immediately noticing. It also asked if the boundaries put in place were age-appropriate. I thought about Melissa simply walking out of the house and getting in TJ's van. We hadn't spotted her until it was too late, but how could we stop her going to her room or to the bathroom, and walking freely about the house? I couldn't stand guard at her door or follow her when she went to the toilet, could I?

I think Lynne could read my mind. Before I said anything she sighed and said, 'I considered all of the practicalities of trying to keep watch and I'm sure you have too. But it doesn't really apply to Melissa, I don't think. She's only twelve but if she wants to go, she'll go. You can't put security guards on the doors day and night. As for the boundaries, we can only do what Social Services tell us, can't we? There are some useful bits here though, but again they may be more useful for other kids and not Melissa. The more I think about it, the more I think she's a bit of a special case.'

Lynne pointed at a boxed-in section of the article labelled 'Help and advice'. I read on. One piece of advice was not to leave the house immediately to look for the child, as they may be hiding and watching and they may enjoy the drama of provoking a 'search'. Far better, it advised, to calmly carry on with what you're doing, or sit down and count to ten. It also suggested that you try to remember what was said immediately before the child went missing, so you could use this in conversation later. For example, you may want to say, 'I could see you were upset when I said you had to be home at the usual time.'

I thought back to my last conversation with Melissa. I remembered how she'd told me she'd love to be in a show and sing on a stage, and I'd suggested she join a choir or a drama group.

'Me? Really, do you think I could do it?' she'd asked.

'Oh my God,' I said to Lynne, suddenly remembering what came next. 'My last words to Melissa were, "You can do anything you want to do if you put your mind to it and work hard enough."'

Lynne rolled her eyes. 'Angela, none of this is your fault and it's not about you, or Jonathan, or what either of you have said or done. She behaved in exactly the same way when she was with Nick and me, remember? I think the best advice that article gives is not to panic, not to blame yourself and to take time to gather your thoughts and prepare for when she does come home. Have a cup of tea and an oat biscuit – because what else can you do?'

'Mmm,' I said, turning to a column headed 'What to do when the child is back home'. The advice here was to avoid an in-depth analysis of why the child had run away. Instead, it suggested showing kindness and understanding, for example, by asking if they were too hot or too cold, needed something to eat or drink or felt tired and needed some rest.

'This is interesting,' I said. '"Is there a link to the past?" Now that's a good question.' I continued reading aloud. '"Ask yourself, was there ever a time when the young person's freedom was restricted? Did they feel constrained or unable to move around as they would have liked to? If so, has this driven the child to push boundaries and run away?"' I paused for breath. 'Well, I wish I knew the answer to all of those questions.' I looked at Lynne and raised my eyebrows. 'What d'you think?'

Lynne shrugged. 'I know very little about Melissa's past – probably exactly the same as you – but maybe there's something in this? It would certainly provide a good explanation if, for example, she was locked in the house as a child. But I was never told about anything like that.'

I thought about the fact Melissa said her stepfather used to hold drunken parties in the house. I wondered if Melissa started running away to avoid going back to the house when she knew he'd be there, drinking with his friends? Maybe it had become a habit, a kind of avoidance tactic, so she didn't have to deal with the mess at home?

Lynne said she thought it was possible Melissa became a runner because her home life was so chaotic. 'Who wouldn't want to run away from home if you lived in a place like that?'

I thought this was a good point, but then again why would she run from Lynne's house, and from ours? We didn't have chaotic houses; we were trying to provide a haven of stability and support.

The final page of the article talked about keeping the peace, avoiding shouting at the child when they returned home and gently encouraging them to talk to you in a calm manner, in the hope they may open up about where they'd been. This was sensible advice, particularly as talking was really our only tool.

'Using "natural consequences" could be worth a go,' Lynne said, though to be honest she didn't sound convinced;

I could tell she was just trying her best to help me in any way she could. She gave me an example of how she'd used this method, telling me about one occasion when Melissa wanted to wear her favourite tracksuit but Lynne had not got round to washing it.

'I told her that I'd spent the previous afternoon driving to and from the police station to collect her, and that was why I was behind with the washing. That actually seemed to get through. She said sorry and I really do think she saw things from my point of view. Not that it stopped her running away again of course, but at least I got through for a short while. I think I did, anyhow. It's very hard to tell what makes a difference, or if anything at all really does get through.'

I took good note of this; imposing 'natural consequences' fitted in with everything we'd been taught on our training course, and maybe if I kept up a steady flow of consequences like that, it might just make Melissa think twice about running away again.

The police phoned just before 9 p.m. to tell us they'd picked Melissa up and she was at a local station. Jonathan and I agreed to collect her, after first making sure my mum could come over and sit with the boys while we were out. Social Services generally advise us not to travel alone in a car with a child if we can avoid it, and if you have no choice you must put the child in the back of the car for safeguarding reasons. We didn't know what state we'd find Melissa in, though we imagined she would be dishevelled and would possibly have had a drink. At the very least she was probably annoyed or angry at being picked up by the police, and in the circumstances neither of us would want to risk being alone in a car with her. As we've been told many times during training, children can lash out or make false accusations about their carers, and it's always best to avoid being alone in a confined space with any child, if at all possible.

Ryan and Marty were ready for bed by the time we got my mum installed in front of the TV. I explained to them that we were going out to fetch Melissa and they didn't miss the opportunity to exploit the situation, asking if they could stay up a bit later so they could spend time with my mum. I agreed, saying they could play a game of dominoes, and they seemed thrilled to bits about this, so much so that they didn't ask any more questions and couldn't wait to get started. I was relieved they didn't quiz us about Melissa, as we wouldn't have been able to give them any more information about why we were going out at short notice like this to collect her; it was her business, not theirs. We were also in a hurry, not wanting Melissa to be in the police station a minute longer than necessary. Jonathan and I hastily put on our shoes, grabbed our coats and dashed out of the door.

'I think we could have told the boys we were going to the moon and they'd have just accepted it,' Jonathan laughed as we climbed in the car and headed into the night.

'I know! I remember being that age myself. Kids will do anything for a later bedtime – especially when a game is thrown in. It's great to see them playing something other than computer games.'

The box of dominoes the kids were playing with was the same one I had as a child. I used to love sitting down on a Sunday afternoon for a game with my parents. We loved all the classic board games, like Monopoly and Cluedo and Snakes & Ladders. Though my dad had his issues with alcohol I have barely any memories of it affecting our lives. With Mum's help and support he managed to stop drinking when I was five years old; something I did not find out for many years.

My parents both worked very hard, running the shop, and Sunday afternoon seemed to be the only time they ever rested. Mum would always make a roast dinner, and we'd invariably be full of beef and Yorkshire puddings and rhubarb crumble and custard when we sat down to play. Dad often excused himself after a short while so he could read the paper or do a crossword, but Mum would sit with me for longer, and I loved spending that special time with her.

Seeing Mum playing with the kids we fostered, and setting up the same old games we'd played together, always warmed my heart. I know a lot of the kids we've looked after over the years had never been taught how to play dominoes or draughts, or any of the board games that most kids grew up with and took for granted. Shockingly, one child we looked after disclosed that she *had* been taught to play a certain game by a male relative, only for it to lead to sexual abuse, as he had told her that if she lost she had to go and lie on the bed and wait for him. When I heard that, it was one of those times when I had to try very hard not to show the child I was shocked, so as not to put her off disclosing anything else in the future. I shed a tear afterwards, in private.

Jonathan and I got lost trying to find the police station. It was a small village station we'd had no reason to ever visit in the past, and in fact we didn't even know it existed until now. Just when we thought it was going to be around the next corner we ran out of directions and spent about ten minutes going round in circles, trying to pick up the route. I'd hastily scribbled down the brief directions I was given over the phone when the police called, and now I was hunting through an old *A to Z* street directory.

'Would you believe it? This map doesn't even go that far!'

Jonathan was very patient, following my directions, even when he thought we should be heading in completely the opposite direction and when I led us down the narrowest roads, pitted with pot holes and with no street lamps. In the end we came out on a main road and decided to pull in at a garage.

I ran in, dodging hailstones, and asked in a rather too loud voice where the police station was. There were a few other people in the garage shop, and it felt like all eyes turned to me. I guessed they must have been wondering what business I had with the police.

'Are you all right love?' the man behind the counter asked, looking a bit embarrassed.

'Pardon?'

'I mean, is everything OK?' He looked towards Jonathan, who was parking the car on the forecourt.

'Oh, yes, I'm fine. I don't *need* the police, I just need to find the police station.'

'Right. It's third left out of here, over the mini roundabout and it's behind the pebble-dashed building a couple of hundred yards up on the right.'

The man avoided making eye contact with me when he spoke and the other customers seemed to look at me sideways as I walked out.

'Honestly,' I huffed when I got back in the car. 'You'd think they'd never seen anyone from out of town before. I think they thought I was some kind of criminal!'

Jonathan started chuckling.

'What?'

'Maybe they just thought you were a bit eccentric.'

'Eccentric? Why?'

He pointed at my neck and I looked down at my scarf. In my haste to leave the house I'd grabbed the first one I put my hand on when I reached in the hall cupboard. The only problem was, it wasn't a scarf at all; it was a large tea towel. My friend had brought it home for me from a trip to Portugal and it had a donkey's face emblazoned on it, and long red tassels. How it had ended up on a peg beside my coat in the hall cupboard I had no idea. Jonathan and I still laugh about that wardrobe malfunction to this day, but all I can say is that these things happen when you are short of sleep, feeling stressed and are called out unexpectedly on a dark winter's night. At least by the time we finally found the police station I'd got over my embarrassment and seen the funny side. We both laughed, and I think it helped release some of the pressure we were experiencing.

'At least you didn't walk into the police station like that,' Jonathan joked. 'Melissa might have run the other way again!'

We parked up and went into the small station. Melissa was in a room with two female officers. She looked at the floor when Jonathan and I walked in.

'We've had a word with her,' one of the officers said gently. 'I think Melissa understands that it's dangerous to run away and go missing.'

Melissa slowly peeled her eyes off the floor and looked at me.

'Sorry,' she said softly.

She was curling a long strand of hair around her finger and looked very young and vulnerable. I wanted to tell her how sorry we were too that this had happened again, and to explain how worried we'd been, but I stopped myself, remembering the advice in the article Lynne had shown me.

'How are you feeling?' I asked. 'Are you hungry?'

'I'm all right. I've eaten well, actually. I've been well looked after.'

She had a coat on her lap and told me one of her friends had given it to her. The other female officer told us that Melissa had been picked up at a flat. The police had been tipped off that a youth they were looking for in connection with a burglary lived there, and when they knocked Melissa answered the door. We learned that the photograph of her that we'd given to the police had been circulated around some of the local police stations in the area, and one of the attending officers had seen it and recognised Melissa immediately. Apparently, she said she didn't realise her friend had done anything wrong, or she wouldn't have stayed in the flat. The female officer also reported to us that Melissa had commented, 'I only went there 'cos my friend didn't want to stay there on her own.'

'Do you want to tell Mr and Mrs Hart anything else? Maybe who the friend is?'

Melissa was not forthcoming and the officer looked at me. 'Melissa was the only girl we picked up. The other girl – her friend – had not been reported missing.'

'Was it Sam?' I asked.

Melissa looked at the floor again and I thought she was going to cry.

The first police officer put her hand on Melissa's arm and gave it a gentle squeeze. 'Look, love, you're too young to stay out at night like this. Just because your friends are allowed out it doesn't mean you are too.'

'I'm sorry. I didn't mean to go missing for so long. I just wanted to see my friends for a bit, and then . . .'

She bit her lip.

'And then?'

'We got invited to Finn's and, I'm sorry . . .' Tears rolled down her cheeks. 'I didn't know anyone was in trouble with the police.'

'Can I give you a hug?' I asked.

She shook her head. 'I'm all right, but thanks. I won't do it again. I'm so sorry.'

The officers thanked us for collecting Melissa, handed her back a bag and wished us the best of luck.

'Don't worry, love,' the first one said sympathetically. 'We all got up to some kind of mischief when we were kids. You're safe now. Just don't do it again, d'you hear?'

Melissa nodded. 'I won't.'

When we got in the car Melissa told us she felt really bad about the worry she'd put us through and promised she was not going to run away ever again.

'Can I see TJ tomorrow?'

My heart sank. It seemed utterly ridiculous that I would even consider sanctioning this after what had just happened. I told her it would be helpful if she would talk to us some more about what had gone on over the last few days. I reassured her that she would not be in any trouble and that I just wanted to keep her safe and to help and support her. Unfortunately, she didn't want to talk about her missing days any more, and so we still had no reasonable explanation about why she'd run away, what TJ's involvement was or whether he had been at the flat she was eventually found in.

'It's late now. Let's talk again tomorrow,' I said eventually. 'Let's just get you back to the house.'

'OK. But I can see him, right? I'm allowed. I know I am. My social worker told me you can't stop me going out.' She said this in a pitiful rather than an accusatory way. I was shocked at her naivety. How could she not realise how inappropriate it was to be nagging us about seeing TJ when she'd just run off with him like this? I wondered what on earth was going on in her head. It was as if the way she behaved had somehow been normalised, when in fact it was completely wrong. I thought of Marty when that word – normalised – came into my head. He had thought it normal to touch other children inappropriately. Melissa seemed to think it was acceptable to keep going out with people who were clearly leading her astray. What had gone on in her earlier life to make her this way, or was it that something was going on in her life now that was pulling her in the wrong direction, again and again? I reckoned it was probably a combination of the two. *What a mess*, I thought. Parents who don't care properly for their children really have no idea how much harm they do, not only in the moment but also for years to come.

Jonathan must have been thinking similar thoughts about Melissa wanting to see TJ. He cleared his throat. 'Melissa, I'm not sure you realise or remember this, but I actually saw you getting into TJ's van, before you went missing. We need to be able to trust that when you see him, or any of your other friends, you tell us exactly what you are doing and where you are going, and you come home at 9 p.m.'

'OK. I promise I'll be back by 9 p.m.' She said this flippantly and in an insincere, sing-songy voice, then reined herself in and whispered, 'Sorry. I promise. I will be back by nine. I won't run away again. It wasn't TJ's fault. It wasn't anything to do with him.'

I repeated that we'd talk about this the next day, and she agreed. She shut her eyes and we spent the rest of the journey in silence.

Back home, Melissa chatted politely with my mum and then said she was very tired and went up to bed.

'What a lovely girl,' Mum said. 'And no trouble at bedtime. When you were that age you were always asking me if you could stay up later.'

I smiled, more to myself than to my mum. If only she knew.

15

'There's something in the sink'

The house was very quiet when I woke on Saturday morning. Jonathan had already gone to work in the shop, though I hadn't heard him get up. When I looked at the clock I was surprised it was eight thirty because I normally woke much earlier, even at weekends.

I sat up in bed and thought about the events of the previous evening. Melissa's behaviour was so puzzling and unpredictable and I wondered what the day would bring. It was the football tournament later, which the boys were looking forward to. Jonathan and I both wanted to take them and had arranged cover in the shop, but what about Melissa? Would she come with us? Mum had offered to come over and sit with her, but what if Melissa ran off?

I climbed out of bed and put on my dressing gown. I felt refreshed, though I remembered lying in bed and fretting about whether Melissa would be there in the morning or go missing in the night. In the end, I must have been so exhausted I fell asleep.

None of the three children were up, and I enjoyed having breakfast on my own. I'd wake them all up at ten if they didn't appear before then. I've always appreciated that growing children – and especially pre-teens and teens – need a bit of a lie-in. Their minds and bodies are going through so many changes. I understand it's a physical need rather than laziness that makes them lie in bed for longer than adults.

Melissa's trainers were where she'd left them in the hall and that put my mind at rest. I also knew Jonathan would have checked that the doors were not unlocked when he went through to the shop, and if he'd had any suspicions that Melissa had done a runner I'd have known about it by now.

I'd enjoyed my cereal and was just putting my empty bowl in the dishwasher when Ryan appeared.

'Good morning!' I said, turning round as I heard the kitchen door creak open. 'Did you sleep well? D'you want a cup of tea?'

Ryan said no very quietly.

'Still waking up?' I looked at him properly now, and caught my breath. He was very pale and looked scared.

'Ryan, sweetheart, are you OK?'

'Er, no, not really. There's something in the sink.'

'The sink?' Confused, I looked across to the kitchen sink. It was empty. 'What do you mean?'

'The bathroom.'

'You mean the washbasin? In which bathroom?'

'Ours.'

'OK. Do you know what it is?'

Ryan shook his head. He looked like he'd seen a ghost.

'Shall I go and have a look?'

'Yes please. Can I stay here?'

'Yes, if you want to.'

I went up to the children's bathroom with my heart in my mouth, not knowing what to expect. When I pushed open the door, in the half-light of the morning I could see deep red splashes in the basin and splattered up the mirror. I gasped, shocked to my core, and put my hand to my lips. What on earth had happened?

I reached for the bathroom light with a shaking hand. I could feel the adrenaline coursing around my body, afraid of what else I was going to discover.

My eyes adjusted to the brightness of the light and I could now see that it wasn't blood, as Ryan must have thought, and as I'd feared. It was nothing more than red hair dye. *Thank God that isn't what I thought it was,* I said to myself, exhaling deeply and immediately taking in a long, deep breath. *Thank God for that.*

I could smell the ammonia now too, and when I put my foot on the pedal bin and the lid popped up I saw the packet of 'cherry red' dye. I immediately thought back to the bag Melissa had been carrying when the police handed her over. The dye must have been in there, as I certainly didn't keep any in the house.

'Melissa,' I said to myself as I opened the vanity unit beneath the basin, pulled on a pair of rubber gloves and took hold of a cloth and some cleaning fluid. Even though I wanted to get back to the kitchen as quickly as possible and explain this to Ryan, I had to clean up first. I didn't want Marty to see this mess and have a shock too. Nor did I want the dye to damage the bathroom fittings, but most of all I wanted to remove all trace of the dye so Ryan didn't have to look at it again. He'd had an awful fright, poor lad.

I had no idea how Ryan's brother had taken his own life. All I knew was that he had been twenty-three years old and had left a note, making accusations about their late parents. I didn't know where Ryan was at the time or what he knew. After this experience I started to wonder whether blood was involved, and precisely what Ryan had seen or heard.

When I returned to the kitchen Ryan was still as white as a sheet and was staring at the wall blankly. He jumped when I came through the door.

'It's OK, sweetheart. I've cleaned up the mess. It was only hair dye. Melissa must have dyed her hair in the night.'

'What?' He looked confused.

'You know, hair dye. That's what was in the washbasin and on the mirror. It was Melissa, or at least I'm assuming it was Melissa.' In an attempt to lighten the atmosphere I added, 'Maybe I'm wrong. Maybe Marty fancied a change and *he's* the one who's dyed his hair cherry red?'

To my relief, Ryan finally grinned. 'I don't think he'd do that. He's a City fan. I'm the Red!'

I smiled. 'Well perhaps it was Jonathan? I haven't seen him yet this morning, he's in the shop. Listen, Ryan, you know that if there's anything you want to talk about you can say anything you want to me.'

'I know. Am I allowed to have hot chocolate?'

'Yes, sweetheart. And do you want some toast or cereal?'

'No thanks. I'll get something later.'

Marty appeared while Ryan was drinking his hot chocolate. Ryan's colour had returned to his cheeks and he appeared to be back to his usual, quick-witted self.

'It wasn't him,' he said, quick as a flash, nodding towards Marty.

'It wasn't me, what?'

'You didn't dye your hair bright red in the middle of the night.'

'Er, no. What are you on about?'

Before either of us had chance to answer him, Melissa bounced into the kitchen. Her auburn hair was visibly redder and I could smell the dye. I introduced her to Marty, realising that they still hadn't met. Then, to break the ice, I jokingly told her we were wondering if he was the one who'd been up in the night dying his hair. Marty looked even more confused now, while Melissa laughed and then greeted Ryan with a playful punch on the arm, saying, 'All right, mate?'

Ryan gave her the thumbs-up and said, 'Sweet.' This made me smile; I always find it endearing when the kids lapse so effortlessly into their own sublanguage. It tells me they are making an effort to get on with each other, and that this is their conversation, and not one for adults to take part in.

'So, didn't you sleep well, Melissa?' I asked eventually, raising my eyebrows and looking at her hair.

'Oh, yeah, I mean no. I did this at about three in the

morning! How mad is that? I was wide awake. I thought I'd give it a go.'

'Cool,' Marty said. 'Now I finally know what you're on about!'

I noticed Melissa had also done something to her eyebrows. It looked like she'd over-plucked them and tried to dye them, though she had such a pale complexion she'd stained the skin beneath her fine hairs. This had the effect of making her eyebrows look tattooed on.

The boys started to talk about football, allowing me to talk quietly to Melissa.

'I wonder why you couldn't sleep, sweetheart? You were very tired last night.'

'I know. I just woke up and – ping – my eyes snapped open and I was wide awake.'

'OK. And how are you feeling now?'

'I'm fine, thanks. I'm sorry about all that. Thanks for picking me up.'

'I'm glad you're safe, that's the main thing. That's what we care about. We want to look after you and make sure you are safe.'

'I know. TJ looks after me, though. You don't need to worry about him. All the boys look out for me. I'm a lucky girl. I have a lot of good friends.'

'They all look out for you?'

'Yeah. Have you got any chocolate cereal? And can I use the phone?'

'No chocolate cereal but there's plenty of others to choose from. Or I can do you some toast, or an egg?'

'Just cereal thanks.'

While I fetched Melissa a bowl and spoon and filled up the jug of milk on the table I told her about the football tournament the boys were going to take part in that day.

'We thought we could all go to the leisure centre together and go for a pizza afterwards. Would you like to do that?'

'Yeah, sounds great.'

I was pleased about this. I really didn't want to leave my mum with the responsibility of looking after Melissa on her own.

'And can I see my friends afterwards?'

My heart tightened in my chest.

'I don't mean TJ, don't worry. I've changed my mind about seeing him. I just want to go out with my mates from school.'

I asked her which friends she wanted to see, and she said Rosie and some other girls were going to the junior disco in the church hall. I would still have preferred her to stay in this evening. I reminded her that the last time she went out with Rosie she was nearly an hour late, and that this was not to happen again. She said that was different, because that time they were out with TJ and Des, but this time it would just be the girls, going to the junior disco. I reluctantly told her she was allowed to go, as long as she stuck to the plans, stayed with Rosie and was in by nine.

'Cool!' she said. 'Thanks Angela. And yes, I won't let you down.'

I can't say I felt completely reassured: I don't think it was possible not to worry about Melissa, whatever promises she made.

She was smiling when she sat at the table with the boys and I was happy to hear her joining in their conversation about football. It turned out she was very knowledgeable about their favourite teams, which impressed them. Everybody was excited about the tournament and looking forward to going out for pizza. The atmosphere was good, and I allowed myself to enjoy the moment, and hope it would last.

'Maybe this is the way forward?' I whispered to Jonathan as we were all about to get in the car to drive to the leisure centre that afternoon. With all three children still in a good mood and getting along well, I was feeling in a positive frame of mind.

'How d'you mean?'

'Keep Melissa busy. Keep her so busy she has less time to think about boys and running off.'

'It's a good thought, but I'm afraid the only thing that would stop Melissa from running away would be to guard her day and night, and we can't do that. I'm already dreading tonight, to be perfectly honest. Despite what she says I don't think we can trust her an inch.'

However much I tried to look on the bright side I couldn't argue with a word Jonathan said. I nodded, and a wave of fear washed over me. Jonathan was normally focused on allaying my concerns and he always tried to look at things positively. His gloomy state of mind showed just how demanding and worrying it was to look after Melissa.

Thankfully, we had a great afternoon; I think we all needed it. It had finally been decided that both boys would return to school the following Monday and Jonathan and I were pleased they had the chance to let off some steam and have fun before they returned to the classroom. As we had hoped, once a date was set for Marty to start at his new school, Ryan hadn't taken long to decide he would go back to his old primary; he didn't want to be left behind and he thought he'd be bored all day without Marty for company.

Happily, the boys were placed in the same team for the football tournament and got through to the semi-finals. Melissa was on the edge of her seat cheering them on, and Ryan and Marty were both awarded medals, which they wore with pride. Their faces were glowing and Melissa clapped and cheered and told them she thought they'd both played brilliantly.

'You're kind, aren't you?' Marty commented, which made Melissa laugh in an embarrassed sort of way.

'I'm telling the truth,' she told him. 'You're really good. You should play for a proper team.'

'I'm going to try to join a local team, when I'm in my next house.'

I had mixed feelings listening to their conversation. On the one hand it was great to hear the kids engaging with each other and being kind and encouraging, but I also felt a pang of pain for Marty. Hearing him use the phrase 'my next house' upset me. He had told me he didn't really know the family he was moving in with very well, even though they were related, and I thought it was a shame he called it a house and not a home. I really hoped it would work out for him.

Melissa used the phone box in the leisure centre before we went for our pizzas, and she told us she'd arranged to meet Rosie at the top of our road at quarter to seven so they could walk to the disco together. 'Is that OK?' she asked. 'Are you cool with that?'

'Yes, sweetheart. That's fine. I remember going to that junior disco myself many years ago. I used to love it.'

'No way! Was it the same one?'

'Sort of. It was in the same church hall, but in our day they called it a dance not a disco.'

She laughed at this, and I told her I'd met Jonathan at a dance when we were both seventeen.

'I can't believe that. Didn't you want to have lots of different boyfriends?'

'No. When I met Jonathan I knew he was the one.'

She thought this was hilarious. 'I'd never be able to pick one. I'd get bored with just one boyfriend!'

We went to a new pizza restaurant that had recently opened up at a retail park on the outskirts of town. It had been heavily advertised and the car park was full when we arrived.

'I think everyone's got the same vouchers we got through our door,' Jonathan smiled.

'Looks like it. Let's hope we can get a table.'

We hadn't been able to book and it was early evening. All five of us walked in and joined a queue of people behind a roped-off barrier that said 'Please wait to be seated.' It took ten minutes for us to reach the front, and the waitress explained that we'd have to wait approximately half an hour.

'Are you happy to wait?' she asked politely. 'As there's five of you I'll try to put you in a booth by the window, over there.'

The wait wasn't ideal, but the three kids all nodded enthusiastically.

'Are you sure?' Jonathan teased. 'I could go home and make you all some beans on toast, and you wouldn't have to wait at all?'

They all sighed and rolled their eyes at Jonathan's 'lame' attempt at humour, as Marty put it. After checking their ages the waitress said all three were allowed to play in the large indoor adventure playground at the back of the restaurant, and she said Jonathan and I were welcome to go through to the restaurant and have a drink while we waited for our table. We agreed to this and, after taking our booking, the waitress said she'd come over to the bar to find us when our booth was ready.

Jonathan went to buy some drinks while I took the three children to the play area. Melissa said it looked 'awesome' and challenged the boys to a race down the slides. It was great to see them all getting on and enjoying themselves, and I was pleased Melissa was joining in so enthusiastically. Given her precocious tendencies it wouldn't have surprised me if she'd considered the play area too childish, but that wasn't the case at all.

I told the children where to leave their shoes before they

disappeared inside a mass of rope ladders, inflatables, plastic slides, swings and ball pits. For an indoor play area attached to a restaurant it was very big. I realised you couldn't see the entrance and exit from the bar so I went over to tell Jonathan I would stay by the equipment, where I could keep an eye on the kids.

'OK,' he said. 'I'll get you a lime and soda and I'll tell the waitress to come and find us over there. What shall I get for the kids?'

'I'd leave it for now. They can order what they want when we sit down. I don't think they'll be bothered about drinks for the time being.'

As I made my way back towards the play area I noticed a small boy running towards his mother in tears.

Poor love, I thought, as he looked really upset and was gulping for air.

'What's the matter Freddie?'

'I hate him!'

'You hate who? Come on, love. Come and have a drink of lemonade.'

I thought to myself, *What a shame. I'm glad it's not Ryan or Marty in tears – or Melissa, for that matter.* Then I immediately wondered who the 'him' was, and hoped that neither Marty nor Ryan had upset this little boy.

When our table was ready I called to Ryan, who I'd just watched coming down one of the slides, and asked him to tell the others we could go and sit down.

'OK!' he said. 'Can we come back in here after?'

'Yes. But come and eat now.'

He gave me a thumbs-up and dashed off to find Melissa and Marty.

He reappeared with Marty moments later but shrugged and said he couldn't find Melissa.

'Oh,' I said, trying to look as unconcerned as Ryan. 'I'm sure she's in there, can you go round once more? She could be behind those red and yellow blocks at the back?'

The boys dashed off together while I stood there wondering if I'd been played like a fiddle. *Has Melissa managed to run away from the restaurant without me noticing?* I thought. *Surely not.*

My mind went back to the leisure centre. She'd made a phone call. I began to worry that she'd arranged to be picked up by one of her boyfriends and had given us the slip amid the chaos of the extremely busy play area.

'Where's our table? I'm STARVING!'

I heard her before I saw her. Melissa appeared from nowhere, pink-cheeked, hurtling towards me, flanked by Ryan and Marty.

'Do we have to put our shoes back on or can we stay like this?'

Relief flooded through me.

'I'd pop your shoes back on and go and wash your hands. I'll come to the bathroom with you, Melissa. I need to wash my hands too.'

The pizzas were well worth waiting for. The children all chose the same thin-crust margherita pizza and then made a joke of asking each other if they wanted to try each other's.

We were all laughing and choosing desserts when a woman approached our table and asked earnestly if she could have a word with me. I recognised her as the mother of Freddie, the little boy I'd seen sobbing.

'Yes, is there a problem?'

'Yes there is,' she said. She looked very nervous. Her face and neck were flushed red and her hands were trembling.

'Excuse me,' I said to the children. I stood up and suggested to the woman that we step away from the booth. Jonathan offered to join us but the woman said she wanted to talk to me, 'mother to mother'. I didn't correct her; it seemed unnecessary to point out I was a foster carer. The last thing I wanted was to inflame what I could already sense was a sensitive situation, and Freddie's mother might be one of those people who had predetermined ideas about kids in care.

We walked to the side of the restaurant, where we were out of earshot of the other diners. I wondered what on earth she was going to say. It was fairly obvious that Ryan or Marty – or possibly Melissa – had been involved in some sort of altercation with Freddie, or at least that he was blaming them for something. However, I was totally unprepared for what she said; in fact, it took my breath away.

'My little boy said he's been . . .' The woman looked embarrassed and as if she had to steel herself to carry on. 'He says your son "touched" him.'

'Touched?' I said, understanding immediately that she meant touched in an inappropriate way. I felt my throat tighten. This was not a good situation, and I immediately thought about Marty, and his past history. How slow of me not to work this out quicker.

'Yes. He put his hands down his pants. That one. The one in the blue shirt.'

Sure enough, it was Marty she was referring to. I stayed very calm and said I was sorry to hear this.

'You should be,' she hissed.

I chose my words carefully, not wanting to admit guilt on Marty's behalf. Despite knowing about the abuse he'd suffered at home and the fact he had touched a younger child inappropriately in the past, I couldn't jump to any conclusions. I hadn't seen what had happened, and as far as I knew nor had Freddie's mother. Also, I'd only heard one side of the story. I waited for the woman to carry on, as I could see she had more to say.

'I could phone the police and my friend said I should, but I don't want to put my son through any more of an ordeal than he's already been through.'

She said Freddie had been 'inconsolable' for the best part of an hour – all the time we'd been at our table – and had only just plucked up the courage to tell his mum what had happened in the ball pit.

'What I want you to do is teach your son right from wrong,' the woman said, her voice trembling. 'He needs to know what the boundaries are and what is acceptable and what is totally not acceptable.'

I wanted to know exactly what had taken place but at the same time I didn't want to ask. The woman didn't volunteer any more information.

'I'm very sorry your son has been so upset,' I said.

'So am I. And I only hope this doesn't scar my little boy for life.'

At that point Freddie appeared. He was grinning from ear to ear, had ice cream around his lips, and asked if he was allowed another drink of lemonade.

'Go and sit down with Tina. I'll be over in a moment.'

I told the woman I would handle the matter and thanked her for talking to me calmly; it was clear she was hopping mad but was succeeding in controlling her anger. 'I appreciate you talking to me this way,' I said. 'And I assure you I'll deal with this.'

Once again I was conscious that I didn't want to accept blame on Marty's behalf, however likely it appeared he'd behaved improperly, as he had done in the past.

'OK. We'll leave it there.' The woman gave me a cold stare.

When I got back to the table Marty looked guilty and worried.

'Is everything OK?' Jonathan asked.

I gave him a little nod so he could see I was OK. 'Now what are we all having for dessert?'

Melissa narrowed her eyes and Ryan frowned but I didn't respond to their sceptical looks. 'Dessert is always the best part of going out for a meal, isn't it? So, do you all know what you're having?'

I didn't look round again and had no idea if Freddie's mother and her party had left after she spoke to me, or whether she stayed and saw us all eating sticky toffee puddings, ice cream and chocolate brownies. If she had I imagine she'd have wondered how we could sit there like that after I'd heard what she'd had to say.

I *was* very concerned about what she'd told me and unfortunately I didn't doubt it was true, but we had three children to take care of and it wouldn't have helped matters if we'd abandoned the meal and left in a dramatic way. I couldn't discuss the allegation with Marty in front of the other children and it would have drawn too much attention to him if I took him to one side in the restaurant and made any kind of fuss. It wouldn't have served any purpose, other than to upset and alarm everyone. Far better, I figured, to finish the meal, keep Marty in my sight and deal with the matter calmly and in the privacy of our home later. That would give me the best chance of encouraging Marty to be as open and honest as possible about what had happened. I hoped he would be.

16

'We're going to end up in an early grave'

While Melissa got ready for the junior disco I talked to Marty, explaining what the lady in the restaurant had said to me.

'I didn't do anything wrong, did I?' Marty had a quizzical look on his face and I felt very sorry for him. Despite his therapy sessions and the support he received from various professionals, I wondered if Marty understood the difference between right and wrong when it came to physical touching. He told me that all he'd done was pull the back of the boy's jogging bottoms down as a joke, not realising this would cause so much trouble. I asked him to think about exactly what had happened next, and told him he could tell me about it, if there was anything else to tell.

'Sorry, Angela,' Marty said. 'I didn't mean to cause trouble. That's all I did. I didn't think his undies would come down too.'

I talked to him about the fact he must never remove another child's clothing again, even as a joke. 'I'm saying this for everybody's sake,' I said. 'I don't want anybody getting upset and I don't want you to get into any trouble of this kind again. The only way to be sure of this is for you to never touch another child in any way that may be seen as inappropriate. Do you understand what I'm saying?'

Marty assured me that he did and said, 'Yes. Sorry. I won't. Thanks for the pizza and everything. It was good.' All that had happened would go in my notes and be reported back to Social Services.

We'd had a phone call while we were all at the restaurant from Rosie's mother, who was called Claudia. Jonathan played back the message and relayed to me that Claudia was going to pick both girls up from the disco at nine and bring Melissa back home.

'Cool,' Melissa said when I gave her the message. 'She's really nice, Rosie's mum.'

I was grateful to Claudia. I wouldn't have wanted Jonathan to go out and collect Melissa on his own and I didn't really want to trouble my mum for babysitting again. Jonathan and I were tired, and we were looking forward to putting our feet up and watching TV for a couple of hours. The boys were shattered too, and I knew they wouldn't be up late after all the football they'd played, and all the chasing around they'd done in the play area.

Melissa went upstairs to get herself ready for the disco and I decided to call Claudia to tell her we'd got the message, and to thank her for picking the girls up. We had the family's home number already, as Melissa had given it to us the first time she hooked up with Rosie. Jonathan had jotted it down and pinned it on a small corkboard next to the phone in the kitchen.

I dialled the number but there was no reply so I tried again later, by which time Melissa was already on her way out to meet Rosie. Still there was no reply.

'Maybe Claudia is out tonight and it was convenient to collect the girls on her way back?' Jonathan suggested.

'You're probably right.'

We weren't concerned; my main reason for calling was to thank Claudia for her kind offer. She'd made a point of saying in her message there was no need to call back, so after one last try we left it at that.

Unfortunately, by ten past nine there was no sign of Melissa and I immediately started to fret. The church hall where the junior disco was held was very close to our house. By car, it was no more than a five-minute drive.

'I'll try Rosie's home number again if they don't turn up soon, see if I can find out what's going on.'

Jonathan looked at his watch and pulled a face, one that said, 'I don't like the sound of this.'

We didn't want to cause unnecessary fuss, but as every minute ticked by, the more of a bad feeling we developed. I inevitably started to wonder if the girls had met up with TJ and Des, or some other boys. By twenty past nine I decided I had no choice but to pick up the phone again. Annoyingly, there was still no reply from Rosie's number. I tried again, and again, before a young girl finally answered.

'Hello, is that Rosie?'

'Yes, it's Rosie here. Who is this?'

'I'm Angela Hart. Melissa is living with us.'

'Oh hi! Sorry. I know who you are now.'

'Is Melissa with you?'

'No, why? Should she be?'

Alarm bells started to ring very loudly in my head.

'I thought your mum was collecting you both and bringing Melissa back to our house after the disco?'

'My mum? No. My boyfriend walked me home.'

'I see. Sorry, there seems to have been some crossed wires. Is your mum there? Can I speak to her?'

'No, sorry. She's out with my dad. They're at a function until late. My grandma's sitting for me and my sister but she's asleep in the chair. Do you want me to wake her?'

Rosie sounded puzzled and concerned, while I felt nauseous, realising someone, somehow must have pulled a stunt and that, once again, Melissa was missing.

'It's OK. I don't want you to wake your grandmother. There's just been a breakdown of communication, I think.'

'Right. But you're worried about Melissa?'

'Well, we expected her home by now. Hopefully she'll be back soon. Do you know who she was with when the disco ended?'

'No. I left a bit before the end. Maybe she's just walking slowly?'

I mentioned TJ, and asked Rosie if she'd seen him.

'No, why would I?'

'Isn't he friends with your boyfriend?'

'No. I've got a new boyfriend. Des wasn't really my

boyfriend. Anyhow, TJ and Des never go to the junior disco. They're too old, but they sometimes hang around outside.'

I thanked Rosie and said goodbye, asking her to ring me if she heard anything. My stomach was doing somersaults and I wanted to talk to Jonathan. He looked at me in astonishment when I told him that Claudia was out all evening at a function. We stared at each other for a moment, scratching our heads. What on earth was going on? We hadn't imagined things. Rosie's mother had definitely called . . . or at least someone had definitely phoned saying she was Rosie's mother, but it couldn't have been her, could it?

There was only one explanation: we'd been duped. For a moment I wondered if Rosie had been talked into pretending to be her mother, to help Melissa stay out later, but I dismissed that idea. Rosie had sounded genuinely confused and concerned about Melissa.

I looked through our answerphone log to see if it had recorded the number we'd received 'Claudia's' message from. It had, but the number was withheld. I quickly called Rosie back and asked if she could tell me if their home number had any restriction on it. She said it didn't, and it would not appear as a withheld number. 'OK, sorry to trouble you, Rosie.'

'No problem. I hope she's OK.'

We replayed the answerphone message. On second hearing, and despite knowing what we did now, it didn't sound fake, even though we knew it had to be. Another one of Melissa's friends must have left this message, yet the voice sounded entirely plausible as that of Rosie's mother, or any mother. I couldn't believe this had happened, or that Melissa had pulled off such a cunning plan.

We waited until ten before going through the familiar routine of phoning the out-of-hours number at Social Services, telling the duty social worker what had happened and being advised to call the police. The officer who took my call listened patiently to all the information I gave and reassured me they'd do their best to find 'our little runaway' and get her back to us as quickly as possible. He sounded pleasant enough to begin with, though he didn't seem unduly concerned, which irritated me. Then he said jovially, 'Leave it with us. Now you go and have yourself a good evening!' I didn't think that was a very fitting thing to say in the circumstances, and it made me wonder if the officer was on autopilot, or was maybe tired out at the end of a long shift. It seemed to me that he'd either not listened properly or had somehow failed to grasp the urgency of the situation: our evening was already ruined, and how could we possibly enjoy the rest of it while Melissa was out in the dark, goodness knows where? I didn't want to be rude, but I couldn't let this go. This was a missing child we were talking about, not lost property. I hated to think this officer might treat other anxious carers or parents in this way.

'Actually, having a good evening is the least of my worries,' I said curtly. 'I can't think of anything but getting Melissa back to us. I hope you find her quickly. I hope she's safe.'

'We'll do our best, madam. These girls are a caution, aren't they? Foster kids, eh!'

I took a deep breath and told myself to remain calm and be polite.

'This girl – Melissa – is twelve years old,' I said firmly. 'It's pitch black outside and freezing cold. I'm extremely worried for her safety. She's been missing for more than an hour and I have no idea who she's with, or where she is.'

'I do understand, madam. Rest assured we'll do our level best to retrieve her and reunite you with her.' I told him she'd dyed her hair a darker cherry red than her natural auburn and he said something about alerting patrols. Then he said very formally, 'I bid you goodnight.'

'Goodnight,' I said, through gritted teeth.

Jonathan and I sat in the kitchen drinking tea. Our nerves were shredded, thinking about the danger Melissa could be in, and we were also feeling wounded and demoralised by her deceitful behaviour.

'What are we doing this for?' Jonathan said. 'It's madness. We're going to end up in an early grave.'

I felt a pang of guilt. It had been my idea to foster in the first place, and I'd stuck to my guns even after we'd both had doubts and wobbles at various times over the previous few years. It was not Jonathan's style to grumble and be pessimistic like this, and I knew he must have been feeling extremely stressed and worried.

'I'm sorry. I didn't think it would be like this.'

Jonathan stood up, put his cup in the sink and walked

to the back of my chair. Then he wrapped his arms around me, resting his chin on top of my shoulder as he did so. *I couldn't do this without you,* I thought. I took hold of his hands and looked down at them. I saw that his fingernails were bitten to the quick and I felt another stab of guilt.

'Don't say sorry,' he said. 'We both thought we knew what we were getting ourselves into. And in any case, it's Melissa we need to be worrying about, not ourselves. I was just letting off steam, that's all.'

The phone rang as we were discussing whether it was worth us trying to get some sleep. It was Lynne, telling me she'd seen Melissa walking past her house.

'I was closing the bedroom curtains when I happened to look out. She was on her own, but she was heading in the opposite direction to your house.' Lynne explained that she didn't want to call to her out of the window or go after her in case she ran, and she thought it was best to phone me straight away. 'I hope I've done the right thing, only from when she was with us I know chasing after her wouldn't have worked.'

I thanked Lynne and very quickly filled her in on what had happened that evening. It was now ten past eleven and I called the police back immediately and told them about the sighting.

'We have a patrol not far away. We'll take a look.'

'Thank you.'

There was a knock on our door about twenty minutes later.

'Thank God!' I said. Jonathan and I both sprang to our

feet and went to answer the door together. A solitary police officer was standing there.

'Good evening, sir, good evening, madam. I'm PC Jones. I've come to take some details about your missing person. For example, do you have a photograph of the said person?'

He was a fresh-faced officer and by the officious way he spoke I imagined he was straight out of training school.

'Please come in. Yes. We do have a photograph of Melissa. I'll go and get it. We've given a copy to the police before.'

'I understand. Thank you very much.'

Jonathan took PC Jones into the kitchen while I fetched the photograph. He explained that he'd had a call on his radio while he was out doing routine patrols, and that it was quicker to come to our house than to return to the station to 'ID the missing person.'

He studied the photograph very seriously.

'Does she try to conceal her appearance or will she look like this, do you suppose?'

We said we'd never known Melissa to attempt to disguise herself but for the second time that evening I pointed out that she'd since dyed her hair a deeper shade of red: 'Cherry red, to be precise.' I added that she might, possibly, use the name Maz instead of her real name.

'Thank you for your time. Please be assured we'll do our best to find her.'

By the time we'd said goodbye to PC Jones it was nearly midnight and we decided we'd better try to get some rest.

'This is ridiculous,' Jonathan said as we got into bed. 'If we didn't have the boys here we could go out looking for her. She was on foot when Lynne spotted her. She can't be far away. Shall I just go out looking?'

'No, not now the police are on the case. We should leave it to them. That's what Wilf would say.'

'Perhaps I should have jumped straight in the car instead of waiting to get hold of the police?'

I told Jonathan not to think like that. 'She could have got into a car and she could be anywhere by now.'

Jonathan harrumphed and turned over, but we both found it impossible to sleep.

'I'm going out to look for her,' he said eventually, getting out of bed and pulling on a pair of trousers.

'What? You can't do that.'

'Look, I won't put myself in any danger, I promise. But the least I can do is go and look for her. I can drive around town and feel like I'm doing *something*. It seems so unnatural to do nothing. How can we just go to sleep?'

I could see that he was adamant about this and I trusted him implicitly to be cautious and remember all the safeguarding rules we'd been taught.

'If you see her, what will you do?'

'I'll pick her up, of course, if she'll let me. But I'll make her sit in the back of the car. I won't be long. Don't worry. I'm just going to go around the town, back past Lynne's house, and have a look along the parade of shops where the takeaways are.'

PC Jones had given us a contact number and I reminded Jonathan of this. I really didn't want him to go out in the dark, driving around the town, but I wasn't going to stop him. I understood how he felt, and he reassured me once more that he would take care of himself.

I listened to the sound of the car firing into life and then the growl of the engine turning into a distant muffled hum. I watched the hands on my bedside clock ticking and ticking and ticking. My eyelids felt so heavy it was as if they were made of metal.

I must have been so exhausted I dropped off for a few minutes, but suddenly I snapped my eyes open. Somebody was coming into the house.

'It's her!' I said, sitting up and reaching over to Jonathan's side of the bed. He wasn't there, of course. I switched on my bedside light and realised it was my husband coming back into the house, not Melissa. I heard him cough as he hung his keys in the box on the wall by the door. I heard him putting his shoes in the cupboard in the hallway. And I heard the familiar sound of his footsteps on the stair carpet.

I was grateful Jonathan was home safe and sound, but at the same time I wished I was hearing the sound of Melissa bounding up the stairs instead, whistling to herself or even grumbling about something or other. Any sound from her would have been welcome. Where was she?

I looked at the clock and saw it was just before one o'clock. As he'd promised, Jonathan had not been long.

'Didn't see a soul,' he said. 'Save for a couple of foxes lurking around the back entrance to the park.'

I told him I'd fallen asleep. 'I'm not surprised. You must be totally shattered. I know I am.'

*

The next time I woke it was five in the morning. Jonathan was asleep and I tiptoed up to Melissa's room and tapped gently on her door before pushing it open. I switched on the light and walked over to the empty bed, where I picked two long red hairs off the pillow. I dropped them over the waste paper basket and watched them float downwards and settle on top of an old tissue and some screwed-up paper. I knew Melissa wasn't there before I looked, but I couldn't stop myself from checking.

I sat on the end of her bed and had a few moments to myself. I thought about how I'd seen so many news reports about missing children. I'd read interviews with parents who feared their child was dead yet never gave up hope. Tragically, I'd heard stories about children who were found dead, and how the parents coped, or didn't, as was usually the case. One story I saw on our local news had always stayed with me. A bereaved mother was interviewed in her young daughter's bedroom, surrounded by disco-dancing trophies, posters of pop stars and a shelf full of birthday cards. One had a big, sparkly badge attached to it, declaring brightly: 'This princess is seven today!' I had sat transfixed – frozen with horror – as I learned that the girl had been killed in a hit-and-run accident. It had taken years for the driver to face trial and finally be jailed. The mother explained that she had not been able to bring herself to move a single item from the room, even though her daughter would now be almost ten years old. The bedroom had become a shrine, and the heartbroken mother said it would always stay that way.

I looked around at the clutter of Melissa's life – the tracksuits discarded on the back of her chair and the floor, a plastic hairbrush that needed a good clean, the holdall she arrived with, thrown in the corner, her small collection of schoolbooks and the new slippers I'd bought her. Her feet were tiny. Size three. The slippers were fluffy with a rabbit's face and floppy ears on either side. *She's a young child,* I thought. *She should be here. She should not be out like this. Why is she missing?* I pushed away dark thoughts that filled my head, trying to stop myself from imagining what danger she was in, and worrying about whether she'd come back unharmed, or even come back at all.

At ten to seven that morning we received a call. I was lying wide awake in bed and I grabbed the phone from my bedside table.

'Is Melissa back with you?'

It was Lynne. I thought it was very early for her to be calling, even in the circumstances. I was immediately on my guard and felt a knot tighten in my stomach.

'No. Have you heard something?'

Jonathan sat up. He looked a bit dazed, as if he'd been woken from a very deep sleep. He rubbed his eyes and mouthed, 'Who is it?' I mouthed back that it was Lynne and he furrowed his brow.

Lynne sounded apologetic and said it was probably nothing, and she was sorry for calling, but she'd heard something from her husband, Nick.

'I'm sorry, Angela. I was really hoping you were going to tell me Melissa was safe and sound, back with you. I shouldn't have called. I don't know what I was thinking . . . I was worried and I should have thought this through but I just had to pick up the phone . . .'

I braced myself. 'What is it, Lynne? What have you heard?'

There was an ominous pause. My heart was racing and now Jonathan was looking extremely worried, his eyes searching my face for answers.

'There's been an accident, on the bypass. Kids, they're saying. In the early hours. I'm sorry, it gave me such a jolt when Nick told me. I just wanted to know Melissa was safe. I was sure she'd be back with you. I was sure she'd get picked up after I spotted her last night. Nick told me I was working myself up about nothing and that I should give you a call to put my mind at rest. I'm sorry. Now I've just worried you too.'

Lynne's husband was a mechanic. The garage he worked for did roadside and motorway recoveries. I knew his job involved removing vehicles that had been involved in accidents and were causing an obstruction.

After quickly telling Jonathan what Lynne had told me I asked her if anyone had been injured. There was another pause.

'I don't know any details. Nick wasn't working this morning, but he's heard it was a bad smash. He heard a teenager died at the scene and the air ambulance was called out.'

I quickly relayed this to Jonathan, then said, 'Teenager? She's not a teenager.'

I knew I was clutching at straws, but Lynne was happy for me to do so.

'Exactly. And honestly, Angela, I'm sure you would have heard if Melissa was involved in any way at all. I'm really sorry. I feel awful now. I bet she's just out with her friends. She's probably asleep in some friend's house, totally fine, and she'll turn up soon as if nothing at all has happened, asking what she can have for breakfast.'

'Lynne, I'm going to call the police. If I hear anything I'll let you know. Please do the same. And don't worry about me. I know you didn't mean to alarm me. Oh, hang on a minute. Jonathan is asking what time it happened, the accident I mean.'

'Around five.'

'OK. Thanks. I'll speak to you later.'

My heart was positively thumping by the time I hung up. It had been five o'clock when I got up and went to Melissa's bedroom. Had I had a sixth sense that something terrible had happened? Is that why my mind had gone back to the tragic stories I'd heard about missing children, and kids who never came home?

Jonathan immediately called the police but couldn't get through. I called out-of-hours and the duty social worker knew nothing about there having been an accident.

'That's good,' I said to Jonathan, trying to convince myself that if Melissa had been involved then the police or the hospital would have identified her as a child in care, and Social Services would have been alerted immediately.

We switched on the radio. The seven o'clock news would

be on any minute. Meanwhile we tried the police again but still couldn't get through.

'Shall I call the hospital?'

'Hang on a minute,' Jonathan said. 'The news is starting. Let's see if there's any more detail.'

He turned the radio up.

The top story was about the accident. Two teenagers had died in the crash, which had happened when what was believed to be a stolen white Ford van carrying six teenagers lost control and hit a tree. No other vehicle was involved. Police were investigating whether the occupants of the car were joyriders. Four teenagers were in a critical condition in the local hospital.

'White Ford van,' I repeated. I felt like I was in a bad dream.

'But a *stolen* white Ford van? TJ *owns* a white Ford van.'

The phone rang shortly afterwards and I nearly jumped out of my skin.

'Mrs Hart? I've got some news. It's about Melissa. Is your husband with you?'

17

'I'm looking forward to seeing my mates again'

It was PC Jones on the phone.

'Yes, my husband is here.' My throat had turned to sandpaper and my voice rasped as I scraped the words out.

'That's good,' the officer said.

I held my breath as I waited to hear what PC Jones was going to say next. Jonathan was padding around the bedroom and he stopped in his tracks and came and stood close to me. He took hold of my hand and gave it a reassuring squeeze.

'We have located Melissa.'

'Where is she?'

The words were sticking to my tongue like sand flies.

'She's here at the station. Would you or your husband be able to collect her?'

I exhaled deeply and felt the grip of my gritted teeth loosen.

'Is she OK?'

'Yes, she's not in the best of moods and is short of sleep.

She may have been drinking last night, or in the early hours. But she has not come to any harm.'

'I can't tell you how good that is to hear. I thought she might have been in an accident . . .'

'No, Mrs Hart. She's perfectly safe. She was picked up by a patrolling officer, in the town.'

I relayed the news to Jonathan, relief flooding from me. His hunched shoulders fell several inches as he looked up to the ceiling and whispered, 'Thank God.' I heard his neck crack; the tension was seeping from him too.

'We heard about that accident on the bypass,' I explained to PC Jones. 'We were worried she'd been involved.'

'I understand. I know it's been all over the news. But I can assure you Melissa is fine. I've just seen her. I'm glad you're both there. Can you come and pick her up now?'

I explained that we had two other children in the house and I'd need to get my mum over to sit with them if we were both to collect her, which was what we'd prefer to do. PC Jones said that was fine; they had nobody available to bring Melissa to us but they would certainly keep her safe until we arrived.

Melissa was in a stark room with two female officers who were busy doing paperwork under the glare of a large fluorescent strip light. They both looked tired and stressed, while Melissa was slumped in her seat, the hood of her sweatshirt pulled down over the top half of her face. She pushed it up and peeped at us from beneath the navy-blue shield. Her green eyes looked slightly bloodshot and she had mud splattered on her trainers and tracksuit bottoms.

The older of the two female officers thanked us for coming. Then, looking over the rim of her glasses at Melissa, she warned her, 'Right young lady, you stay out of trouble. We don't want to see you in here again. We've got quite enough to do already.' She spoke to her in a forceful but reasonably friendly way; firm but fair, I thought.

Melissa peeped anxiously at Jonathan and me and thanked us for collecting her. Then she stood up and shuffled towards the door. She'd taken her hood down now and she stifled a yawn as she ran her fingers through her matted ponytail. I tried to engage her in conversation as the two of us stepped into the corridor. Meanwhile Jonathan hovered back: he wanted to ask the officers if there was anything they could tell us about Melissa's disappearance, as we'd been given almost no information.

'What have you been told?' the younger officer asked.

'Nothing, except that she was picked up by a patrolling officer in the town.'

'OK. She was picked up at the taxi rank at the corner of the market square. Congregated with a gang of youths including two other MPs. The time was . . .' she consulted some paperwork '. . . 06.28 and, yes, she was brought into the station by one of our patrolling officers.'

'MPs?'

'Missing persons. Both teenagers. Both also returned home this morning. A successful resolution all round. Thank you for coming to collect Melissa, and good luck with her. She's not a bad kid.'

Both officers had resumed their paperwork before Jonathan had walked out of the door. He met Melissa and me in the corridor and we all walked to the car together. She muttered that she was sorry and then blamed one of her friends for the fact she'd gone missing after the junior disco.

Here we go again, I thought. *This is sounding like last time, when she said she only stayed in that flat overnight because her friend didn't want to stay there on her own.*

'One of the girls is going out with a taxi driver and he offered us a lift home from the disco. He took us for a spin and then we kinda lost track of time. Sorry.'

'Have you been drinking?'

She didn't look drunk but I could detect alcohol on her breath and stale cigarette smoke on her clothing and hair. She also had black rings under her eyes.

'Just a bit, but that was hours and hours ago. I'm fine now. I'm just tired. Can we stop talking about it? I'm fine, honest.'

I said we'd stop talking for now, but that we'd need to have a chat later, after she'd had some rest.

'OK, that's fine.'

Melissa slept in the back of the car. When we got home she opened her eyes just long enough to see her way up the stairs and into her bedroom, where she collapsed in a heap on the bed. I gave her a pint of water in case she was dehydrated, encouraged her to try to drink as much as she could then left her to go to bed and get some sleep.

I checked on Melissa every few hours. Each time, she was sound asleep with the duvet pulled up right over her head. She didn't wake up until mid-afternoon, when she sidled into the kitchen in a crumpled tracksuit and said she was really hungry. We'd had a roast at lunchtime and there was plenty left over, but she said she didn't fancy it. Instead, she made herself a bacon and cheese sandwich. She smothered it in brown sauce and mayonnaise and devoured it in a flash, washing it down with a large glass of milk. It looked revolting but she said it was delicious, and then asked if she could have a packet of crisps. I'd run out so she settled for a slice of apple pie and custard.

Despite sleeping for most of the day, Melissa still looked extremely tired and said she felt 'wiped out'. As soon as she'd eaten she went back to bed. I wondered if she'd taken drugs because she seemed a bit spaced out. I made a note of this to pass on to Social Services the next day.

I'd called the out-of-hours social worker number when we got back from the police station to make sure they knew Melissa had been found. Nowadays there are Social Services policy and training documents that are pages and pages long, complete with intricate instructions – flowcharts even – that explain in fine detail each and every step that has to be taken when a child in care goes missing. Back then, however, things were different. There were far fewer rules and regulations about the procedures the various professionals had to follow, and as a result there was also a far greater risk that a crucial link in the chain might break. For this reason, I always called the out-of-hours duty social worker if the police called me with news, just to be sure Social Services were fully up to speed and their records were updated.

After imposing on my mum to babysit early that morning we had invited her to stay for Sunday lunch with us. She happily accepted, and while Melissa was still sleeping Mum had played some board games with the boys. This meant Jonathan and I could cook together and get some jobs done, which we were grateful for.

The weather brightened up a bit in the afternoon and Ryan and Marty did some football drills and shooting practice in the garden. Jonathan then explained that he'd won some sporting trophies and shields in his younger days and that they were now gathering dust on a shelf in the garage. The boys were very keen to see them, which Jonathan was really pleased about.

Both boys talked about starting back at school the next day, and we got the impression they were quite looking forward to it. Melissa was finally returning to school too, on the same day. She was meant to have started sooner but the date had been pushed back to this Monday, because she'd been missing.

The plan was that Marty and Melissa would have taxis collecting them, and I was going to walk Ryan to his primary school. As he was in his final year and the journey was straightforward on foot, on the second day I'd let him walk by himself or with his friends. I had reminded

Melissa about the arrangements, but she had looked uninterested.

'Whatever,' she shrugged.

Once again I dared to hope that her return to school would be a turning point for her, but I have to admit I was now less optimistic than I had been.

'I'm sure you'll enjoy it once you're back. You're tired today and I understand you may not be feeling up to it, but I think you'll be fine in the morning.'

'I suppose.'

I had encouraged Melissa to talk about her disappearance on Saturday night but she resolutely refused to give any details or further explanation. I told her that we were confused about the phone call we'd received from the person who had claimed to be Rosie's mum.

'I don't know what you're talking about. I thought Rosie's mum was collecting us. If she had, I wouldn't have got in Marco's taxi, would I?'

She yawned and rubbed her eyes. I told her I'd found out that it was never the plan for Rosie's mum, Claudia, to collect her from the junior disco and that I could only imagine that someone must have pretended to be Claudia, because what other explanation was there.

'What do you mean?' Melissa looked genuinely confused. 'I'm going to my room. I can't deal with this. Sorry, Angela, but my head's aching. I need to go back to bed. Like you say, I've got school tomorrow. At this rate I won't be able to cope. Can I have a painkiller?'

I supervised her while she took one headache tablet, gave

her a fresh glass of water and let her go back up to her room. Melissa's story didn't stack up. I wasn't sure if she was being honest about expecting Claudia to collect her, but I could tell I wasn't going to get any closer to the truth today, if ever at all.

To my surprise, Melissa appeared in the kitchen shortly after seven the next morning, looking bright and breezy and with a wide smile on her face. She'd got up as soon as I tapped on her door at twenty to seven, had a shower and was already dressed in her school uniform. *What a difference a day makes,* I thought.

'How are you feeling?'

'Good, thanks. I'm looking forward to seeing my mates again.'

'I'm glad to hear it,' I said. To tell the truth, I wasn't sure whether it was a good thing or not that she was going to be mixing with all her old friends again. I wondered if it might be better if she started afresh with a completely new group of friends, in a completely new school, but I kept that thought to myself.

'Yeah, I'm sorry I've caused you and Jonathan so much hassle. I didn't mean to. I honestly didn't plan for things to work out how they did on Saturday night.'

'Thanks for saying that. Today's a new day and a fresh start. I'm sure you'll feel better once you've settled back into school again.'

'Yeah, I reckon I will. Thanks.'

*

It was a wet morning but the taxis arrived on time for both Marty and Melissa, and it was just after nine by the time I'd returned from taking Ryan to school on foot. We'd huddled under umbrellas and Ryan couldn't resist splashing in a few puddles. It didn't matter: his school shoes were sturdy and he'd arrived at school dry, and in very good spirits.

Jonathan was in the shop when I arrived home and I made myself a coffee and sat down at the kitchen table, snatching a few minutes to myself. There were no messages for me, and I sighed with relief. Everything had worked like clockwork for a change, and knowing that all three children would be safely in school by now was comforting. I generally find that children do so much better when they have a routine and are being educated as they should be. Their self-esteem grows, they tend to have more confidence and they usually eat and sleep better. Their overall behaviour often improves too, because they are tired when they get home and don't have the time and energy to challenge you as much as they do when they are bored and spending too much time in the house. Having said that, with younger children sometimes the opposite is true: they behave like angels at school and turn into little devils the minute they are out of the gates and feel able to let off steam. I remember one little boy in particular. At parents' evening his teacher complimented him, and us, on his impeccable behaviour.

'I wish they were all like him,' she said. 'Is there a secret you can share with me, Mr and Mrs Hart?'

Jonathan and I were speechless. This child had a habit of rampaging around the house, shouting and kicking doors. He never listened to us when we asked him to stop and calm down, and often the best we could do was make sure he was not harming himself while we allowed him to vent his pent-up tension. Invariably, he'd stop after about ten minutes of intensive protest, then flake out on the sofa and drink a large glass of water, panting like a puppy and seemingly feeling so much better. When we told the teacher this – out of earshot of the little boy, who had lapped up her praise – she was surprised but not entirely shocked, as she recalled that this was a pattern of behaviour she'd learned about at teacher training. It was not uncommon, but she'd never come across such an extreme example as this little boy.

I sipped my coffee and thought how nothing beats being in a warm and cosy kitchen in the winter, hands wrapped around a hot mug while rain trickles down the window panes. I wondered what all the kids were doing at school and looked forward to hearing all about it. Inevitably, I couldn't help thinking more about Melissa than the boys. *She's such a worry*, I thought. She'd be in her first lesson by now. She'd looked very smart in her uniform. I pictured her with her hair all neatly plaited and her shoes freshly polished, as they had been. I really hoped she was settling back in quickly. Maybe she would start to move in some different circles now she'd had a break? Maybe she would find a boyfriend of her own age, or even find herself so busy with her studies that she stopped being so boy mad? I dared to hope so, but I couldn't push my fears completely out of my head.

It was playing on my mind that Melissa had had a pregnancy scare – whether or not it was a genuine one – at such a young age. It seemed wrong that the authorities appeared to have no real strategy in place for dealing with this. As far as I could see, Melissa had been treated in exactly the same way as a girl over the age of consent would have been. How was that allowed to happen? She was twelve, and people in authority knew she was seeing older boys. It didn't seem right at all that more questions weren't asked by Social Services or the GP, and I had an uncomfortable feeling every time I thought about it. As foster carers our only power was words, as Jonathan and I had conceded on more than one occasion. I'd spoken to Melissa about the pregnancy scare when it happened and I would talk to her again, if and when I saw the opportunity. That was all I could do. I had absolutely no evidence that Melissa had had sex with a boy over the age of sixteen, and it was next to impossible to stop a couple of underage kids from experimenting sexually with each other if that's what they wanted to do when they were out of your sight.

Valentine's Day was coming up. It was always one of our busiest times in the florists; we had lots of special displays to put up and orders coming out of our ears. I finished my coffee, quickly did a few household chores and went through to the shop to help Jonathan.

'Well this is a rare treat,' he joked when I fished under the counter for my work apron and asked him what I could do to help.

'What do you mean, a rare treat?'

'I've barely seen you in here. You've been skiving of late, Mrs Hart.'

I laughed. Jonathan was pulling my leg, of course; the truth was I'd been so busy with Melissa, Marty and Ryan being at home full time – or practically full time, in Melissa's case – that it had been impossible for me to put in the hours I normally did in the shop.

I always loved the build-up to Valentine's Day and this year was no exception. I enjoyed putting the finishing touches to the window display, going through the order book and seeing which bouquets needed making up, and reading the messages customers wanted on their gift cards. Some of them were sweet and tender while others were funny and cheeky.

'This is a treat for me, more like,' I said. 'It's heart-warming, reading all these lovely messages. Just the tonic I need!'

During the course of the morning we had some good news. One of our relatives was getting married and we were invited to the wedding, which would be in a beautiful village church. The venue for the reception was a former stately home set in rolling countryside. I immediately started thinking about my outfit, and the fact the occasion would give me a great incentive to lose some more weight. I'd been on a diet for several months and had lost a stone, but my goal was to lose another stone and a half. Picturing myself looking trim in a new dress on the lawn of the stunning mansion house was exactly the goal I needed.

'Do you know, I think I might buy a fitness video,' I said to Jonathan as I tidied a large drawer full of coloured ribbons. I'd been to some step aerobics classes in the previous few months and really enjoyed them, but I'd missed a lot of sessions recently because of our fostering commitments. It was never easy to get out on a regular basis in the evenings. We often had to ferry the children to their various clubs, and I didn't like to leave Jonathan in sole charge unless it was unavoidable. Unfortunately, men are at greater risk than women of having malicious allegations thrown at them by unhappy children, and we're constantly taught to minimise the likelihood of this happening by sticking together as much as possible. Fortunately this suited us both, and still does.

I think the job of fostering would be a million times harder if Jonathan and I didn't work so well together. We've known other couples to buckle under the pressure of running a business at the same time as fostering demanding children, but Jonathan and I have always seen the world in the same way, and we've always been prepared to roll our sleeves up and do whatever it takes. I can't think of a single time when we've disagreed about anything to do with our fostering commitments, and knowing we can rely on each other for support has definitely helped us to carry on fostering year after year.

'A fitness video?' Jonathan said. 'Sounds like a great idea.

If I buy myself a leotard and a pair of leg warmers can I join in?'

We both laughed and then looked up to see an embarrassed-looking teenager standing in front of us. For a moment I thought he'd heard Jonathan's jokey remark, but I realised he was probably blushing because he was feeling self-conscious, as he was ordering Valentine flowers for his girlfriend. He was crimson by the time he'd agonised about what to write on the card, finally settling on 'Happy Valentine's Day with love from Timbo XXX'

'Love Is in the Air' came on the radio a few minutes later. The shop was empty now and I began swaying from side to side as I swirled a shiny white ribbon around a bouquet of red roses.

'Shall we ask your mum to babysit so we can go out for a meal for Valentine's?' Jonathan asked.

'Yes, I'd love that,' I said, though I must admit that my first thought was about Ryan, Marty and Melissa, and whether I really wanted to leave them for a whole evening. Was it fair on my mum, and what if Melissa pulled one of her stunts and ran off somewhere?

'I'm glad you said that, because I've already booked us a table.'

'Really? That's lovely, thank you. Which restaurant?'

'Your favourite – where else? You know how busy they get. I didn't want to miss out.'

'Lovely! I guess the diet will have to go on hold until February 15th!' As I spoke I was still worrying about leaving my mum babysitting, but I told myself not to spoil Jonathan's treat. I knew it was the right thing for us to go out; we've been told so many times by social workers and fostering professionals that carers must make time for themselves in order to thrive in the job. Besides, Mum would enjoy it. Whenever she babysat she always told us that seeing the different kids we had staying with us kept her young, and we hadn't come across any child who didn't take to my mum straight away.

The phone rang once again, and it was another one of our relatives, cooing over the beautiful wedding invitation she had also received in the post that day. With no mobile phones back then, we always diverted calls from the house into the shop whenever Jonathan and I were both on duty in the florists. This was a blessing and a curse: we were nearly always contactable, which was essential for our fostering work, but it also meant that friends and relatives often interrupted our working day. On this occasion I didn't mind at all. My elderly aunt was very excited and I enjoyed talking to her about the wedding, although I eventually had to stop the flow of chatter about bridesmaids and flowers to politely explain we had several customers browsing in the shop and I ought to go and help Jonathan.

I put the phone down and was chuckling and saying, 'Thought she was never going to stop talking!' when it immediately rang again.

'That'll be another excited wedding guest!' Jonathan quipped.

I was smiling when I answered the phone, giving the name of our shop and brightly asking how I could help.

'Hello. I'm calling from Ridgebrook School. I'm trying to get hold of Mrs Hart. Is this the correct number for her?'

A lump bulged in my throat and the smile froze on my face.

'It's Mrs Hart speaking. How can I help?'

Jonathan turned to look at me: he said later he could tell immediately that something was wrong. I indicated that I'd step out of the back of the shop to continue the call on the wireless handset and he nodded. This was a routine we'd been through on countless occasions before, given that we often took calls from schools, Social Services, social workers and support workers when we were in the shop. All our fostering colleagues knew their phone calls would be diverted through if one of us was not at home, and we told them to always leave a message if a shop assistant was on duty and we were both out. The system worked well. Additionally, all the social workers we worked with knew to come into the florists if they called at the house and there was no answer at our door. Many took this opportunity whenever they were passing, because they didn't want to miss the chance of making an extra check on how things were going, although it has to be said that some were less generous with their time than others. We had the feeling certain social workers saw 'popping in' to the shop when it suited them as an easy way of ticking off one of their routine visits. 'I'll put this down as a visit' was the phrase that typically gave them away, though I'm happy to say this was not the norm, and most of our social workers gave us as much of their time as they could possibly afford in their busy schedules.

'It's Mrs Bishop. I'm the attendance officer at Ridgebrook. Melissa has failed to attend her second lesson this morning.'

The words choked all the joy out of me; it felt like I'd stepped out of sunshine and into the teeth of a storm.

18

'Girls love bad boys, don't they?'

Doreen had explained to me that Melissa's school attendance would be very closely monitored because of her previous record. She had to be signed in to every lesson, rather than simply being registered at the start of morning and afternoon sessions like the other pupils. If she failed to turn up for a timetabled lesson, her teachers had been instructed to alert the office immediately. She was also to stay in at lunchtime, as in the past she had a habit of simply not returning after being allowed out of school for lunch.

'She's not turned up for her second lesson? Is she still on the school premises or do you mean she is missing?'

I already knew the answer before Mrs Bishop said, 'I'm afraid she is missing. There is no sign of her on the premises. We believe she has walked out of school, during the changeover between periods one and two.'

Mrs Bishop went on to explain that the school was on a split site and Melissa had to cross the quadrangle to get from the science block to the music department; it's possible she simply carried on past the music room and exited via the service entrance at the back of the building. The gates had been deliberately left open as it was bin collection day, apparently.

I didn't know the set-up at Ridgebrook School at all; Doreen had been the point of contact and had made all the arrangements for Melissa to return there. As we were only looking after Melissa on a short-term placement, and the school was some distance away, we were told there was no necessity for us to visit or meet the teaching staff before Melissa started back there. I regretted this now. I wished I'd had the chance to check the school out for myself, if only so I didn't feel the way I did now, not even being able to picture the buildings and the layout of the school, and feeling completely in the dark about the surrounding area and where Melissa might have gone.

Though I was angry and upset that this had happened – and so quickly – I tried hard not to blame the school. Jonathan and I had failed to keep Melissa in the house and we only had three children to look after. Ridgebrook School had more than a thousand pupils to keep tabs on and, unfortunately, we'd learned that when a child is determined to escape, there is a good chance they will succeed.

In the early nineties most schools didn't have any of the sophisticated security measures they have in place today. Door entry controls and CCTV now routinely used to safeguard children – both by keeping kids inside and accounted for, as well as keeping intruders out – were virtually unheard of in state comprehensive schools. It meant that if a child set their mind on sneaking off the premises undetected, it really wasn't very difficult for them to succeed. The only way to 'catch' truanting kids was retrospectively, when the register was taken and a teacher then raised the alarm if a child failed to show up to a lesson, which is exactly what had happened with Melissa. There was another flaw in the system too, in my opinion. In those days schools tended to rely heavily on detentions or suspensions for tackling truanting. The emotional support, counselling or mentoring that a truanting child may be offered today was far less common – it was a case of meting out a punishment or exclusion, or threatening kids with expulsion, rather than attempting to get to the bottom of why they were skipping school in the first place. When we'd discussed Melissa's return to school with Doreen, the social worker had touched on the subject of detentions and suspensions and was clearly not sold on using them as sticks to tackle truanting. She had commented that she believed the detentions Melissa had had in the past had made her rebel further, while the suspensions were sometimes welcomed by her. 'What d'you do with a child who runs away from school?' Doreen had said cynically.

'I don't know, what d'you do with a child who runs away from school?' Jonathan had replied, seeing where she was going with this.

'Tell them they're not allowed to come in for a week, and then watch them whoop with delight.'

This turn of events had taken me completely by surprise.

Melissa had done a very good job of convincing me she was looking forward to returning to school, and I'd also seen how she was interested in her schoolwork. I really hadn't thought she would run away from school, at least not on the very first morning. Besides, when she went missing from home, it wasn't because she was avoiding things. From what I'd seen, she ran away because she was running *to* something, not *away* from it. In my opinion, *what* she was running to was the real problem; that was what we needed to get to the bottom of. She was running to be with friends, boyfriends, parties and goodness knows what else. She wanted to grow up fast. Often she ran at night, and in Lynne's experience she usually ran under cover of darkness. Who would she be with on a Monday morning? I'd been naive, of course, but I had not expected Melissa to disappear from the school premises after one lesson, and in broad daylight too. She'd given me the distinct impression she was going to make a go of settling back into school and I'd trusted her. How wrong I'd been.

I asked Mrs Bishop exactly how long Melissa had been missing. She reiterated that Melissa hadn't been seen since the end of her first lesson, when she apparently told her friends she was going to the toilet. Though only about fifteen minutes had passed since then I was aware she could have travelled miles in that time if one of her friends or boyfriends had picked her up in a car or van.

In true British style I politely thanked Mrs Bishop for phoning and letting me know what the situation was, though by the end of the call I really felt like screaming. It was incredibly frustrating that Melissa had been able to slip away undetected like this. She was a child who was on the radar, with a history of absconding from school, and she'd escaped after only one lesson. One lesson! It wasn't even break time or lunchtime. Surely it should not have been so easy for her to simply walk out of the gates? Why didn't a large comprehensive school have a better system in place to keep tabs on kids at risk of absconding? I knew the reasons and reminded myself not to blame the school. Melissa simply couldn't be monitored every second of the day. She was a schoolgirl, not a prisoner. The school had put a 'return to school' plan in place for her and nobody had done anything wrong, apart from Melissa. I really did not blame the school, but still I couldn't help feeling the way I did.

I let Wilf know what was happening. We left it for almost two hours before calling the school back to check if they'd heard any more, and then phoning Social Services and the police to report Melissa missing.

The afternoon dragged horribly. I felt like my bubble had well and truly burst and I felt so foolish for daring to hope Melissa's return to school was going to help turn her life around.

'I don't know what we expected,' I lamented to Jonathan. 'By the sound of it she's walked out of school as easily as she walked out of our house and got in TJ's van.'

'I know. It shows what an impossible task it is to stop a runaway from running.'

I agreed, but of course could take no comfort from this.

I spoke to Doreen and Elaine, who once again offered

sympathy, told us not to worry and reiterated that this was nobody's fault but Melissa's. Neither was as surprised as I was that this had happened so soon.

'I'm sorry this is happening to you,' Doreen said. 'She's such a silly girl. Why can't she learn? I guess it's an age-old problem. Girls love bad boys, don't they? I'm assuming she's gone off with another boy. That always seems to be what's behind her escape acts.'

Elaine said, 'I can't understand Melissa at all. How can she do this to you when you've been so kind? I don't understand it. She has no idea which side her bread is buttered, does she? Please let me know if there is anything I can do to help.'

I appreciated their support and their kind words, but I certainly wasn't looking for any sympathy, or compliments for that matter. It was very upsetting and unsettling for us to be in this situation, but I was focused only on Melissa's wellbeing, not mine or Jonathan's. As supportive as Doreen and Elaine were, whatever anybody thought about us as carers was completely secondary at this moment in time. I wanted Melissa to be found and I wanted to stop this from happening again. That was all I could think about, but how could we make her see sense and stop running?

As usual I let off steam talking to Jonathan.

'Sometimes it feels like Social Services are more interested in adhering to policies than anything else. Nobody will lose their job over this. The social workers have done nothing wrong. We've done nothing wrong. The school has followed Melissa's return to school plan to the letter, as far as we know. Everyone's in the clear. Melissa is the only one at fault. We can all just sit back and wait for her to return, knowing we've done nothing wrong. How marvellous—not!'

Jonathan was drumming his fingers on the counter, his eyes darting around the shop, making sure no customers were in earshot.

'I feel totally useless,' he whispered back. 'It's not even as if we can go out and look for her. We don't even know the area around Ridgebrook, and as you say she could have got into a friend's car and travelled to goodness knows where.'

He looked up as a woman we'd known for years approached with a lovely selection of flowers she wanted gift-wrapped.

'Thank you, Mrs Carter. You've chosen well. Is there a special occasion?'

'Yes. My daughter's moved into her new house today.'

'Congratulations! It doesn't seem five minutes ago when she was still at school. I remember her coming in here in her Brownie uniform.'

'The Brownies! Yes, Caroline was an Imp, and how fitting that was. She was such a cheeky little thing, always up to no good! She used to have me run ragged and worried sick! I thought she'd never grow out of it, but they all settle down in the end, don't they?'

'Yes, they do,' I said, thinking to myself, *I'm not sure that's true of everybody, unfortunately.*

'Are you still fostering?'

'Yes, we are.'

'Really? Good for you. How many children have you got staying with you at the moment?'

Jonathan hesitated. 'Er, three.'

Mrs Carter chuckled. 'You don't sound too certain!'

Jonathan laughed and I gamely joined in as we shared a look that said, 'There's a good reason for that.'

I spoke to Wilf about Melissa's taxi. I was worried about it making a wasted journey to the school that afternoon and wanted to warn the taxi firm that Melissa might not be there. He told me to call the cab office direct and explain the situation. He said to tell them they would still be paid by Social Services regardless of whether Melissa showed up or not. We certainly wouldn't cancel it, just in case she did happen to turn up.

When I made the call a very chatty woman called Gaynor answered the phone. 'It isn't a problem, darling. Happens all the time, and it's always the girls. I don't know what they get up to, little madams! It's the parents and carers I feel sorry for. You must be worried sick when they bunk off like this. Of course, the kids don't care, do they? They go off and have their fun and come back when they're hungry or have run out of money. Still, I was no angel at that age. Blooming kids! All right, darling, I'll let the driver know and I'll make sure he checks in with me. If she shows up, d'you want me to give you a bell?'

'That would be great, thank you.' I gave her our number.

'No problem at all, my love. Always happy to help. And don't you worry too much. They always turn up.'

The way Gaynor made this sound so commonplace concerned me, prompting me to ask some questions. 'How common is it, if you don't mind me asking?'

Gaynor sounded happy to continue our chat. I explained that I'd been fostering for several years and had never encountered this problem before, despite the fact many of the children who stayed with us had been taken to and from school all over the surrounding areas by taxi.

'Like I say, happens all the time these days. It never used to. It seems to be certain schools – Ridgebrook is just one of them – and it's like it goes in waves.'

'Waves? How do you mean?'

'I mean, like one school has a spate of truancies, then all of a sudden it's a different school all the kids are bunking off from. I think once one girl starts doing it her mates think it's smart to follow suit. It's what kids do, isn't it? It's usually the big comps that have the biggest problems, but that's hardly surprising. Too easy for the kids to walk out and not be noticed. And if they're near the town, that's even worse.'

'Yes, I can imagine. More temptations, I suppose.'

'Exactly right, my love. No point bunking off school if you're stranded in the countryside, is it? But if you can go to the shops and all that, or hang around the arcades, then the problem's always gonna be worse. Stands to reason, doesn't it?'

I explained that I didn't know the area around Ridgebrook School but was aware it was fairly close to the town.

'Close to the town? You're not wrong there. It's a hop, skip and a jump to the shopping arcade, and that place is like a rabbit warren. Go in there and you could be lost all day, even if you didn't want to be! Anyhow, darling, I'll give you the heads up if your girl turns up. I'll tell the driver what's what and he'll be there on time regardless, just in case.'

'Thanks. And I'll call you if we hear any more in the meantime.'

The day dragged after that, and I was watching the clock and the phone non-stop. I called the taxi firm at quarter past four, not long after I'd collected Ryan and we'd walked home together. By then it was obvious Melissa was not going to turn up for her lift home, and Gaynor confirmed that the driver had checked with the school office before leaving with an empty cab, after waiting for almost half an hour. I said I'd give them plenty of notice about the following morning, so Melissa's taxi to school didn't show up unnecessarily.

'All right darlin',' Gaynor said. 'I won't cancel it until you give me the word. If I don't hear, the cab will be there. Best to look on the bright side, eh? I bet she'll be back tonight when her stomach's rumbling!'

Ryan heard me on the phone and asked if everything was OK. I simply told him Melissa hadn't met her taxi after school.

'Oh,' he said, narrowing his eyes. 'Do you think she didn't like the driver? Maybe she's getting a lift off a friend?'

'We'll see.'

'But she's coming back tonight, right?'

'I'm afraid I can't answer that, Ryan.'

'That sucks,' he said. 'You're a really nice lady, Angela, and I think it's mean of Melissa to make you worried.'

This touched me and I thanked him for his thoughtful words. Kids have a habit of taking you by surprise – in good and bad ways – and I was really grateful for Ryan's unexpected show of support.

Ryan and I had a hot drink together in the kitchen and he chatted about his school and told me a new supply teacher was taking his class the next day, as his form teacher had to go into hospital.

'I'm sorry to hear that.'

'So am I. She's got grown-up toenails.'

'Oh, you mean in-growing toenails? They can be quite nasty.'

'That's it, yeah. In-growing. Urgh! Sounds disgusting. Do you want to hear a joke?'

'Yes please, I'd love to.'

'Why did the biology book have to go into hospital?'

'I don't know. Why did the biology book have to go into hospital?'

'Because it broke its spine!'

'D'oh! Have you got any more?'

'Why wasn't the geometry teacher in school?'

'Go on.'

'Because she sprained her angle!'

Ryan was doing some homework at the kitchen table when Marty arrived home.

'How did school go?'

'OK.'

'How was the journey?'

'Quite long.'

'Did you settle into the class OK?'

'I suppose.'

'What was the best thing about the day?'

'I dunno.'

'What did you have for lunch?'

'The lunch was awesome. We had macaroni cheese and salad and you could go back for seconds. And the pudding was chocolate sponge and ice cream. We never had chocolate sponge and ice cream in my old school. The puddings were rubbish.'

'I'm pleased you liked the food.'

I wanted to ask about the teachers, but because of his history Marty was being shadowed by a one-to-one support teacher for the time being. I didn't want to mention this in front of Ryan, so instead I asked about his lessons.

'What subjects did you have?'

'I can't remember.'

'What's your favourite subject?'

'I dunno.'

Marty scratched his head. 'We played football at break, though. They have this awesome field and I'm going to do a trial for the school team. There are thirteen boys in the class who all support the same team as me. How cool is that? What are we having for tea? I'm starving. And can I play football later?'

I smiled to myself. Food and football. They were obviously the best ways to Marty's heart, bless him. He didn't mention Melissa's absence so nor did I.

On Valentine's Day, by which time Melissa had been missing for nearly a week, a huge bouquet was delivered to our door. I was taken aback; it came from a rival florist and of course I was not used to being sent flowers. Jonathan often joked that the fact we ran a florists had saved him a fortune over the years, as he'd never once bought me flowers as a present, for my birthday, Valentine's or anything else. More often than not we had lots of lovely flowers in the house; the ones that had gone slightly over and were not perfect enough to sell in the shop but were too good to throw away.

This bouquet was for Melissa, the delivery driver told me. I took the flowers into the house, filled up the sink in the utility room and placed the stems in the water. I had a cupboard full of vases but I didn't feel like displaying these flowers. There was no note, and there was no Melissa either.

It was the weekend now, and Melissa had been missing since Monday morning. There hadn't been a single sighting of her and I was fed up to the back teeth of being told by the police and Social Services that there was nothing we could do and we shouldn't trouble ourselves: the professionals had it all in hand.

I called the out-of-hours and told them about the delivery of flowers, giving the name of the company and asking if they thought we should try to trace the sender. I knew it was unlikely the florist would give out the name of the person who'd ordered the flowers if I called them: in our shop we had a policy not to give out any details of our customers over the phone. The out-of-hours social worker told me that, yes, of course it would be helpful if the sender could be traced, but then – rather annoyingly – she started to explain about customer confidentiality and told me that I should leave this to the police and not try to do any 'detective work' myself. She made me feel like I had been trying to be some kind of Miss Marple, attempting to solve the mystery from my kitchen table when really I should be leaving it to people who knew what they were doing. This irritated me, as I knew all about customer confidentiality already and had not been suggesting that I break this myself!

I called the police and spoke to a kindly but rather bemused older officer. 'Thank you for the information. Forgive me, but the person who sent the flowers must not realise she's missing, wouldn't you say?'

'I did think about that, but it's a lead I still think is worth chasing up. This person may have information, even if they aren't aware Melissa is missing.'

The officer agreed and said he'd put someone on it right away, but unfortunately we never heard any more on the subject of the flowers or the sender. I was so desperate for any snippet of information that might lead me to Melissa that I daydreamed about ringing the rival florist myself and pretending to be her, but I soon pushed that thought from my mind. I'm one of those people who find it impossible to lie, and even if I tell the gentlest of white lies it's always very obvious. Besides, I thought again about how I would never give out any customer's information to a member of the public if someone phoned our shop. Even if I got away with pretending to be Melissa I was unlikely to be told who had sent the flowers. As desperate as I was for news, I conceded this was a matter best left to the police.

'I don't feel much like celebrating,' I said to Jonathan as we got ready for our Valentine dinner that evening.

'I know what you mean, but the table's booked and your mum's on her way over to sit with the boys. Let's make the most of it.'

As I blow-dried my hair I thought about the first day Jonathan and I met Melissa, when she said she'd have escaped from the secure unit if she were Rapunzel, as the lads there had nicknamed her. I also thought about her dyeing her lovely auburn hair cherry red, and how she tied it up with fancy ribbons and scrunchies. 'I've told them that if I was really Rapunzel I wouldn't still be here, would I? A prince would have come to my rescue!' That was exactly what she'd said; I could hear her very young-sounding voice; she was just a child. Was she with a boy right now? A boy she thought was her prince? Was she trying to be all grown up, staying in someone's house, drinking, smoking, having sex? What if she really did get pregnant?'

'You look lovely,' Jonathan said, admiring my reflection in the dressing table mirror.

'Thanks!' I stuttered, having jumped when he walked up behind me. It was obvious my mind was elsewhere but Jonathan knew better than to offer a penny for my thoughts;

we were going out and there really was no point in spoiling the evening by picking over how horrendous it was to be in limbo like this, waiting for news of Melissa.

All week long my sleep had been disturbed. I'd woken in the dead of night to the sound of Melissa opening the back door, climbing the stairs, creeping into bed. But it wasn't Melissa, of course. It was a tree branch creaking in the garden, an air bubble in the plumbing working itself through the pipes, or one of the boys getting up to use the toilet. I'd dreamed of Melissa appearing in the kitchen with a sheet of shimmering red hair tumbling down her back, looking like one of the cartoon princesses she had on some of her socks and clothing. I'd also 'seen' her in what can only be described as a nightmare. I woke with a start, thinking all over again that Melissa had been involved in that horrific car crash, only this time PC Jones was not calling to tell me Melissa was safe and well – the police were knocking at the door to tell me they had the worst news.

Before we went out for our meal, Jonathan and I went into the lounge to say goodbye to Mum, Ryan and Marty. To our dismay, Ryan was as white as a sheet, Marty was sitting on his hands and looking awkwardly at the floor and Mum was apologising and saying she hadn't meant any harm.

'Whatever's the matter?' Jonathan said.

Ryan and Marty looked away and Mum launched into a description of what had just gone on.

'I'm really sorry. I seem to have upset Ryan but I really

didn't mean to. I only suggested a game of . . . well, I won't mention it again. Shall we play dominoes instead?'

'Can we just play our computer game?'

It was Marty who spoke.

Jonathan and I looked at each other and then at Mum. Jonathan replied, 'That's fine by me, as long as you're OK with that, Thelma.'

'It's fine by me. I've never much liked ha—, I mean that game much in any case. And there's a good weepie on TV.'

Ryan gave us a thin smile and I was pleased to see he already had a bit of colour back in his cheeks. Jonathan looked at his watch. We really did have to leave now if we were going to make our table.

'OK boys, you can have an hour on the game. You both have school tomorrow, so it goes off at half eight. And please be in bed on time.'

They both grinned and ran down to the dining room, where the computer was plugged in.

'What game was it, Mum?' I asked when the boys had disappeared.

'Hangman. I'm quite sure those computer games are far more offensive!'

Jonathan caught my eye. As I've said before, we had not been told how Ryan's brother had taken his life. After the upset with him thinking Melissa's red hair dye was blood I'd had my suspicions, but now it was impossible not to have other ideas. However Ryan's brother had died, I thought how terribly sad it was that a boy as young as Ryan had experience of such a devastating tragedy.

I reassured Mum that she mustn't worry. 'The boys seem perfectly happy now. We'll just not mention that game again. Here's the number of the restaurant. Don't hesitate to call us if you need to get hold of us. We won't be late.'

'OK dear. You two have a lovely meal. I'm glad you're going out. I thought you might not have bothered.'

'Why?'

'I thought you were on a diet, dear.'

'Yes, Mum. I am. But I'm having a night off.'

'Oh, is that allowed?'

Mum had never had any trouble with her weight and didn't really understand the world of dieting. I was an expert, having dieted on and off ever since my teens, but nevertheless Mum often pulled me up on my habits, thinking she knew best. This wound me up sometimes, but I knew she didn't mean any harm.

'Yes it is allowed!' I said. 'Cheat days are the latest thing – didn't you know? See you later, Mum!'

We left her shaking her head and saying, 'Well I never!'

Jonathan and I were just about to order dessert when the restaurant manager came over to our table, saying my mother had called and was holding the line. Fortunately, we'd known the manager for many years and he also knew my mum, as when my dad was alive he used to take Mum to the same restaurant on special occasions.

'Thanks, I'll take it,' Jonathan said, immediately getting to his feet. 'Probably one of the kids!' he added, smiling apologetically at the manager.

'No problem, Mr Hart. Happy to help. Please, step this way.'

I hoped to goodness Mum hadn't inadvertently run into any more problems with Ryan, or with Marty, for that matter. As Jonathan crossed the restaurant I had a fantastic thought, immediately followed by a negative one. Had Melissa turned up? Or what if Mum had suggested another game that might trigger bad memories for Ryan? I pictured all the games we had. What about Cluedo? Oh no, there was the rope and . . . my mind spun. I'd have to talk to Wilf about this issue. Maybe I should have made an exception in Ryan's case, and confided in my mum about his history, so she wasn't at risk of saying or doing the wrong thing? Of course, that would have gone against our confidentiality training and I wouldn't have done so without taking advice. I thought that it was probably too late now in any case, given that both boys were moving out very soon, but I'd still mention it to Wilf so it could be passed on to others involved in Ryan's care.

I'd been torn between the banoffee pie and the raspberry sorbet before we were interrupted. I'd completely lost my appetite by the time Jonathan returned from taking Mum's call. On balance, I'd decided this was most likely to be bad news and I braced myself for what he had to say.

'It's Melissa,' Jonathan said, unexpectedly. 'She's been found. The message from your mum is that the police want us to go and fetch her.'

I couldn't believe my ears and I grinned with delight. That was the best news I could have had.

'Is she OK?'

'She's safe. She's with the police. That's as much as I can tell you.' He finally allowed himself to smile: poor Jonathan had also thought we were going to receive bad news and was still trying to take this latest news in.

19

'Do you know why your head's busy?'

'I think we should go straight there,' I said, without hesitation.

'Are you sure you don't want to nip home first?' Jonathan gestured towards our clothes. I was in a dress and a pair of heels and he was wearing his best shirt and jacket. We hadn't dressed for the cold night at all. I only had a thin coat with me, and Jonathan had a mac in the car but no winter coat, as we'd driven and knew there was ample parking right in front of the restaurant.

'Yes. It makes sense to go straight away. Mum is already babysitting and we can be on our way as soon as we've paid the bill. The quicker we get to Melissa, the better.'

And that is exactly how our Valentine's night out ended – or should I say, how it panned out. The manager knew we were foster carers and probably guessed there was some drama with the kids. We didn't enlighten him, but he generously told Jonathan to feel free to use the restaurant phone if he needed to make any other calls. After quickly speaking to my mum again to warn her we'd be later than we first expected, Jonathan called the police. He spoke as quietly as he could in the noisy restaurant, trying to be as discreet as possible as the phone was right at the front, on a small desk where taxi and table bookings were made. A group sitting near the entrance looked up and stopped talking when they heard Jonathan asking to be put through to the duty sergeant. In return he gave them a big, generous smile; he says that's always the best way to deal with nosy parkers!

It seemed Melissa had turned up at her auntie's house. From the name the police gave we knew this was the same auntie whose stepson Melissa had described as a 'weirdo' and had disgusted her with his comment about wanting to 'do it' with her. That was all we knew as we set off on the hour-long drive to collect her from the police station, where she was now being looked after.

'It's lucky I hadn't had a drink,' Jonathan said, though the truth was he very rarely had one. He preferred to drive rather than take taxis, and he always said he liked to have his wits about him, as you never knew what might crop up with the kids. I'd had a glass of sparkling wine as the restaurant offered all guests a complimentary drink with the Valentine's menu that evening.

'It's not luck, it's good judgement,' I said. I was glad I'd only had the one glass, but wished I hadn't bothered.

As we headed out of town we went past a parade of shops, outside which a large gang of youths was congregated. Some were smoking and a couple of the older-looking boys were drinking from cans, while a few had spilled over onto the road. Two boys were leaning up against a large black sports car that had a silver spoiler on the back. Jonathan slowed down to a snail's pace in order to steer past the gang as safely as possible. As he did so I spotted TJ with a petite blonde girl. He had his arm around her and was gazing into her eyes. They looked very much like an item, despite the fact the girl looked even younger than Melissa. In the centre of the group was a man who looked to be in his twenties. He had a thick black beard, but what really made him stand out was the fact he was dressed in a flashy designer Puffa jacket and had a gold baseball cap on his head. He was clearly the leader of the pack; kids were swarming around him, laughing and taking cigarettes from the packet he was passing around. TJ didn't notice us; he was kissing the blonde girl now. Jonathan accelerated as we left the group behind us and headed in the direction of the motorway.

'D'you think we should stop and call the police?'

'And say what?' Jonathan said wearily.

'Well, you know, one of those young girls could be missing from home. It's clearly one of those gangs Melissa gets caught up with.'

Jonathan sighed. 'I think we'll have to leave the police to do their job. What crime would we say they are committing? Hopefully a routine patrol will pick up on them.'

I knew Jonathan was right. They weren't making enough noise to be accused of breaching the peace or causing a public nuisance. It was impossible to know for sure, from a brief glance, which of the kids who were smoking and drinking were too young to do so. As for the fact the girls appeared to be younger than most of the boys they were hanging around with, that wasn't a crime either – at least not as far as we could see. On the face of it they were simply a group of young people hanging around the streets and letting their hair down a bit, as kids had always done. I had to agree that we couldn't feasibly call the police out to report this gang. Just like Social Services, the police were already stretched to breaking point and were far too busy to speculatively investigate a group of kids like this. Still, I didn't like what I'd seen. Even if no criminal activity was taking place, those young girls were clearly in a vulnerable position.

Once we were on the motorway and had worked out which junction we had to come off at, Jonathan and I started to talk about Melissa.

'Why on earth did she go to this auntie's house if what she says about the stepson is true?'

'Maybe he's not living there any more? He could have moved out. Mind you, we don't even know what age he is, do we?'

This was true – we had no idea if the stepson was a child or an adult. We knew very little about Melissa's family and extended family. We also had no information about who else lived in her auntie's house, if anybody. With the scant detail we had, it was impossible for us to work out how and why Melissa had left school on Monday morning and turned up at this auntie's house today. She'd been gone for six days, and her movements in that time were a mystery to us.

As Jonathan commented, trying to work it out was 'like trying to solve a Rubik's cube with one hand tied behind your back.'

Nevertheless, we talked of nothing else, all the way to the police station. It would have been fruitless for us to try to talk about anything else.

We found the station easily, as it was on the approach road to the town and was large and well lit. Jonathan and I pulled on our inadequate coats and hurried across the car park, bracing ourselves against the needles of rain and biting cold. I shuddered, feeling the freezing air on my legs and wishing I was wearing trousers and flat shoes rather than barely there tights and kitten heels.

It took a few minutes for us to be seen at the desk and explain who we were. By that time I'd just about started to defrost. I felt less physically tense as the stuffy warmth of the well-heated station filtered through my body. Finally, I unfolded my arms, which I realised had been clamped tightly into my chest.

We were taken through to the room where Melissa was waiting for us, and the moment I saw her I felt myself freeze and tense all over again, my muscles tightening and my throat narrowing as I stifled a gasp.

'Sweetheart, are you OK?'

Melissa was in a terrible state. She had a split lip and a cut on her forehead. Her tracksuit was filthy and her whole demeanour was of someone who was completely dishevelled and probably hadn't had a good night's sleep or a shower in days.

She stared at me, saying nothing.

'How are you?' I asked. 'How did this happen?'

'You really don't want to know,' she said slowly, shaking her head. Looking me up and down, she added meekly, 'You look lovely, Angela.'

I half smiled; this was sweet of her, but in the circumstances it was completely out of place for my appearance to be the topic of conversation.

An officer told us Melissa had turned up at her auntie's house 'after the altercation' earlier that evening. We didn't point out that we hadn't been told about an altercation; he was in full flow and we waited to hear what else he had to say. It seemed that Melissa had confessed to her auntie that she had 'absconded from care' and her auntie had phoned the police.

'I asked her not to,' Melissa interjected, looking intently at her trainers. 'I don't want to go back in care. I don't like being in care.'

The officer looked at us with pity and shrugged. I saw Jonathan swallow hard: it's always painful when kids say they don't want to live with you, but unfortunately it's par for the course when you're a foster carer. The vast majority of kids want nothing more than to return to their family or extended family, regardless of how dire their circumstances were prior to being taken into care.

'Melissa,' I said. 'You won't be in care forever. Everyone

is working hard towards moving you in with your Auntie Cathy, as soon as possible. Then, hopefully, you won't have to move again. That will be your home.'

'So what's the hold-up?' She shot me a look that was part accusatory and part pleading. I felt very sorry for her.

'I honestly don't know, sweetheart. What I do know is that you have to come back home with us tonight. I will ask Social Services to fix up an urgent review meeting and Jonathan and I will do all we can to help you move on as soon as possible. For this to happen we need you to co-operate with us, it's for your benefit.'

She rolled her eyes and sighed but didn't say anything else.

Jonathan asked if 'the altercation' would result in any legal proceedings.

'Yes. Melissa wants to press charges against the two girls who assaulted her. My colleagues have already dealt with this.'

I asked if there were any more details we could have.

'Not a lot to say. Girls fighting over their boyfriends. All got a bit heated, evidently.' He jutted his chin towards Melissa and looked pointedly at her split lip and the cut, which had bled into her right eyebrow.

'They're nasty pieces of work,' Melissa suddenly spat. 'Lying cows!' Then she winced and touched her lip and said pitifully, 'Ow, that really hurts.'

That was Melissa in a nutshell: trying to act cool and tough, but not being able to hide the fact she was really just a vulnerable little girl who was easily harmed.

It took fifteen minutes to persuade her to get in our car, and that was only after the police officer winked discreetly at Jonathan and told her he would go and see if there was a cell free for the night if she wanted to stay there instead.

'All right. I'll go. But I'm not going to stay. I'm calling Social Services myself, first thing in the morning!'

We thanked the officer and picked up some paperwork that we'd need to pass on to Social Services. Melissa trudged slowly to the car. Then she slumped on the back seat and folded her arms in a huff.

'Why are you all dolled up, anyway?'

'We were out having a meal for Valentine's Day when we got the call from the police.'

'Oh. Sorry.' She actually did sound sorry, and once again I thought what a contradiction Melissa was. How could a girl who was naturally sweet and kind switch to behaving like a street fighter and a brat? Brawling over boys was the problem, according to the police. Boys, boys, boys. They seemed to be at the heart of all of Melissa's troubles.

Once home, I think she was too tired to keep up her protest. Melissa said she wanted to go to sleep but her face hurt and she was worried the pain in her lip would keep her awake. We went into the kitchen and I asked if she was hungry or needed a drink, and she politely told me she'd eaten at her auntie's house earlier, then asked if we'd managed to eat our meal at the restaurant.

'Yes thank you. We didn't manage dessert, but I guess that's a blessing.'

'Why?'

'I'm trying to lose weight.'

'Well I'm not,' Jonathan quipped. 'And I had my eye on the banoffee pie, I'll have you know.'

Melissa managed a little smile; she knew he was only teasing.

Jonathan finally ran my mum home. She'd been watching TV and the boys had been sound asleep for hours by the time we got back. As he escorted Mum out, Jonathan deliberately bypassed the kitchen where Melissa was sitting nursing her lip with a damp tissue. I fetched her a bowl of salt water and some cotton wool, which she used to dab the cut above her eyebrow. Fortunately, it wasn't deep and looked like it would soon heal.

I heard Jonathan chatting about this and that and apologising for keeping Mum up so late. She said it was no bother at all. 'Is everything all right now?'

'Yes. Thanks to you we could sort it out quickly.'

'That's good. If you built a granny annexe for me, it would be even easier, you know?'

Mum was still very sprightly and independent at the time and was only joking, though it's something we did give some thought to in years to come.

While Jonathan was out I stayed in the kitchen with Melissa, checking if her lip was all right and generally trying to make her feel at home and as comfortable as possible.

'I'm having a cup of tea, would you like one?'

'No thanks. Can I have hot chocolate?'

'Yes, good idea. I can find you a big straw to drink it through. That'll be better for your lip.'

While I made the drinks I told Melissa about how Jonathan and I had been at the same restaurant that my dad used to take my mum to for Valentine's, and for their wedding anniversary and other special occasions. I didn't expect her to be particularly interested in this and was only making conversation, hoping it would encourage her to relax.

'I think you're dead lucky,' Melissa said. 'I'd love to get married and have a husband who loved me and took me out for nice dinners. That's all I want. But not all boyfriends are nice, are they? I think it's hard to find a good one. I want the best one.'

I wanted to talk to her about the fact she was only twelve and the world was her oyster, but I was afraid I'd stifle the flow of conversation if I said anything she might conceive as being preachy.

'I know I'm lucky. Jonathan is a great guy. You are right to want the best. Don't settle for anything less.'

There was a pause. 'It was Veronica Smith who had the idea, you know.'

'The idea?' I kept my tone even, though I felt a surge of hope and relief that she was starting to open up about her latest disappearance.

'Of inviting me to the pictures, with her and her boyfriend and his mates. I never thought we'd stay out so long. I missed the taxi so Veronica said I could stay at hers. I should have told you, I'm sorry.'

I realised Melissa was talking about Monday, when she left school in the morning and never returned. I couldn't be sure if any of this was true, but even so I went along with her story and gently asked her if Veronica's parents were home when she went to stay there. 'Er, yes. They didn't mind me staying. They just went to work really early the next day, leaving us to get ourselves to school. You can walk to school from their house. Then we bumped into Degsy and Oz and then—'

'Degsy and Oz?'

'I know! What were the chances of that? They were just walking past the school the next morning, with two other lads. I didn't realise one of them was going out with Sharon Slater.'

'And so you didn't go into school on Tuesday. You went out with the boys?'

'Yes, me and Veronica didn't go to school,' she said. 'But you know that already, don't you?'

'Yes, but I didn't know the reason.'

'So, we went out with the boys. Oz had his car. His mate fancied me and that's what led to the scrap with Sharon Slater and Kim Fletcher.'

It was a bit confusing, but I was committing all of this to memory. I imagined Veronica's parents had had no idea Melissa was missing, but even so I questioned how you could allow a young girl to stay in your home on a school night and not attempt to contact her parents or guardians. No doubt the girls had spun a yarn to stop this happening, but who knows?

I encouraged Melissa to keep talking and said she could tell me anything she liked. I said we were on her side and that we wanted to help keep her safe and ensure she didn't get into fights or come to any more harm. I took care not to look shocked or judgemental, instead staying calm and giving her an understanding nod and an encouraging word, hoping she'd carry on talking. I wanted to find out what happened for the rest of the week. Had she continued to stay with Veronica or had she stayed somewhere with Degsy and Oz, or somebody else?

Unfortunately, Jonathan returned very quickly from dropping off Mum, and Melissa clammed up as soon as she heard him come in. I signalled to him to leave us alone when he popped his head around the kitchen door, but the moment was gone. Melissa left half of her hot chocolate, said she was tired out and went up to bed.

I told Jonathan everything she'd said and wrote it all down. I was deeply suspicious of how Oz and Degsy had 'just turned up' at the school, which to my knowledge was not in their neighbourhood, but again I had no idea if Melissa's version of events was true.

Jonathan and I finally went to bed ourselves, feeling absolutely shattered. It was a school day tomorrow. By the time we'd got Melissa home it had been far too late to organise her taxi for the morning. Though we always hate it when kids miss their education, in the circumstances Jonathan and I decided not to rush Melissa back to school. She needed to recover, and we didn't want her immediately absconding again. I'd made up my mind to call Social

Services first thing and push for the emergency review I'd spoken about with Melissa. We simply couldn't go on like this, and I was worried sick she'd come to worse harm than she already had done, perhaps falling pregnant or disappearing off the radar completely.

I could hear Melissa pacing around but I left her to it, assuming that as she was very tired too so it couldn't go on for long. I drifted off for what felt like a short while, and when I woke up I could still hear Melissa padding around. It sounded like she was moving furniture. I glanced at the clock. It was 3 a.m.

Jonathan was asleep so I quietly swung my legs out of bed and tucked my feet into my slippers. It was cold and I shivered, feeling for my dressing gown in the dark. Our bedroom door creaked as I eased it open. Jonathan stirred but didn't wake. I tiptoed up the stairs to the top floor of the house. Melissa's bedroom light was on; I could see a wand of light beneath the door. I tapped gently.

'Melissa?'

No reply.

'Melissa, sweetheart, are you OK?'

'Yeah.'

'Good. Can I come in?'

'Er, OK.'

I pushed the door open and saw Melissa sitting cross-legged on the floor, elbows on her knees and her chin cupped between her hands. It reminded me of the first time I saw her, sitting on the floor of her room at the secure unit, only that time she'd had her knees hugged to her chest. She was still dressed in the dirty tracksuit she'd had on earlier and didn't look like she'd made any effort to go to bed.

'Can't you sleep?'

'No.'

'I thought you'd be exhausted.'

'I am, but I can't sleep. My head's busy.'

'Do you know why your head's busy?'

'Dunno.'

'Have a think.' I gave her a friendly smile, one I hoped would remind her that she could talk to me if she wanted to.

She sniffed loudly and I walked over to reach for a tissue from the box on her bedside table. As I passed the tissue to her I glanced down and noticed some packaging on the carpet. I recognised it immediately as part of a pregnancy testing kit.

'Melissa,' I said. 'Are you worried about anything?'

'No.'

'What about this?' I picked up the packaging.

'What? Oh, that was Stacey's.' She said this in a blasé manner, as if she were barely interested.

'What do you mean?' I'd never even heard her mention her friend Stacey before.

Melissa sighed and paused for a moment, obviously deciding whether she was going to enlighten me.

'Sorry, yeah. What happened was, she thought she was pregnant and she wanted to keep the baby.'

'She wanted to keep the baby? OK. I'm still not sure I understand why you have this testing kit.'

Melissa sighed again.

'So, Stacey's dad would have gone mad and made her get rid of the baby. He doesn't like her boyfriend at all, not at all.'

'And so how come you have this test here?'

'Oh, yeah, I get that this is confusing. Sorry Angela. Right, what was going to happen was that I was going to do the test for her, so she could tell her dad that she wasn't pregnant and prove it by showing him the negative test. He's quite scary, Stacey's dad. He'd have battered her boyfriend. But it turns out she isn't pregnant anyway. She's quite cut up about it really. She wants to have a baby.'

Melissa yawned and rubbed her eyes.

'Have I got this right? You did the test for Stacey, thinking she was pregnant, and trying to help her cover it up?' Again, I couldn't be sure that Melissa's tale was truthful, but I did want to make sure that she herself wasn't pregnant.

'Yeah, I did the test but Stacey didn't need it. So all's well that ends well. Here, do you want to have a look?' To my surprise she pulled the stick from the box and showed me the blue 'negative' sign in the indicator window. Then buttoned her lips and busied herself with plaiting her hair.

This story didn't seem to stack up. I'd have noticed this testing kit on the floor while Melissa was missing. It had only appeared this evening, yet for this explanation to make sense Melissa had to have done the test *before* finding out that Stacey wasn't pregnant after all. I figured that meant she must have done the test then called Stacey tonight. This seemed unlikely but of course it wasn't impossible. She could have called her while I was asleep, I supposed. I'd check the call log on our landline tomorrow; I was too tired to think straight at this point, and the main thing was that Melissa wasn't pregnant.

'I think you should try and get some sleep now, Melissa.'

'Yeah, you're right. I'm shattered. I'm sorry, you must be too.'

'Yes, I am, but that's hardly surprising. It's the middle of the night.'

'I like the dark,' Melissa said dreamily. 'Don't you?'

'I like looking at the stars,' I said. I told Melissa about the camping trips I used to go on as a child, when my parents used to point out the constellations and encourage me to make a wish.

She went to the window, pulled back the curtains and peered into the sky for a few moments.

'No luck tonight,' she said. She whistled softly to herself as she traced the shape of a star on the inside of the window pane.

I told her it was best to turn off the light in order to see the stars from inside the house. I switched off her bedside lamp but still there was no sign of a single star in the sky. I thought about how I grew up associating the stars with hope and possibility. Inevitably, the blackness outside did nothing to allay the creeping fears I had about Melissa, and what would happen to her.

She drew her curtains and tucked herself into bed, still

wearing her tracksuit. I let that go, though I hated to see a child sleeping in grubby clothes, and I doubted she'd even cleaned her teeth. Her eyes closed as her head touched the pillow. I said goodnight, crept back to bed and finally fell into a deep sleep.

20

'I don't believe it!'

'Did Melissa come home?' Marty asked.

He was coming down the stairs for breakfast and he spotted her muddy trainers discarded by the front door.

'Yes, sweetheart. She did.'

'That's good.'

'Yes, it is.'

'Is she going to school?'

'Not today.'

'Do I have to go?'

'Yes!'

'That's not fair! If I run away, does that mean I don't have to go to school?'

'Marty, Melissa is very tired and—'

Thankfully Marty interrupted me, saying he was only joking and that he liked being back at school.

I had a banging headache, having had so little sleep. Jonathan had gone out very early to the wholesaler and had commented that he felt 'like death warmed up' when he left the house in the dark. His six o'clock alarm had woken me up and I told him about Melissa being up in the night, and the pregnancy test. He kissed me on the forehead. 'Try not to think about it now. Get a bit more sleep, you need it. I'll see you later. We'll deal with it all, don't worry.'

I always say you should sleep on things, and that problems that often seem huge at night or in the early hours don't seem so bad in the morning, when you've had some rest and time to let things settle in your mind.

'Thanks, you're right. I'll try to grab a bit more sleep.'

I shut my eyes and had managed to sleep for another half hour or so, before I got up to help first Marty then Ryan get ready for school.

Marty's taxi arrived on time and I was still in my dressing gown when I waved him off. Ryan was eating his breakfast by then and I was glad we'd have a bit of time to talk privately, as I wanted to make sure he was OK after the incident with the hangman game the night before.

'How are you this morning?'

'Fine. How are you?'

He didn't seem at all disturbed, thank goodness. He'd already showered and was in his uniform, and he seemed full of beans as he started telling me all about the Year Six trip he would be going on later that year. He was looking forward to being able to choose which friends he'd share a room with, and there was going to be archery and kayaking at the outdoor activity centre they were staying at. He didn't stop chattering, and the time slipped by.

Glancing at the clock on the cooker I suddenly realised I was running a bit late.

'Oh look! We need to leave in fifteen minutes. You'd better go and clean your teeth, and don't forget you need to take your PE kit today. And that library book needs to go back.'

Ryan looked at the clock too and got to his feet straight away. 'I didn't realise the time,' he said, heading for the kitchen door.

I'm normally much more vigilant about timings in the mornings. I like to teach all the kids the importance of punctuality and I try to get them into good habits of building in enough time and avoiding last-minute rushes. I'd slipped a little this morning, no doubt because I was so lacking in sleep I was doing everything at a slightly slower pace than normal.

I put the dirty plates and cereal bowls in the dishwasher and then dashed upstairs to have a very quick shower and get dressed, suddenly feeling all at sixes and sevens. *At least Ryan's OK,* I thought.

As I got myself ready I realised I hadn't had a particularly good start to the day in terms of my diet either. Instead of the porridge and skimmed milk or yoghurt and fruit I normally made the effort to prepare, I'd eaten a thick doorstep of toast with strawberry jam. I needed the sugar kick, I justified. I'm never at my best when I'm short of sleep and that morning I definitely felt on the back foot as I rushed around.

Jonathan was back from the wholesaler just before Ryan and I left the house to walk to school.

'Any sign of Melissa yet?'

'No, but I don't expect she'll be up much before lunchtime.'

Ryan had also made a remark about the fact it wasn't fair Melissa was allowed a day off school but, like Marty, he didn't really mean it. I could see he was looking forward to his day. When we left he had quite a spring in his step as we walked along, wrapped in warm coats, gloves and hats. I told him the story about me mistaking the donkey tea towel for a scarf and he laughed his head off.

'What do you get when a donkey eats a porcupine?'

'I don't know,' I replied, telling him I was impressed that he always managed to tell a joke that somehow tied in with what we were talking about.

'A pain in the ass!'

He delivered the punchline loudly and I hoped none of the small children walking in front of us heard. Then I had to gently tell him that although I could see the funny side, it was best not to tell that joke again, as the word ass was a bit rude.

'Ass isn't a swear word!' he said, even louder this time.

Some of the kids in front turned around and giggled and one of the mums caught my eye and smirked: I think she'd heard the whole conversation.

'No, it's not a swear word, but it's not a polite word. Your teacher would tell you off if you used it in the classroom.'

'Well I tell you this, Angela, it's hard to be funny without offending *anyone*.'

There's a lot of truth in that, I thought. Ryan was a great little character and good company, and I'd miss him when he was gone.

While I did the school run Jonathan sat at the kitchen table with a stack of invoices and a pot of tea. We had cover in the shop that morning, and he was still in the kitchen when I returned.

'Cuppa? I've just boiled the kettle again.'

'Yes please. It's cold in here, I think I'll turn the heating up. Been any sign of Melissa?'

'No,' Jonathan replied, yawning as he spoke. 'Not a peep.'

'Lucky her, having a lie-in.'

'Indeed. Let's hope it's the tonic she needs and she wakes up feeling more positive.'

'Yes, let's hope so, hey? I'll just go and check on her.'

I turned up the temperature on the central heating thermostat in the hall and went up the stairs. It was shortly after 9 a.m. when I tapped gently on Melissa's door. There was no reply.

'Are you OK? Can I come in?'

Still there was no response.

'I'm going to come in, sweetheart.'

I would never have gone into Melissa's room without giving her any warning, and even though I presumed she was so fast asleep she wouldn't hear me, I still told her what I was going to do. I pushed open the door and winced when it creaked. *This needs oiling,* I thought. It was very dark in the room as the curtains had a blackout lining.

Melissa was snuggled down under the duvet. From my position in the doorway she looked like she was bundled up like a little hamster in a nest, wrapped up so well I couldn't even see her head. *Bless her,* I thought. *There is no way she could have gone to school this morning.*

I thought the room felt a bit airless with the central heating on and so I decided to open the air vent above the window, figuring that Melissa would benefit from having some fresh air, particularly as she was buried under the duvet. I tiptoed across the carpet and silently slipped my hand behind the curtain, reached up above the window and slid the air vent open. As I did so I turned and glanced at the bed, and that's when I realised something was wrong. From this angle it looked like Melissa wasn't in the bed at all. Surely I was seeing things? I held my breath and slowly reached for the top of the duvet.

'Are you there, Melissa?' I said quietly. 'I'm turning down the duvet.'

I gasped. Underneath the duvet was a pile of her clothes. My stomach turned over. *How could I have been so stupid?* I ran down the stairs and into the kitchen.

'Melissa's not here!'

'What? What do you mean?'

'She's not in bed. She must have slipped out.'

'But how? Are you sure she's not in the bathroom or somewhere else?'

I explained about the clothes and that she'd tried to make it look as if she was tucked up in bed, to fool me. 'You were first up. Were the doors still locked this morning?'

'Yes! Are you absolutely sure she's not in the house?'

'Yes! Well, no. MELISSA! MELISSA!'

We both searched the house from top to bottom. No keys

were missing and we couldn't work out how she could have left the house locked up if she'd escaped in the night. Her trainers were still in the hallway too.

The very last room we checked was the utility room. A blast of cold air hit us as soon as we opened the door. The window was swinging open and a space on the worktop had been cleared, no doubt so Melissa could climb up there before she lowered herself out of the window and ran off.

'I don't believe it!' Jonathan exclaimed. He already had black circles under his eyes; now he had a face like thunder. He thumped the worktop. He's never an aggressive person, but he had to vent his frustration somehow. His anger was immediately replaced by worry and fear. He held his head in his hands. 'What a silly, silly girl. Why is she doing this to herself? What's going to happen to her this time?'

I wanted to cry. I thought I'd made some progress with Melissa in the early hours, encouraging her to open up as I had done. She was tired out and her face was cut. I wanted to look after her, nurse her back to school and then send her on the next step in her life in the best possible state. Now what?

Later that day, in Melissa's absence, we had an emergency meeting with everyone involved in her care. We were told that unfortunately the auntie she was meant to move in with – Auntie Cathy – could not give her a home immediately, and so in the circumstances a different aunt and uncle had agreed she could move in with them as soon as she was found. This would mean Melissa would have no school place, as this family lived in a different county, many miles away. However, the general consensus was that Melissa's safety was the top priority. Getting her as far away as possible from the people she was mixing with and the towns she gravitated towards was of the utmost importance: we'd reached crisis point.

Before I'd called Social Services and the police that morning I'd quickly checked the log on our landline. Sure enough, a call had been made from our phone in the early hours of the morning – presumably during the very small window of opportunity Melissa had had when Jonathan and I were both asleep. I imagined she must have kept herself awake for as long as possible, waiting to creep into the lounge and make the call only when she was certain we were sound asleep and wouldn't disturb her. Mind you, even if we had caught her using the phone, no doubt she'd have come up with some excuse or other about why she was calling someone at that hour.

I didn't recognise the number she'd called but I made a note of it and gave it to the authorities. I explained about the conversation we'd had about Stacey and the pregnancy test but said I had no idea if the number Melissa had called was Stacey's or somebody else's. I emphasised that I agreed with the decision to relocate Melissa across the country.

I felt that as long as she could call the friends she was associating with, presumably to arrange a place to meet them nearby or to be picked up in a car or van, then she was in danger. The only solution was to fix it so that these arrangements were extremely difficult, if not impossible, for her to make. We couldn't stop her using the phone or going out to meet her friends locally, we couldn't patrol the perimeter of her school, and at night we had to get some sleep. As previous foster carers had found out, we simply couldn't guard her every minute of the day and therefore we could not stop her running away. Moving Melissa far away from the people who led her astray seemed the only solution. I couldn't imagine she would run away to be on her own in a place where she knew nobody but her aunt and uncle; at least I dared to believe she wouldn't. I sincerely hoped the strategy would work.

I was incredibly grateful to the relatives who had stepped in. Nowadays, 'kinship carers' like Melissa's aunt and uncle would need to go through an assessment process, similar to but less rigorous than the F Form assessment foster carers have to undergo. I don't know if things were different back then; we were given no further details about Melissa's aunt and uncle. Unfortunately, her placement with us had come to an abrupt halt and our job was now done.

The Social Services manager who presided over the meeting thanked us for having taken Melissa in, knowing she was a runner. 'It was always going to be a challenging placement. You have coped admirably.'

Wilf and Doreen were both at the meeting and they seconded this, praising us for our patience. The manager was also keen to point out that we'd barely had a chance to get to know Melissa, as she'd spent more time away from us than with us during the length of her placement. 'You are certainly not at fault,' she said. Jonathan and I appreciated the support. We'd heard other foster carers talking about how disheartening it was when a placement broke down. The manager made it clear that this was not a breakdown. She said it was only ever going to be a short placement and what had happened was more of a curtailment than a breakdown. It was kind of the professionals to attempt to soften the blow as they did, but Jonathan and I still felt extremely bruised by what had happened.

One youth worker at the meeting – someone we'd never met before – talked about a project that had been set up in our county to deal with the growing problem of runners and missing children. She mentioned that the project was for all kinds of missing children – not just runaways like Melissa, but also 'child prostitutes'. She explained that these were children who fell into the clutches of 'pimps'. I remember feeling disturbed by that term. It was such a shocking concept and it made me realise that even though Melissa's situation was bad, it could have been a whole lot worse.

It was icy outside and I slipped and fell in the car park of the Social Services office. I landed on my right hip and right forearm. Jonathan helped me up and wrapped his arms around me. I tried to laugh it off; the embarrassment I felt hurt more than the pain. *Thankfully nobody saw me*, was the first thing that crossed my mind.

'It's not my day really, is it?'

'You know what they say – things can only get better.' Jonathan was trying to cheer me up but I could tell he was feeling as crushed as I was. I sat in the car, my hip and arm starting to smart. I'd been buckling under the strain of caring for Melissa – or trying to care for Melissa – and now the placement had officially collapsed. The fall felt symbolic.

'I hope you're right. I really do hope that things can only get better, but the way I'm feeling, I'm worried something else will go wrong. Things happen in threes, don't they?'

'We've already had three things today,' Jonathan said. 'Ryan saying "pain in the ass" at the top of his voice on the school run, Melissa disappearing and you falling over.'

'Nice try,' I said, 'But I'm not sure the first one counts.'

I hoped to God Melissa would turn up safe and well and it was not too late to save her. It didn't matter that we were no longer her foster carers, I still cared deeply for her and hoped that someone would let us know as soon as she reappeared. It was arranged that Doreen would come to the house to collect her belongings, and I hoped that when she did she would bring good news.

'Melissa always turns up,' Jonathan said. 'It's only a matter of time.'

'I know. But the waiting is awful. I can't stand it. I really hope she isn't in danger. I want her to have a totally fresh start – it's the only way forward for her, I really believe that.'

Melissa's aunt and uncle lived in a beautiful part of the country and I dared to picture Melissa walking by the sea, the wind in her hair and the demons of the past being blown away. I kept hold of that image while we waited and waited.

Epilogue

About six or seven years ago I was lying in the dentist's chair having a filling replaced. The sound of the drill was reverberating around my skull and I was clenching my fists into tight balls, even though the pain and discomfort was nowhere near as bad as I expected it to be.

The radio was playing in the background and the national news headlines came on. The dentist stopped drilling long enough for me to hear the main story. It was about a gang of men convicted of trafficking underage girls for sex. I shuddered. The drill started up again and I thought how horrific this was, especially as it had happened in a part of the UK I was familiar with. In my mind, trafficking was something that happened in foreign countries, or at least the perpetrators of such crimes came from overseas. Girls were drugged and smuggled across borders. They were poverty-stricken, desperate youngsters from families who didn't have the means to protect them, or girls who were orphaned in wars and had nobody to save them, and no means of protecting themselves. It was not something that happened in our country, to our young people; that's what I thought.

When I heard that news report it had been almost twenty years since we'd had Melissa staying with us. I'd never forgotten her; I don't forget any child who stays with us, and my memories of Melissa were clearly etched on my mind.

I can remember the bittersweet moment when her social worker, Doreen, called at our house to collect her clothes and the few other possessions she'd brought with her. I was incredibly relieved that she had been found. Two weeks after she went missing she had been picked up in a B&B with one of her friends. Their boyfriends had paid for them to stay there, it seemed, and the landlord raised the alarm when he saw how young the girls were.

Packing Melissa's bags was very upsetting. She was such a young girl, as her belongings attested. The Disney designs on her clothing, the childish hair bobbles and her little fluffy rabbit slippers pulled at my heartstrings. She was too young to be involved in the grown-up world she seemed so addicted to, running off with her friends and loving the thrill of going out with older boys as she did.

When I emptied the contents of Melissa's bedside drawer I found instructions for the discarded pregnancy test that was still in her room, the long list of names I'd seen before and a cigarette lighter, which was hidden under a pair of *Beauty and the Beast* socks. There was also a packet of hair dye, a pair of tweezers and an old cinema ticket. I noticed it was for a film she should not have been allowed to see;

it was a 15 classification. I discovered her school shoes were missing: presumably, she'd worn those deliberately on the day she absconded, so as to leave her trainers on display in the hall.

I felt terrible for failing to realise for so many hours that she'd done a runner. From the timing of the phone call she made from our landline, we reckoned Melissa could have been gone for over four hours before we worked out she'd climbed out of the utility room window. Everyone I spoke to was extremely kind about this. The other foster carers at our support group – Lynne included – said we had done everything in our power to keep Melissa safe and had nothing to feel guilty about. I knew this deep down, but it didn't stop me having regrets and feeling foolish, wishing I'd done more to stop her escaping like that.

Telling Ryan and Marty that Melissa was not coming back was also tough. They said kind things about her, and I felt bad that they'd been subjected to the disruption she'd caused in the house, both having their own issues to cope with as they did. I liked both boys, and when they moved out shortly after Melissa's departure I missed having them around, though the house wasn't ever empty, as more children came to stay. I heard that both Ryan and Marty did very well in their new homes, and while he was still at the primary school I saw Ryan in the playground occasionally, when I was taking other children in. He never failed to give me a cheery hello and often told me a joke.

*

A couple of years ago I bumped into Elaine, Melissa's former support worker. I was attending a safeguarding conference and she was working there as a volunteer. She was sitting at a table, signing people in and giving out name badges. I recognised her straight away and went over to say hello. Elaine must have been in her early seventies by then. I asked her if she remembered me, and if she had ever heard what became of Melissa. She hesitated for a moment before saying, 'I do remember you, you've barely changed.' I thanked her for the compliment: I'd turned sixty and had been in my thirties when I first met Elaine. 'Do you know, I saw your names on the list earlier and they rang a bell. How silly of me not to realise straight away that it was you, and Jonathan, of course. How is he?'

I was itching to hear if she knew what had happened to Melissa. I'd tried to keep in touch with Elaine in the aftermath of Melissa's move across the country, but had been told that she'd left her job and gone to work for another authority. Doreen moved on too, and in all these years we'd never found out what became of Melissa.

'Jonathan's fine. We've both often wondered about Melissa. I'd love to know if you ever heard how she got on.'

'Melissa? Yes, she was the one with the beautiful red hair. That was the best thing that could have happened to her, moving away.'

'Did you keep in touch?' I was on pins now, hoping for positive news after all this time.

'No, I didn't. But, now then, let me think.'

Elaine scrunched up her eyes and placed her hands on her temples, as if trying to summon up some deep-rooted memories.

'Yes, Melissa. Yes, I do recall . . . I was told the move was very successful. She stayed with her relatives – an aunt and uncle, wasn't it? – and I heard her file was closed, which was music to my ears. Given what we know now, it's possible she had a very lucky escape.'

'That's so good to hear,' I said. Though so much time had passed it was still a huge relief to me to hear that. Jonathan and I always try to stay in touch with the children we foster, but of course Melissa's placement ended very abruptly, without us even having the chance to say goodbye. I was absolutely delighted to hear her move had worked out, and that she'd stayed with her relatives. The fact her file had been closed was a very good sign. In hindsight I wasn't sure what Elaine meant by the phrase 'given what we know now' and there had been no time to ask: a queue was forming behind me. I thanked Elaine and went to find Jonathan to tell him the good news.

'A lucky escape?' he said, delighted. 'It's wonderful to hear that.'

That day I picked up an information leaflet about trafficking and the problems of child sexual exploitation (CSE), and around this time I was also starting to hear more in the news about so-called 'grooming gangs.' When I got home from the conference I googled CSE. I wanted to find out more about it, and how to spot the warning signs that a child may be at risk. This was clearly something foster carers like us needed to be educated about, and I always follow up on all the latest research and information available about anything and everything to do with child safeguarding. We'd been told we would receive CSE training during the course of our ongoing specialist fostering training, which continued to provide us with regular backing, information and support, though we were still waiting for it. In the meantime, I wanted to educate myself as much as possible.

I sat at my computer and read details that made me shudder. The reports online said it was mostly white British girls who were being groomed by older men – predominantly of Asian heritage – who often aimed to traffick the girls for sex. They plied them with drink and drugs or both, and they tried to impress them with cars and money. Melissa was fresh in my mind, having talked about her that day. I thought back to her friend Sonia and her son Kazim, remembering how she had talked about his dad, Buzz, and the fact he was of Asian heritage. Melissa had had a thing for his friend Tommy, who was also of Asian origin. I didn't want to jump to conclusions on flimsy evidence, but my mind was making some disturbing connections.

I spoke to Jonathan about this at length. 'Melissa wasn't being groomed, was she?'

He looked at me in horror. 'Melissa? No, of course not.'

I hoped he was right and that I was worrying unnecessarily, but I couldn't let this go.

Together, we picked over what we knew about the types

of boys Melissa hung around with, and what she got up to when she mixed with the wrong crowds. To our knowledge, her boyfriends were white boys, older than her but still in their teens. Though she'd fancied Tommy, we weren't sure if he was ever her boyfriend. Boys like TJ, Degsy and Oz were all white and didn't fit the profile of the abusers being described in the media, and although we knew Melissa smoked and dabbled with alcohol, we never witnessed her being drunk, at least not in the way you would imagine a person who was 'plied' with alcohol would be.

Gradually, more information about grooming was trickling through to foster carers, and to health care professionals, social workers, teachers and in fact anyone involved in the care and safeguarding of young people. I was learning that no child is immune from the risk of CSE, and that it was an international problem affecting an incalculable number of children. It didn't matter how well-cared-for a child may be; the men who groomed children were highly skilled at manipulating them and brainwashing them. They knew exactly what to say and do to lure a vulnerable child into believing they were boyfriend and girlfriend, not abuser and victim, and that it was OK to have underage sex with someone you were going out with. I read how once the child was drawn into the 'relationship', the next step would be to encourage them to commit crimes and cut themselves off from their families and the people who cared for them.

They would soon be sucked so deep into their abuser's world they couldn't escape. They might be too scared or ashamed to cut ties and go back to their loved ones, or they might be threatened with violence, making it impossible for them to break free. The abuse might escalate, and the girls might be assaulted verbally, physically and sexually if they don't comply with their abuser's demands. In some cases, the girls - or boys, as they are victims too - might be forced to have sex with other people, for the perpetrator's gain.

The more I read about CSE the more I thought back over Melissa's time with us. I couldn't get the thought out of my head that she might have been a CSE victim without us ever suspecting it.

'What if she actually was being groomed and we simply didn't realise?' I said to Jonathan one day. 'What if it was going on right under our noses, and under the noses of everyone in authority?'

We wrung our hands and racked our brains once more. As we'd done before, we discussed the fact the boyfriends we knew about were white males, and that this didn't fit with the profile of the local men who were under investigation or already in jail. Melissa didn't have a criminal record either, whereas victims of grooming were very often coerced into committing criminal acts by their abusers. Understandably, Jonathan and I wanted to convince ourselves that this had not happened to Melissa, but knowing what we did now about CSE and the tactics used, I continued to have nagging doubts, and I kept digging for more information.

*

Last year I had another chance encounter, this time with a former Social Services manager I used to work with, who also used to work in children's homes in the nineties.

'Isn't it terrible?' Hilary said. 'If only we knew then what we know now. So many missed opportunities. So much wasted time.'

She went on to say how dreadful it was that young girls who were having sex with older men were once viewed as 'child prostitutes' and their abusers described as 'pimps.'

'How can you have a child prostitute?' Hilary asked, throwing her hands in the air. 'There is no such thing. These were abused children, not the precocious little madams they were made out to be. Thank God this problem is finally being seen for what it was – and what it is.' My mind darted back to the emergency meeting we'd had when Melissa's placement with us ended. That was the first time I'd heard the term child prostitute, but nobody suggested that was a world Melissa was caught up in, or did they? Did Social Services have their suspicions and is that why that youth worker attended the meeting? I thought hard. *No, they didn't.* I could remember clearly that the youth worker had said the missing person project she worked on was 'not just for runaways like Melissa,' but kids caught up in child prostitution.

Hilary and I talked about the fact the CSE problem was ongoing and that, unfortunately, it looked like the cases that had come to light were just the tip of the iceberg.

'Education is key,' she said.

I agreed with this and told her I wish I'd known a lot more, and a lot sooner.

'Do you think this has happened to a child you've cared for?'

Without naming Melissa I explained that Jonathan and I had our doubts and suspicions about one particular girl but weren't convinced, largely because the boys she hung round with didn't fit the profile of the convicted abusers and the vast majority of grooming gangs that had been identified. Hilary considered this for a moment. Then she went on to tell me that older teenage boys used to hang around the children's homes she worked at, befriending young girls. These boys did not fit the profile of the predators making headlines in the media either. They were white and typically much closer in age to their victims – maybe seventeen or eighteen. They were the ones who initially introduced the girls to cigarettes, alcohol and drugs – typically cannabis, to begin with. They introduced them to sex, too. Often, these boys worked as drug runners for the older men who controlled the grooming gangs.

My blood ran cold. Hilary went on to explain that she believed these teenagers may have been out of their depth themselves, operating in a world they didn't plan to enter or even recognise for what it was. 'Nevertheless, they were in it, and they played a critical role. They gained the girls' trust and, whether they knew what they were doing or not, they normalised underage sex, illegal drinking, experimenting with drugs and criminal behaviour.'

I was horrified at what I was hearing, and I wondered how many other people were in the dark, given that the teenage boys themselves might not have realised the full extent of what they were involved with. Carers, parents, healthcare professionals, social workers, teachers – so many of us had been left scrabbling around for answers, out of our depth and ill-equipped to deal with an epidemic that hadn't yet been diagnosed. The warning signs were there, but the knowledge we have today was not. I had a creeping realisation that the children who were trapped at the centre of the abuse could not possibly have recognised the complexity or sheer evil of what was happening to them. Had Melissa been in the dark too? Had she been a victim, one with no idea of what she was a victim of?

I was hanging on Hilary's every word as she continued to describe the grooming process.

'Catastrophically these teenage boys introduced the girls to their older, richer and much more sophisticated "friends",' she said. 'And they were predominantly men of Asian heritage. People have been afraid to say that for fear of sounding racist, but that is a fact. The girls trusted the older men because they were not strangers, they were friends of friends. And the girls couldn't believe their luck; suddenly they were going to adult parties, being driven around in flashy sports cars, having food bought for them and a free supply of alcohol and cannabis on tap, which they were encouraged to lap up. The men knew everything about the girls, but often the girls only knew the men by their nicknames, or which car they drove or business they ran. Takeaways and taxi firms, a lot of the time.'

The more Hilary spoke, the more I started to realise this

could definitely have been happening to Melissa, to some extent. I began to feel quite sick as I thought about TJ, Degsy and Oz. I could see that they could have been part of the grooming chain; they fitted the profile of the older teenage boys who made the introductions to the abusers to a tee. Once again I thought of Sonia, and Kazim's father, and how he'd been friends with Tommy. Buzz and Tommy both used nicknames. They chose names that were easier for the girls to say than their real names, but why were older men like them so keen to do this, and to befriend young girls? Some of the names on that list Melissa kept in her bedroom had puzzled me. She had Ozzy Osbourne and Tom Jones written down. I'd thought it was unlikely that a twelve-year-old girl would be a fan of those singers, but now I wondered if they were nicknames for other boys or men. I wished I knew the answer, or that the police or Social Services had had the intelligence and resources to investigate this at the time. Melissa had described Tommy as a 'proper sophisticated guy' who had a 'really good car'. There were links to takeaways and taxi firms too. TJ worked in a takeaway, and I realised the fact Melissa seemed to be able to get picked up at all hours, whenever she made a call from our landline or a call box, meant she probably had access to free rides. She was certainly given free food, alcohol and cigarettes; it was obvious someone else was paying, as she only received a few pounds a week in pocket money. Her friends had older boyfriends too – including those who came from good, caring families, like Rosie. *No child is immune from the risks.* I'd read that chilling warning several times now and I couldn't get the phrase out of my head.

I asked Hilary for her honest opinion about Melissa. She didn't know her and couldn't possibly be sure, but after listening to more of my recollections she told me, 'I think that crisis review meeting probably saved her skin. I imagine at the time you felt like a failure. But that final time she absconded meant that she was uprooted. From what you've told me, she would have been cut off from the gangs who operated in our area, and in the neighbouring counties. The fact her Social Services file was closed is a very good sign. She got away before she was in too deep. I can't say for sure, as unfortunately CSE is a nationwide problem, but it certainly sounds like she had a lucky escape from the gangs operating in this part of the country.'

I remembered what Elaine had said at that conference – she had also described Melissa as having had a 'lucky escape'. Had Elaine had the same suspicions about Melissa and, if so, when? I had no idea, and it was frustrating to be trying to piece everything together so many years on. I truly wished I had a time machine and could go back to the nineties, armed with the knowledge I had now, and that I could find out exactly what had gone on.

Today, all things considered, I'm afraid I do believe that Melissa was subjected at least to the early stages of grooming. The thought of it devastates me, but when I look back it would explain so many of the mysteries that surrounded her. I always had a very strong feeling that she was not running *away* from care, but running *to* something. I also sensed that she somehow felt compelled to run off; it was like she'd been put under a spell by her friends and boyfriends. She was a naturally sweet-natured girl, so we were baffled by how easily she seemed to transform into a devious, thoughtless and reckless runaway. It was like she was being brainwashed, and I'm afraid I think she was.

I cling to the hope that the chain was broken before one of her teenage boyfriends was replaced with an older abuser, or someone who may have trafficked her for sex. I don't believe that happened, but I can't be sure. Every time I think of Melissa I remind myself that her Social Services file was closed after she started a new life on the other side of the country. I want to believe that she broke free. I try to convince myself she would no longer have felt compelled to run away once she'd cut ties with the network of boys and men she was involved with. I hope that is true.

This has been a difficult story to recollect and write, but I hope it may help others to recognise the signs of CSE, and keep more children safe. If I had a child like Melissa staying with me now I'm confident I'd identify the early signs of child sexual exploitation. I'd feel able to report suspected CSE to the authorities immediately, safe in the knowledge I'd be listened to. I'd like to think that no police officer, social worker or youth worker would ever treat a child victim as a tearaway, a naughty truant or a precocious 'little madam,' as they did in the past.

Twenty-five years have passed since I last saw Melissa.

She'll be in her late thirties now and I truly hope she is a happy, healthy and wise woman who is enjoying her life, perhaps with a family of her own to care for.

Nobody knows how many children have been victims of CSE. Over 2,400 children in the UK were victims of sexual exploitation by gangs and groups from August 2010 to October 2011. For more information, help and advice visit nspcc.org.uk.

Missing People is a national organisation offering assistance to people who go missing or run away, and their families and carers. In the UK 180,000 people are reported missing every year – 80,000 of them children. One in ten children in care is reported missing each year, compared to one in two hundred not in care. Visit missingpeople.org.uk.

Other stories by foster mum Angela Hart . . .

The Girl With Two Lives

A Shocking Childhood. A Foster Carer Who Understood.
A Young Girl's Life Forever Changed

As I stepped back into the kitchen, Danielle looked very proud as she held her notepad up for me to see.

'Finished!' she declared cheerfully. I was surprised to see that the surname Danielle had printed wasn't the one I'd seen on her paperwork from Social Services, and so I asked her casually if she used two different names, which often happens when children come from broken homes.

'Yes,' she said. 'But this is the surname I'm going to use from now on, because it's the name of my forever family.'

Danielle has been excluded from school and her former foster family can no longer cope. She arrives as an emergency placement at the home of foster carer Angela Hart, who soon suspects that there is more to the young girl's disruptive behaviour than meets the eye. Can Angela's specialist training unlock the horrors of Danielle's past and help her start a brave new life?

Available now in paperback and ebook.

The Girl and the Ghosts

The true story of a haunted little girl and the foster carer who rescued her from the past

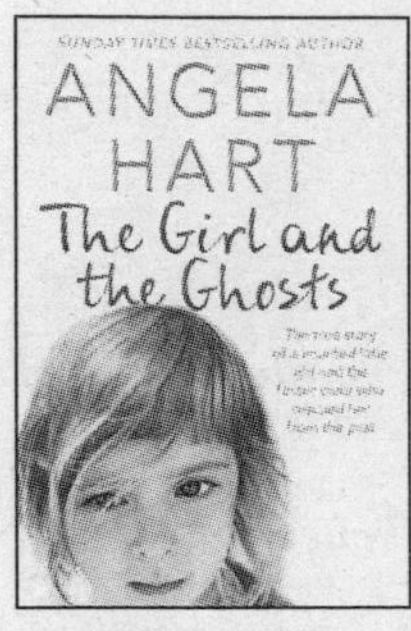

'So, is it a girl or a boy, and how old?' Jonathan asked as soon as we were alone in the shop.

My husband knew from the animated look on my face, and the way I was itching to talk to him, that our social worker had been asking us to look after another child.

I filled Jonathan in as quickly as I could and he gave a thin, sad smile.

'Bruises?' he said. 'And a moody temperament? Poor little girl. Of course we can manage a few days.'

I gave Jonathan a kiss on the cheek. 'I knew you'd say that. It's exactly what I thought.'

We were well aware that the few days could run into weeks or even longer, but we didn't need to discuss this. We'd looked after dozens of children who had arrived like Maria, emotionally or physically damaged, or both. We'd do whatever it took to make her feel loved and cared for while she was in our home.

Seven-year-old Maria holds lots of secrets. Why won't she tell how she got the bruises on her body? Why does she run and hide? And why does she so want to please her sinister step-father?

It takes years for devoted foster carer Angela Hart to uncover the truth as she helps Maria leave the ghosts of her past behind.

Available now in paperback and ebook.

The Girl Who Just Wanted to be Loved

A damaged little girl and a foster carer who wouldn't give up

The first time we ever saw Keeley was in a Pizza Hut. She was having lunch with her social worker.

'Unfortunately Keeley's current placement is breaking down,' our support social worker, Sandy, had explained. 'We'd like to move her as soon as possible.'

We'd looked after more than thirty youngsters over the years, yet I never failed to feel a surge of excitement at the prospect of caring for another one.

Sandy began by explaining that Keeley was eight years old and had stayed with four sets of carers and been in full-time care with two different families.

'Why have the placements not worked out?' I asked.

'Both foster carers tell similar stories. Keeley's bad behaviour got worse instead of better as time went on. That's why we're keen for you to take her on, Angela. I'm sure you'll do a brilliant job.'

Eight-year-old Keeley looks like the sweetest little girl you could wish to meet, but demons from the past make her behaviour far from angelic. She takes foster carer Angela on a rocky and very demanding emotional ride as she fights daily battles against her deep-rooted psychological problems. Can the love and specialist care Angela and husband Jonathan provide help Keeley triumph against the odds?

Available now in paperback and ebook.

Terrified

The heartbreaking true story of a girl nobody loved and the woman who saved her

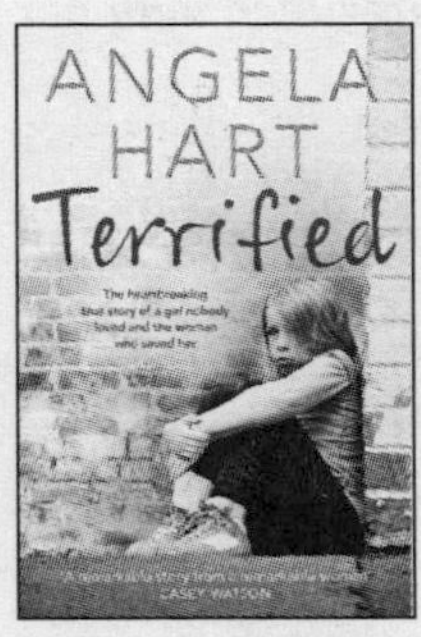

Vicky stared through the windscreen, her eyeballs glazed like marbles. She was sitting completely rigid in her seat, frozen with fear.

I took a deep breath and then asked Vicky as gently as possible, if she was all right.

'I'm here, right beside you, Vicky. Can you hear me? I'm here and I can help you.'

She still didn't respond in any way at all. Her normally rosy cheeks had turned ivory white and the expression of terror on her face was like nothing I'd seen before: I had never seen a child look so scared in all my life.

'Take a deep breath, love. That's what I've just done. Just breathe and try to calm yourself down. You're with me, Angela, and you're safe.'

Vicky seemed all self-assurance and swagger when she came to live with Angela and Jonathan as a temporary foster placement. As Vicky's mask of bravado began to slip, she was overtaken with episodes of complete terror. Will the trust and love Angela and her husband Jonathan provide enable Vicky to finally overcome her shocking past?

Available now in paperback and ebook.

The Girl With No Bedroom Door

A true short story

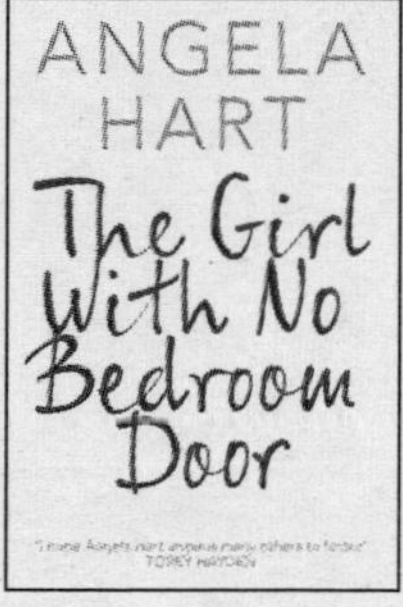

Fourteen-year-old Louise has been sleeping rough after running away from her previous foster home. Unloved and unwashed, she arrives at foster carer Angela Hart's door stripped of all self-esteem. Can Angela's love and care help Louise blossom into a confident and happy young woman?

Available now in ebook.

Read on for an extract from the first chapter of *Sunday Times* bestseller

The Girl Who Wanted to Belong

The True Story of a Devastated Little Girl
and the Foster Carer Who Healed her Broken Heart

'I'll be very, very good,' she told me. 'I won't make Wendy cross with me.'

'I'm pleased to hear you're going to be well behaved, sweetheart. By the way, have you remembered she prefers you not to call her Wendy?'

'Yes. I need to call her Mum. I don't like calling her Mum, but I will. Mum, Mum, Mum.'

Lucy is eight years old and ends up in foster care after being abandoned by her mum and kicked out by her dad's new partner, Wendy. Two aunties and then her elderly grandmother take her in, but it seems nobody can cope with Lucy's disruptive behaviour. Social Services hope a stay with experienced foster carer Angela will help Lucy settle down. Lucy is desperate for a fresh start back home, but will she ever be able to live in harmony with her stepmother and her stepsister – a girl who was once her best friend at school?

Available now in paperback and ebook.

1

'So many questions!'

'That's wonderful!' Jess exclaimed. 'I'll let the social worker know right away. Thanks *so* much. This is great news for Lucy. Please thank Jonathan from me. What would I do without you two? I shudder to think!'

Jess had been our support social worker for some time and we'd got to know each other well. She was a good ten years younger than my husband Jonathan and me – we were in our forties now – yet Jess always seemed wise beyond her years. She was extremely efficient at her job and had a way of always saying the right thing, even when she was completely snowed under with work.

'Thanks, Jess. We look forward to meeting Lucy. It'll be nice to have another little girl in the house.'

'Lucy's very fortunate,' Jess replied, sounding relieved. 'I think you are the ideal foster carers for her. Let me make the arrangements and I'll call you back as soon as I can. Hopefully we'll get her to you tomorrow. Is that OK?'

'Perfect.'

When I put the phone down I felt supported and appreciated, just as I always did after talking to Jess. I was also excited, apprehensive and slightly nervous about meeting our new arrival. To this day those emotions still collide whenever a new child is due to start a placement. I love the sense of anticipation, wondering what the child will be like, how we will get along and how we will be able to help. I immediately start thinking about how to make him or her welcome when they turn up at our door; I want them to feel comfortable from the moment they arrive, although that's not always possible. No child comes to us without issues and I always have underlying worries about what state they will be in, what problems we may need to deal with and whether or not we really will be the right foster carers for the job.

Lucy had recently turned eight years old and Jess had explained to me on the phone that she was described by family members as being 'disruptive', 'aggressive', 'belligerent' and 'totally impossible to live with.' She had support in the classroom, which suggested she had some special educational needs, but there were no further details. Her mum was off the scene – Jess didn't know the details – and Lucy was left with her father, two brothers and her little sister. Problems started when her dad moved his new partner and her young daughter into the family home. Lucy clashed with her 'stepmother' so badly she was sent to live with two different aunties, miles out of town. They either didn't want her or couldn't cope and so Lucy was packed off to stay with her elderly grandmother who lived even further away, in a different county. Lucy had missed a lot of school during this period and it was her struggling gran who had reluctantly called Social Services, asking for help after finding herself unable to cope.

Jess also told me that Lucy's placement would be short term. The little girl missed her daddy and siblings and desperately wanted to go home, despite the issues she had with her new stepmother. It would be our job to help integrate Lucy back into the family unit. Her father and stepmother and possibly some of the children would be given support in the form of family counselling, to help pave the way for Lucy's return. Lucy would see a psychologist and also take part in group family therapy. It was expected the whole process would take two or three months, although understandably nothing was set in stone.

Jonathan and I are well used to taking in children at short notice and not knowing how long they will be staying. We'd been fostering for more than a decade at this point in time. We'd looked after dozens of kids and many had come to us as emergency cases, at even shorter notice than Lucy. I was delighted we could offer Lucy a home, and as soon as I'd finished talking to Jess I went to sort out a bedroom for her, to make sure she would feel as welcome as possible.

The following day Lucy arrived with a social worker called Brian. I was standing on the pavement in front of our flower shop, helping to take in the last of the displays, when they pulled up in a bright red Mini. To my amusement Brian looked exactly like Rowan Atkinson; the likeness was uncanny. As he got out of the car and shook my hand I thought to myself, *I'm glad his car's not green or I'd have thought Mr Bean had arrived!*

'May I present Lucy,' Brian said very brightly as the small and very slender little girl climbed out of the back of the car.

I was struck by Brian's energy. He had collected Lucy from her grandmother's house, which I'd been alarmed to discover was more than a hundred miles away. He must have been driving for hours and it was a Friday too and so the traffic can't have been great, especially in the afternoon rush. Nevertheless, Brian was all smiles and looked as fresh as a daisy. Lucy appeared remarkably bright in the circumstances too. She gave me a broad grin and said hello enthusiastically, which I was very pleased about. As she smiled I noticed she'd lost her two front teeth; her adult teeth were just starting to push through the top gum. Lucy looked very young for her age and she could have passed for a child of seven or maybe even six. She was very pretty, with bright blue eyes, a sprinkling of pale freckles on her nose and beautiful honey-blonde hair that framed her little face and bounced on her shoulders. I grinned back at her, thinking how appealing she looked and how friendly she seemed. It was almost as if she'd come for a social visit, rather than arriving for a foster care placement, which was very heartening to see.

'I'm Angela. It's lovely to meet you Lucy. Come and meet my husband Jonathan, he's in the shop.'

'Is this your shop?'

'Yes. It's a family business. We've been running it for a very long time. My mum ran it before us. You'll meet her soon enough, I'm sure.'

'I thought you were just foster carers. Wow! Do you own all these flowers? What's your mum's name? Where does she live? Does she live with you as well?'

Lucy was standing in the middle of the shop now, taking everything in, her eyes darting everywhere.

'So many questions!' my husband said cheerfully, stepping from behind the counter. 'Hello Lucy, I'm Jonathan. Very pleased to meet you.'

She said hello politely and I introduced Jonathan to Brian. 'Decent journey?' Jonathan asked.

Before Brian could answer, Lucy was off again. 'What do you do with all the flowers you don't sell? Where do you grow them all? You must have a big garden. Who does the gardening? I like gardening. Have you got flowers in your house? Do you have to water them all? Does it take ages? It must take ages. What's this stuff for?'

'We try not to have too many flowers we don't sell, but if we do have any going past their sell-by date we often put them in the house, so we can enjoy them. Jonathan goes to collect them from the wholesalers, we do have a garden, but we don't grow any of the flowers for the shop. Yes, they all need watering, and that green foamy stuff is for making flower arrangements. It's called oasis and it helps the flowers stand up and stay in place. You push the stalks into it, to keep them upright. Does that answer your questions?'

'Er . . . I think so.'

'My mum's called Thelma, by the way,' I said. 'She lives nearby and she loves to meet all the children who stay with us. She babysits for us sometimes.'

'Oh! Do you have a baby?'

'No, I mean she looks after the children we foster for us sometimes.'

Lucy nodded and seemed to approve. 'I like the smell in here. Can I help you? I'd love to work in a shop!'

'Indeed you can, but not right now,' Jonathan said. 'We're about to shut up for the evening and you must be tired after all that travelling. Let's go through to the house.'

We left our assistant Barbara to finish closing the shop. She'd been working with us for many years and was well used to seeing different children coming and going.

'I'll see you again soon, by the sound of it,' Barbara said kindly, and Lucy gave her a smile.

Jonathan and I led Lucy and Brian through the storeroom at the back and into our adjoining town house. Her eyes were everywhere still and she continued to ask lots of questions. I glanced at Brian, thinking, *I wonder if he's had this for hours on end in the car? That man deserves a medal!*

'Do you have children?' Lucy asked, looking me directly in the eye. 'Who else lives here? Do I have to share a room?'

I told her we had another girl living with us called Maria, who was just a little bit older than Lucy. Maria was upstairs in her bedroom and no, Lucy would not have to share a room.

'We have three floors and your bedroom is on the top

floor of the house, next to Maria's. I've got it all ready for you but I haven't put the duvet cover or pillow cases on yet as I thought you might like to choose which colour set you want.'

'OK. Thanks. Have your own children left home?'

'No, we don't have children of our own.'

'Oh.' She narrowed her eyes. 'Is Maria adopted?'

'No, we are fostering her too, just like you.'

'Oh. Do you like fostering then?'

We went into the kitchen, and as Lucy and I continued to chat – or, should I say, Lucy continued to interview me – Jonathan fetched everyone a glass of water. It was an unusually warm, sunny day in early spring and Brian said he needed a cold drink after driving for so long in the heat.

'Thirsty work, wasn't it Lucy?' he said jovially, which made Lucy burst out laughing. There was obviously an in-joke going on here, but they didn't elaborate.

Lucy carried on quizzing me and Brian tactfully took the opportunity to run through the routine paperwork with Jonathan, talking quietly on the other side of the kitchen. By now Lucy had moved on to ask me lots of questions about our garden and what was in the shed she could see from our kitchen window. I was happy to keep chatting while Brian went through the formalities, handing over all the usual forms with contact numbers on, emergency Social Services numbers and so on. Sometimes kids sit in silence during this initial handover, which is never ideal and always makes me feel uncomfortable.

Brian didn't have a great deal of background information on Lucy. This is not uncommon on the first day of a placement, and Lucy had never been in care before so there were no old records on file. In any case, Brian was not Lucy's actual social worker and had simply been drafted in to transport her to our house as he was based in the county where her grandmother lived. She would be assigned a social worker from the area her parents lived in as soon as possible.

As they filled in the paperwork Brian told Jonathan that he had stopped for a cup of tea with Lucy's grandmother. 'She seems like a lovely, sweet old lady,' he said. 'She told me she's very sorry she's had to get Social Services involved and wishes she could care for Lucy herself, but she's too old and frail. I felt sorry for her, to tell the truth. I told her she'd done the right thing.' Brian was aware of the fact that Lucy's schooling had been disrupted with all the moves she'd made between relatives' houses.

'Do you happen to know how much school she's missed?' Jonathan asked.

'All in all I reckon she's missed about half a term from what she's said, but don't quote me on that.'

'I see. I don't suppose you know if she's statemented? Our support social worker mentioned she had help in the classroom. Was anything said to you along those lines?'

'Nothing official, but Lucy told me she always had a lady helping her in her old school, so I guess she must be.'

'OK. That's good to hear. Hopefully it won't be too difficult to find her a school place here.'

As a leader in recognizing the role of stress in illness, Dr. Johnson helped reduce many patients' fears of the unknown with his publication in the early 1970s of *Docubooks,* the first series of books clearly describing the risks and rewards of people's tests and operations.

From 1974 to 1979, Spencer Johnson created *ValueTales,* a book series to help children develop a better self-image and grow into healthier adults. His books became the largest-selling new children's book series of the decade.

As co-author of the international best sellers *The One Minute Manager* in 1982 and *The One Minute $ales Person* in 1984, he has shown people a healthier way to work.

Dr. Johnson's education includes a B.A. degree in psychology from the University of Southern California, an M.D. degree from the Royal College of Surgeons in Ireland, and medical clerkships at Harvard Medical School and the Mayo Clinic.

He has served as director of communications for Medtronic, the first manufacturer of cardiac pacemakers, as research physician at the Institute for Interdisciplinary Studies, a medical-social think tank, and as a consultant to the Center for the Study of the Person and the University of California School of Medicine, San Diego.

There are now over ten million copies of Spencer Johnson's books in use in twenty-four languages.

:01® About the Authors

Constance Johnson has many years' teaching experience in public, parochial, and private schools, including two years with the Peace Corps in the Middle East at the University of Bahrain, College of Education, where she taught English as a second language and supervised student teachers. During this time she also worked with the Bahrain Ministry of Education.

In the United States, she has been a guest lecturer on "Parents as Educators." For school accreditations she has served on visiting committees for the Western Association of Schools and Colleges.

Constance Johnson earned her Bachelor of Arts degree from the University of Vermont, and her Master of Education from California State University at Northridge. She is a member of Phi Delta Kappa (UCLA chapter).

As co-author of *The One Minute Teacher,* she adopted the principles of communication discovered by the millions of readers of *The One Minute Manager* and applied them to education, using insights based upon her years of experience with students, teachers, and administrators at all levels in public and private education.

Dr. Spencer Johnson helps people gain better health through better communications.

He has pioneered the field of medical communications for over twenty years, by taking seemingly complex technical subjects and making them more understandable and usable for millions of people.

His work reflects the changing focus in medicine: from physicians to patients to "well beings."

In the mid-1960s, he created *Moments with Medicine,* a series of books to help his fellow physicians learn technical information more quickly.